Higher Education, State and Society

Bloomsbury Higher Education Research

Series Editor: Simon Marginson

The Bloomsbury Higher Education Research series provides the evidence-based academic output of the world's leading research centre on higher education, the ESRC/RE Centre for Global Higher Education (CGHE) in the UK. The core focus of CGHE's work and of The Bloomsbury Higher Education Research series is higher education, especially the future of higher education in the changing global landscape. The emergence of CGHE reflects the remarkable growth in the role and importance of universities and other higher education institutions, and research and science, across the world. Corresponding to CGHE's projects, monographs in the series will consist of social science research on global, international, national and local aspects of higher education, drawing on methodologies in education, learning theory, sociology, economics, political science and policy studies. Monographs will be prepared so as to maximise worldwide readership and selected on the basis of their relevance to one or more of higher education policy, management, practice and theory. Topics will range from teaching and learning and technologies, to research and research impact in industry, national system design, the public good role of universities, social stratification and equity, institutional governance and management, and the cross-border mobility of people, institutions, programmes, ideas and knowledge. The Bloomsbury Higher Education Research series is at the cutting edge of world research on higher education.

Advisory Board:

Paul Blackmore, King's College London, UK; Brendan Cantwell, Michigan State University, USA; Gwilym Croucher, University of Melbourne, Australia; Carolina Guzman-Valenzuela, University of Chile, Chile; Glen Jones, University of Toronto, Canada; Barbara Kehm, University of Glasgow, UK; Jenny Lee, University of Arizona, USA; Ye Liu, King's College London, UK; Christine Musselin, Sciences Po, France; Alis Oancea, University of Oxford, UK; Imanol Ordorika, Universidad Nacional Autónoma de México, Mexico; Laura Perna, University of Pennsylvania, USA; Gary Rhoades, University of Arizona, USA; Susan Robertson, University of Cambridge, UK; Yang Rui, University of Hong Kong, Hong Kong; Pedro Teixeira, University of Porto, Portugal; Jussi Valimaa, University of Jyvaskyla, Finland; N. V. Varghese, National University of Educational Planning and Administration, India; Marijk van der Wende, University of Utrecht, The Netherlands; Po Yang, Peking University, China; Akiyoshi Yonezawa, Tohoku University, Japan

Also available in the series:

The Governance of British Higher Education: The Impact of Governmental, Financial and Market Pressures, Michael Shattock and Aniko Horvath

Changing Higher Education for a Changing World, edited by Claire Callender, William Locke, Simon Marginson

Changing Higher Education in India, edited by Saumen Chattopadhyay, Simon Marginson and N.V. Varghese

Changing Higher Education in East Asia, edited by Simon Marginson and Xin Xu

Forthcoming in the series:

The Governance of European Higher Education, Michael Shattock and Aniko Horvath

Universities and Regions, Michael Shattock and Aniko Horvath

Higher Education, State and Society

Comparing the Chinese and Anglo-American Approaches

Lili Yang

BLOOMSBURY ACADEMIC
LONDON • NEW YORK • OXFORD • NEW DELHI • SYDNEY

BLOOMSBURY ACADEMIC
Bloomsbury Publishing Plc
50 Bedford Square, London, WC1B 3DP, UK
1385 Broadway, New York, NY 10018, USA
29 Earlsfort Terrace, Dublin 2, Ireland

BLOOMSBURY, BLOOMSBURY ACADEMIC and the Diana logo are trademarks of
Bloomsbury Publishing Plc

First published in Great Britain 2023
This paperback edition published 2024

Copyright © Lili Yang, 2023

Lili Yang has asserted her right under the Copyright, Designs and Patents Act, 1988, to be identified as Author of this work.

For legal purposes the Acknowledgements on p. xiv constitute an extension of this copyright page.

Series Design by Adriana Brioso
Cover image © Setthasith Wansuksri/EyeEm/Getty Images

All rights reserved. No part of this publication may be reproduced or transmitted in any form or by any means, electronic or mechanical, including photocopying, recording, or any information storage or retrieval system, without prior permission in writing from the publishers.

Bloomsbury Publishing Plc does not have any control over, or responsibility for, any third-party websites referred to or in this book. All internet addresses given in this book were correct at the time of going to press. The author and publisher regret any inconvenience caused if addresses have changed or sites have ceased to exist, but can accept no responsibility for any such changes.

A catalogue record for this book is available from the British Library.

A catalog record for this book is available from the Library of Congress.

ISBN: HB: 978-1-3502-9343-4
PB: 978-1-3502-9347-2
ePDF: 978-1-3502-9344-1
eBook: 978-1-3502-9345-8

Series: Bloomsbury Higher Education Research

Typeset by Deanta Global Publishing Services, Chennai, India

To find out more about our authors and books visit www.bloomsbury.com and sign up for our newsletters.

Contents

List of Illustration vi
Series Editor's Foreword vii
Foreword xii
Acknowledgements xiv

1 Introduction 1

Part I: Cultural and Philosophical Foundations

2 The Higher Education-Related Chinese Tradition 25
3 The Higher Education-Related Anglo-American Tradition 48
4 A New Common Template for Comparison: The Five Key Themes 75

Part II: The Individual, Society, State and World in Higher Education

5 Student Development in Higher Education: *Xiushen* (Self-Cultivation) and *Bildung* 87
6 Equity in Higher Education: *Gongping* and Equity 107
7 Academic Freedom and University Autonomy: *Zhi* (the Free Will) and Liberty 127
8 The Resources and Outcomes of Higher Education: The *Gong*/Public and *Si*/Private 144
9 Global Outcomes of Higher Education: Global Public/Common Goods and *Tianxia Weigong* (All under Heaven Belongs to/is for All) 172

Part III: Trans-Positional Approaches to the Public (Good) in Higher Education

10 Comparison and Combination: Complementarities, Hybridizations and Synergies 193
11 Conclusion 218

References 227
Index 255

Illustration

Figures

1.1	The *yin–yang* symbol or *taiji*	19
2.1	The broadening process of the individual in Confucianism	29
3.1	Anglo-American spheres of social action	64
5.1	The expanding entities and *xiushen*	90
10.1	An outline of the comparison and complementarity between *xiushen* and *Bildung*	194
10.2	An outline of the comparison of (social) *gongping*/equity between the Chinese and Anglo-American traditions	200
10.3	An outline of the comparison between *zhi* (the free will) and liberty	205
10.4	An outline of the comparison between the Chinese *gong* and the Anglo-American public	211

Tables

1.1	The scholarship examined for the Chinese and Anglo-American traditions	8
2.1	Smaller self and larger self in the Chinese tradition	32
4.1	Moving from Chinese lexicon to Anglo-American lexicon	76
4.2	Moving from Anglo-American lexicon to Chinese lexicon	78

Series Editor's Foreword

Higher Education, State and Society: Comparing the Chinese and Anglo-American Approaches is the fifth book to be published in the Bloomsbury Higher Education Research book series. This series brings to the public, government and universities across the world the new ideas and research evidence being generated by researchers from the ESRC/OFSRE Centre for Global Higher Education.[1] The Centre for Global Higher Education (CGHE), a partnership of researchers from eleven UK and international universities, is the world's largest concentration of expertise in relation to higher education and its social contributions. The core focus of CGHE's work, and of the Bloomsbury Higher Education Research series, is higher education, especially the future of higher education in the changing global landscape.

Each year this mega-topic of 'higher education' seems to take on greater importance for governments, business, civil organizations, students, families and the public at large. In higher education much is at stake. The role and impact of the sector is growing everywhere. More than 235 million students enrol at tertiary level across the world, four-fifths of them in degree programmes. Over 40 per cent of school leavers now enter some kind of tertiary education each year, though resources and quality vary significantly. In North America and Europe that ratio rises to four young people in every five. Universities and colleges are seen as the primary medium for personal opportunity, social mobility and the development of whole communities. About 2.5 million new science papers are published worldwide each year and the role of research in industry and government continues to expand everywhere.

In short, there is much at stake in higher education. It has become central to social, economic, cultural and political life. One reason is that even while serving local society and national policy, the higher education and research sectors are especially globalized in character. Each year six million students change countries in order to enrol in their chosen study programme, and a

---

[1] The initials ESRC/OFSRE stand for the Economic and Social Research Council/Office for Students and Research England. Part of the original ESRC funding that supported the Centre for Global Higher Education's research work was sourced from the Higher Education Funding Council for England, the ancestor body to the OFS and RE. Research England continues to provide financial support for the research.

quarter of all published research papers involve joint authorship across national borders. In some countries fee-based international education is a major source of export revenues, while some other countries are losing talent in net terms each year. Routine cross-border movements of students, academics and researchers, knowledge, information and money help to shape not only nations but the international order itself.

At the same time, the global higher education landscape is changing with compelling speed, reflecting larger economic, political and cultural shifts in the geo-strategic setting. Though research universities in the United States (especially) and United Kingdom remain strong in comparative terms, the worldwide map of power in higher education is becoming more plural. A larger range of higher education practices, including models of teaching/learning, delivery, institutional organization and system, will shape higher education in future. Anglo-American (and Western) norms and models will be less dominant, and will themselves evolve. Rising universities and science in East Asia and Singapore are already reshaping the flow of knowledge and higher education. Latin America, South East Asia, India, Central Asia and the Arab nations have a growing global importance. The trajectories of education and research in sub-Saharan Africa are crucial to state-building and community development.

All of this has led to a more intensive focus on how higher education systems and institutions function and their value, performance, effectiveness, openness and sustainability. This in turn has made research on higher education more significant – both because it provides us with insights into one important facet of the human condition and because it informs evidence-based government policies and professional practices.

CGHE opened in late 2015 and is currently funded until October 2023. The centre investigates higher education using a range of social science disciplines including economics, sociology, political science and policy studies, psychology and anthropology, and uses a portfolio of quantitative, qualitative and synthetic-historical research techniques. It currently maintains ten research projects, variously of between eighteen months and eight years' duration, as well as smaller projects, and involves about forty active affiliated individual researchers. Over its eight-year span it is financed by about £10 million in funding from the UK Economic and Social Research Council, partner universities and other sources. Its UK researchers are drawn from the Universities of Oxford, Lancaster, Surrey, Bath and University College London. The headquarters of the centre are located at Oxford and there are large concentrations of researchers at both Oxford and UCL. The current affiliated international researchers are from Hiroshima University in Japan, Shanghai Jiao Tong University in China, Lingnan University in Hong Kong, Cape Town University in South Africa, Virginia Tech in the United States and Technological University Dublin. CGHE also collaborates with researchers from many other universities across the world, in seminars, conferences and exchange of papers. It runs an active programme of global webinars.

The centre has a full agenda. The unprecedented growth of mass higher education, the striving for excellence and innovation in the research university sector, and the changing global landscape pose many researchable questions for governments, societies and higher education institutions themselves. Some of these questions already figure in CGHE research projects. For example: What are the formative effects on societies and economies of the now much wider distribution of advanced levels of learning? How does it change individual graduates as people – and what does it mean when half or more of the workforce is higher educated and much more mobile; and when confident human agency has become widely distributed across civil and political society in nations with little state tradition, or where the main experience has been colonial or authoritarian rule? What does it mean when many more people are becoming steeped in the sciences, many others understand the world through the lenses of the social sciences or humanities and a third group are engaged in neither? What happens to those parts of the population left outside the formative effects of higher education? What is the larger public role and contribution of higher education, as distinct from the private benefits for and private effects on individual graduates? What does it mean when large and growing higher education institutions have become the major employers in many locations and help to sustain community and cultural life, almost like branches of local government while also being linked to global cities across the world? And what is the contribution of higher education, beyond helping to form the attributes of individual graduates, to the development of the emerging global society?

Likewise, the many practical problems associated with building higher education and science take on greater importance. How can scarce public budgets provide for the public role of higher education institutions, for a socially equitable system of individual access and for research excellence, all at the same time? What is the role for and limits of family financing and tuition loans systems? What is the potential contribution of private institutions, including for-profit colleges? In national systems, what is the best balance between research intensive and primarily teaching institutions, and between academic and vocational education? What are the potentials for technological delivery in extending access? What is happening in graduate labour markets, where returns to degrees are becoming more dispersed between families with differing levels of income, different kinds of universities and different fields of study? Do larger education systems provide better for social mobility and income equality? How does the internationalization of universities contribute to national policy and local societies? Does mobile international education expand opportunity or further stratify societies? What are the implications of new populist tensions between national and global goals, as manifest, for example, in the tensions over Brexit in the United Kingdom and the politics of the Trump era in the United States, for higher education and research? And always, what can national systems of higher education and science learn from each other, and how can they build stronger common ground?

In tackling these research challenges and bringing the research to all, we are very grateful to have the opportunity to work with such a high-quality publisher as Bloomsbury. In the book series, monographs are selected on the basis of their relevance to one or more of higher education policy, management, practice and theory. Topics range from teaching and learning and technologies, to research and its organization, the design parameters of national higher education systems, the public good role of higher education, social stratification and equity, institutional governance and management, and the cross-border mobility of people, programmes and ideas. Much of CGHE's work is global and comparative in scale, drawing lessons from higher education in many different countries, and the centre's cross-country and multi-project structure allows it to tap into the more plural higher education and research landscape that has emerged. The book series draws on authors from across the world and is prepared for relevance across the world.

CGHE places special emphasis on the relevance of its research, on communicating its findings and on maximizing the usefulness and impacts of those findings in higher education policy and practice. CGHE has a relatively high public profile for an academic research centre and reaches out to engage higher education stakeholders, national and international organizations, policymakers, regulators and the broader public, in the UK and across the world. These objectives are also central to the book series. Recognizing that the translation from research outputs to high-quality scholarly monographs is not always straightforward – while achieving impact in both academic and policy/practice circles is crucial – monographs in the book series are scrutinized critically before publication, for readability as well as quality. Texts are carefully written and edited to ensure that they have achieved the right combination of, on one hand, intellectual depth and originality and, on the other hand, full accessibility for public, higher education and policy circles across the world.

Simon Marginson
Professor of Higher Education, University of Oxford
Director, ESRC/OFSRE Centre for Global Higher Education

Foreword

In a time of geopolitical tension, with fears of another Cold War, anxiety and stress around an ongoing pandemic and a deepening climate crisis, the question of how universities should respond to these issues could not be more important. Of particular concern is the question of how universities can serve to bridge the deep divides in thought and understanding that characterize responses to each of these crises. Given China's status as a rising world power and increasing global presence, it is appropriate that the book has an early chapter on the Sinic tradition of higher education that takes the reader back to higher institutions long pre-dating the European university that consolidated China's role as the 'central country' (中國 *Zhongguo*) receiving tribute widely until challenged by European powers. One of the core themes that runs through the book is the distinction between the public good and the broader concept of the common good recently put forward by UNESCO, and resonating with China's concept of 'all under heaven being shared' (天下為公 *tianxia weigong*), which is elaborated in Chapter 9.

Chapter 3 introduces the Anglo-American tradition, with its roots in European philosophical thought quite distinct from the Confucian, Daoist and Legalist traditions that shaped Chinese higher education. Given the dominant influence of this tradition on the current global research university, it is helpful to have a discussion of how the German concept of *Bildung* found its way into the Anglo-American tradition through thinkers such as John Dewey and Amartya Sen. Sen's work has also been valuable in suggesting trans-positional analysis as an approach to comparison across these two traditions whereby concepts on each side are set against each other in ways that make it possible to see both what is shared and what is divergent. This is the genius of a volume that enables the reader to grasp where common ground is already evident, also to be challenged to a deeper understanding of differences that need to be bridged in a shared commitment to the common good.

Of the five themes that are explored in Part II, perhaps the greatest common ground is found in Chapter 5, the area of student development, with a fascinating juxtaposition of the Confucian notion of self-cultivation (修身 *xiushen*) and the German concept of *Bildung*. The implications of these two concepts are explored in terms of the university's responsibility for forming global citizens true to themselves while also responsible to both the local and global community. Chapter 7 takes up the more contentious issue of academic freedom and autonomy, a key focus of the Anglo-American tradition and one often misunderstood in Western views of state control over Chinese higher education. The elaboration of the Chinese term for moral autonomy (志zhi) as a parallel to liberty in the Western context enables the reader to understand how Chinese scholars have used their intellectual authority to speak truth to power with great courage, in spite of the absence of a legal charter giving the institution protection from direct state intervention until most recently. Three further themes are transposed in other chapters, enabling readers to explore how issues of social equity are interpreted in each tradition, the distinction between public and private on each side and finally the ways in which the ideas of the common good and the public good both differ and overlap.

This brings us back to the current demands facing universities in the Sinic and Anglo-American worlds to find pathways of cooperation that enable scholars on both sides to enter into relationships of profound mutual respect and deepened understanding of the other, as they join hands to collaborate in teaching, research and service for the common good. On the geopolitical side, cooperation in the fields of history and the social sciences may be crucial to preserving and consolidating peaceful coexistence across deep divides. On the side of the natural sciences, the serious threats both to human health and the health of the planet call for unprecedented levels of joint exploration into causes and potential solutions for climate change and all of its impacts. The effort made in this volume to bridge the Sinic and Anglo-American worlds of thought and understanding thus could not be more timely! The reader also needs to be aware of the rich connotations of the Chinese concepts that are introduced and explained and the impossibility of finding English terms that can encompass all of their dimensions.

Ruth Hayhoe, Professor, University of Toronto
President Emerita, The Education University of Hong Kong

Acknowledgements

Working on *Higher Education, State and Society: Comparing the Chinese and Anglo-American Approaches* was an adventure to the unknown, full of joy, excitement, as well as uncertainties. This research was set out with no predetermined destinations. What would the Chinese and Anglo-American traditions tell us about the state, society, higher education and the intersections between them? What are the differences between the two approaches? Do they share similarities? Are there possibilities for combinations? How can that be achieved? These were the guiding questions throughout the whole journey. In my eyes, this book is a result of listening to, following, having conversations with and critiquing ideas in the two rich traditions.

The research was inspired by the notion that creativity is often sparked by the collision of ideas from different cultures, traditions and civilizations. The Chinese and Anglo-American traditions, as two important human traditions, not only have much to offer by themselves but have the potential to lead to fruitful outcomes when being compared and combined. In a world marked by arms race mindsets today, one of the most important and urgent things for us is to understand, respect and appreciate ourselves and others. To quote Chinese intellectual Fei Xiaotong's words:

Find your beauty,
And that of others;
Share the beauty;
And achieve harmony.
(各美其美，美人之美，美美与共，天下大同)

The book is the culmination of a doctoral project that took place in the University of Oxford and two other universities (University College London and the University of Hong Kong). It has been a true pleasure and privilege to work between and engage with the East and the West, physically and epistemologically, though through the lens of a specific focus and with a limited scope. Working on the book was rewarding too. It shaped my thinking, identities and the commitment to moving between the Eastern and Western intellectual traditions.

Acknowledgements

In carrying out this research, I have received tremendous support, help and advice from my doctoral supervisors, mentors, colleagues and friends. I owe a huge debt to my two doctoral supervisors at the University of Oxford, Simon Marginson and Alis Oancea, who provided continuous encouragement, intellectual inspiration, critique and detailed comments. Simon introduced me to this rich research field, read everything line by line as soon as it was written and changed each version of the drafts for the better. I also thank Simon for supporting me in preparing and delivering this book as the series editor. Alis is always caring and sympathetic. She has set a magnificent example of how to conduct conceptual research with rigour and pushed me to rethink things that I took for granted. Vincent Carpentier also supervised and helped me in conducting this research in the early stage.

I am deeply thankful to Yang Rui for his inspiration, mentoring, guidance, support and help. Rui was the external co-supervisor of the doctoral project and provided me with huge support during my exchange study at the University of Hong Kong. In each of our conversations, I had the feeling of *ti hu guan ding*, literally meaning to be filled with wisdom. His scholarship attitudes and true love for the Chinese culture are always inspiring. I also wish to express my sincere gratitude towards Ruth Hayhoe who is an exemplar scholar with a truly warm heart. Ruth is encouraging and generous with her advice and comments. I appreciate her feedback that helped me to improve the work and thank her for kindly agreeing to write a foreword for the book.

I would like to thank Andy Green, Tristan McCowan, James Robson, Lynn McAlpine, Heath Rose, Thomas Brotherhood, Arzhia Habibi and Xu Xin for providing useful feedback and comments at different stages of the work. Special thanks also to colleagues of Project 1.1 and later Project 8 at the Centre for Global Higher Education, including Liu Niancai, Huang Futao, Tian Lin, Carolina Guzman-Valenzuela, Krystian Szadkowski, Aline Courtois and Kiyomi Horiuchi, for many constructive discussions. The book also benefited from conversations with and suggestions from Marijk van der Wende, Maia Chankseliani, David Mills, Susan Robertson, Shen Wenqin, Mok Ka Ho, Wen Wen, Steven G. Brint, Shi Zhongying, Yuan He, Soyoung Lee, Giulio Marini, Zheng Gaoming, Ma Ying, Li Mengyang, Xie Meng, Ruan Nian, Lin Cong, Yusuf Oldac, Jihyun Lee and Wongyong Park. I ask for forgiveness of anyone else whose name I have unintentionally omitted. This work has received financial support from the UK Economic and Social Research Council, Department of Education and Linacre College of the University of Oxford and University College London-Institute of Education.

Equally important is the support I have received of other kinds. I am thankful to my master's supervisor Yuan Bentao who passed away before I finished this book, my dear colleagues and friends, Wang Dingming, Wang Chuanyi, Ning Ke, Wang Fangfang, Zhang Yun and Kang Yuyang. This research also received help from administrative staff at the Centre for Global Higher Education, including Trevor Treharne, Eleanor Gaspar, Carolyn Gallop and Anna Philips. I am grateful to Bloomsbury editors Alison Baker and Anna Elliss for their excellent work in processing this book.

I would like to express my deepest gratitude to my family, including my grandparents, parents and husband, for their immense and unconditional love. I was stuck in my hometown in Hubei, China, for nine months in 2020 when the Covid-19 pandemic broke out. It was during this time that the first draft of the book was written. I thank my grandparents and parents for tolerating my exclusive focus on writing and for feeding and mentally supporting me meanwhile. Special thanks to my husband, Xiangwei, for the life shared while the work was being done. I could not have finished this book without the unending love, patience, support and encouragement from them. To me, they are the *ai de gang wan* (harbour of love).

I thank several publishers for permission to incorporate previously published material, which has been revised accordingly and integrated into the overall line of argument:

- Springer in relation to Chapter 5, largely published in the article 'Student Formation in Higher Education: A Comparison and Combination of Confucian Xiushen (Self-Cultivation) and Bildung in *Higher Education*'.
- Elsevier in relation to Chapter 6, largely published in the article 'Social Equity and Equity in Higher Education: A Comparison of the Anglo-American and Chinese Political Cultures in *International Journal of Educational Development*'.

Lili Yang (杨力苈)
The University of Hong Kong
Hong Kong SAR
8 February 2022

1

Introduction

1.1 What This Book Is About

The title of this book is *Higher Education, State and Society: Comparing the Chinese and Anglo-American Approaches*. As the title suggests, this book investigates and compares approaches to higher education, state and society in the Chinese (Chinese civilizational) and Anglo-American traditions. The central focus is *the public (good) of higher education*, which is understood and explored through the intersections between higher education and four primary spheres of social action, including the individual, society, state and world. These two traditions are each profoundly influential in the world today and are also very different, though there are also important overlaps. By comparing the approach taken in the Chinese and English-speaking worlds, the aim is to establish a broader and more comprehensive understanding of the public (good) of higher education that can work on a cross-cultural basis and facilitate mutual understanding and cooperation in higher education between contexts across the world.

Higher education plays a public role and produces public goods (J. Williams 2016). However, there has long been a lack of clarity about what this means in each single tradition, and the lack of clarity is compounded at world level by the very different understandings between the traditions. This affects cooperation and common action. For example, what do we mean when we say 'higher education and research should contribute to the global public good'. What is the global public good here? As the book will demonstrate, understandings and practices of the public (good) of higher education are closely related to political and educational cultures, including assumptions about the responsibilities of government, state–university relations and the relations between individualism and the collective good. Because these aspects are understood differently in different cultural contexts, there are varying approaches to the public (good) of higher education. This leads to differences in educational and institutional practices in the respective university and college systems. But it is also possible to identify suggestive and fruitful parallels, overlaps and intersections between the different approaches.

This book goes beyond superficial comparisons of East and West. It works at the foundational level of the core ideas in each tradition, unpacking the similarities, differences and potential for conceptual complementarities, hybridizations and synergies between the guiding traditions in the Chinese world and those in the English-speaking world, especially Britain and the United States. The core ideas in each tradition are not just words, they shape contemporary higher education systems and institutions. In both traditions, higher education has a key role in the public good, but this has a partly different meaning in each case. On one hand, there is the Anglo-American tradition of the English-speaking countries in which the state is separated from civil society and the market. On the other hand, there is the Chinese tradition, in which the state has a comprehensive role that takes in all aspects including higher education. These differences are associated with differences in educational culture as well. Together, each package of cultural ideas, in politics and education, has led to different ideas about the public good of society and the way this should be pursued in higher education. The differences and similarities between the traditions really matter, because arguably, these are the two most influential sets of ideas in the world today, not only in relation to evolving higher education systems but more generally in government and society. There is much at stake in the differences, similarities and relations between China and Anglo-America.

To undertake the comparison, the book employs a *two-step trans-positional comparative methodology*, built on Amartya Sen's trans-positional analysis. Following an account of that methodology, the book starts with an exploration of broad cultural and philosophical ideas underlying the public (good) of higher education in each case. The exploration reveals the social imaginaries of the two traditions, which vary in their understandings of four primary spheres of social action – the spheres of individual, society, the state and the world – and the relations between the four spheres. The book compares the two social imaginaries and then examines how higher education interacts with the four spheres of social action. Five key themes of the public (good) of higher education are identified in this process, demonstrating the intersection between higher education and the individual, society, the state and the world.

The five key themes are *individual student development in higher education, equity in higher education, academic freedom and university autonomy in higher education, the resources and outcomes of higher education, and cross-border higher education activities and higher education's global outcomes*. Each theme, and the comparison between the two traditions in each theme, is captured by a pair of terms consisting of a Chinese term and an English/Western term: *xiushen* (self-cultivation) and *Bildung*, *gongping* (equity) and equity, *zhi* (the free will) and liberty, *gong*/public and *si*/private, and *tianxia weigong* (all under heaven belongs to/is for all) and global public/common goods. *Bildung* is a German term widely used in English-language education. The conceptual investigation of the public (good) of higher education in the two traditions centres around the exploration of these five themes. The comparison and search for complementarities, hybridizations and synergies are also organized around the five themes. The comparison and combination further lead to five trans-positional arguments concerning of the public (good) of higher education.

1.2 The Investigation

Education is essential to the renewal and continuation of societies – 'education, and education alone, spans the gap' between generations (Dewey [1916] 2011: 6). With more than 235 million students enrolled in tertiary education across the world in 2020 (UNESCO 2020), higher education has become a powerful sector with the potential to shape societies.

Higher education plays numerous social and public functions. This is realized through the interactions between higher education and various spheres of social action including the individual, society, state and the world. For example, higher education produces research-based new knowledge and advances technologies, provides channels for upward social mobility and contributes to social equity, and transforms students and prepares them to become desirable members of societies. Higher education is also shaped by those spheres of social action. The state/society/higher education assemblage to a large extent determines higher education's missions, organizations and activities. The existence and development of higher education largely rely on the pattern of financial investment from the individual, government and society. Higher education organization and governance need to align with the political structure of the society it is embedded in. The responsibilities and functions of higher education are relevant to the social expectations of higher education. The ways of higher education being shaped reflect how diverse approaches to the public (good) across contexts can mould higher education variously.

However, it remains ambiguous about what the public (good) means in higher education, especially in the context of higher education undergoing multiple transformations amid globalization and the changing role of the state. The idea of public (good) derives historically from the formation of nation-states and political theories about the state's responsibilities and obligations (Neubauer 2008). Nevertheless, the public (good) idea still points to an interesting and important approach to understanding higher education – that is primarily concerned to (re-)imagine higher education through its interaction with the wider society by exploring political and educational cultures of the society in which higher education is embedded. This is what this book attempts to achieve.

There is not a universal political and educational culture. Yet, the mainstream of the existing discussion of the public (good) of higher education arguably mainly assumes the political and educational cultures in Anglo-American societies. A distinctive example is the influential economic formula raised by Samuelson (1954) of public/private goods, which is based on the imaginary of capitalist societies. However, problems may arise when societies attempt to employ the Anglo-American-based interpretations of the public (good) in higher education, particularly in contexts marked by alternative political and educational cultures. For example, Samuelson's formula assumes a minimal state that steps in only when the market fails. This assumption is at odds with the state/society/market relations as configured in, say, Nordic social democracies or Chinese socialist society.

There also exist different languages and ideas to understand and interpret the public (good) of higher education across cultures. Not all languages have the equivalence of the English term of 'public (good)'. Varied understandings have led to distinct approaches to public policy and funding, university governance and autonomy, and quality and accessibility of higher education (Filippakou and Williams 2015). Investigations of the public (good) of higher education need to embed in a certain political and educational culture.

Nevertheless, higher education is globally connected in the same global common space. The mere embeddedness in a single political and educational culture is not enough to explain higher education phenomena, especially those involving cross-border research collaboration, international knowledge sharing and individual mobility (Marginson 2018c). The existing divergences regarding the political and educational cultures not only limit the understanding of the public (good) in higher education from different perspectives but also form ideological and practical gaps that hinder international cooperation between worldwide higher education systems and institutions. We need to transcend the mere embeddedness in a single political and educational culture, and aim to establish narratives that may work on a cross-cultural basis. Understanding similarities and differences between political and educational cultures in order to devise a cross-cultural approach to the public (good) in higher education is a possible means to better explain relevant higher education phenomena, facilitate cross-cultural dialogue and understanding, and help each context to better understand themselves. Better mutual- and self-understanding will further assist in building closer cooperation between universities across the world.

The Chinese and Anglo-American traditions are selected for many reasons. From Samuel Huntington's (1996) statement of 'the clash of civilizations and the remaking of world order' to the judgement that 'our century will be an Asian century' (Maçaes 2019: 1), it is almost a truism that the Chinese and Anglo-American traditions are two key civilizational traditions in understanding the future of our world. In higher education, modern university models and higher education systems, which have been implemented in different societies, are largely shaped by the models of the Anglo-American research university and the Anglo-American ways of organizing higher education (Altbach and Balán 2007). China, however, is developing at an extraordinary rate and is arguably a rising star in the global research system (Marginson 2018a). Instead of entirely employing the Anglo-American or Western university models and higher education systems, China is exploring a new approach to developing higher education with 'Chinese characteristics (*zhongguo tese*)'. Arguably, the two types of the higher education system and university model are either already influential or may become more globally important in the future. Comparing the two traditions is expected to have high relevance in worldwide higher education.

The two traditions are also different in many aspects, as the book will demonstrate. The differences make the comparison likely to lead to more generative results than comparisons between those traditions with more similarities – say, between the Anglo-American and the French traditions. While the comparison can help the two traditions better understand themselves, it is also possible to derive new ways of addressing the existing problems by combining ideas from the two traditions.

1.3 The Two Traditions Relevant to the Public (Good) in Higher Education

Tradition refers to a 'repeated pattern of behaviours, beliefs, or enactment passed down from one generation to the next. Traditions are culturally recognised and sustained' (McCormick and White 2011: 1198). It emphasizes the continuity and passing down of ideas, values and customs (including implicit ones) throughout generations. Although these ideas, values and customs were created in the past, their influence is maintained and still apparent in the present. Tradition's present influence is one of the main reasons why it is worth exploring. However, it can be challenging to try to fully capture traditions that have emerged and persisted over a long span of time.

For the traditions that have been passed down for hundreds or even thousands of years, the content of, and the present influence of, the traditions can be complex. Further, the ways that different traditions have progressed with engagements and contributions from multiple generations can vary greatly. For example, although there is a classic Greek foundation of liberalism, and there are liberal thinkers who frequently refer back to classic Greek philosophy, liberalism arguably can be understood as a post-Reformation school of thought in the Anglo-American tradition (Ryan 2012; see later discussion). Differently, the origin of the Chinese tradition, comprising of, for example, Confucianism and Daoism, needs to be dated back to at least the Zhou Dynasty (around 1046–256 BCE). In terms of Confucianism, the later revision and development of classic Confucianism such as Neo-Confucianism and New Confucianism still centre around the classic Confucian texts, and aim at renewing and reinterpreting those texts in the context of the day. Notably, in this book, the two traditions are examined by focusing on these schools of thought in relation to higher education, which embody important beliefs and tenets of the traditions.

In the English-speaking world, there are various approaches to understanding the 'public (good)' in higher education that are sourced in economics and political philosophy/science respectively, but both draw on a common heritage: the political culture of the limited liberal state, civic republican tradition and an emphasis on individual liberty (Marginson 2018b). The Chinese tradition of 'the public (good)' in higher education originated in China at an earlier time than the post-Reformation and Enlightenment period in England. The Chinese approach to higher education is grounded in the Confucian anthropocosmic worldview and the tradition of having a comprehensive state that is often supreme in relation to the market and society (see more about this in Chapter 2).

Regardless of the differences in approach, both traditions have strengths as well as limitations in capturing and explaining the public (good) in higher education. They are facing conceptual and methodological difficulties. While being successful in terms of capturing economic benefits of higher education, the Anglo-American tradition faces difficulty in explaining higher education's non-pecuniary public goods such as social goods and public-related values (Marginson and Yang 2021). Meanwhile, it also shares with the Chinese tradition methodological difficulties in quantifying the amount of 'public goods' of higher education (Marginson 2018h). Another limitation of the Anglo-American tradition lies in the global dimension. It under-recognizes higher education's contributions to the global public good (Marginson 2018h). This limitation, as the book argues, can be mitigated by taking into account the Chinese idea of all under heaven (*tianxia*), which anticipates a global ecological imagining.

In contrast, the Chinese tradition is more comfortable with higher education's social and cultural goods in addition to economic goods. It draws on a wide range of virtues that higher education may contribute to, such as public-related values and social cohesion and harmony, though these are often visualized inside the state because of a long history of the state supervising and limiting the communicative social dimension. However, there is a long-standing neglect of the private good in the Chinese tradition – the public-private boundary is blurred (Huang and Jiang 2005: xi). Meanwhile, since the mid-nineteenth century, the Chinese tradition has been experiencing changes and transformations, under the influence of Western ideologies such as (neo-)liberalism and Marxism-Leninism. The Chinese interpretation of the public (good) of higher education itself remains unclear. While the comparison can help the two traditions better understand themselves, it is also possible to derive new ways of addressing the existing problems by combining ideas from the two traditions.

However, before getting into details about how the two traditions approach the public (good) in higher education, it is necessary to explain what the Chinese tradition and the Anglo-American tradition refer to in the book. To clarify, the book does not intend to comprehensively review and explore the broader philosophical and social traditions. The aim is to confine the inquiry to what each says about matters bearing on conceptions of the public (good) in higher education that may help explain relevant higher education phenomena across contexts.

1.3.1 The Higher Education-Related Chinese Tradition

The term 'Chinese tradition' is often used in the literature to represent the tradition that has been greatly influenced by ancient Chinese civilization, especially Confucianism (Reischauer 1974). In this book, the notion of Chinese tradition is used in an abstract and idea-centred way, rather than as a geopolitical designation. It emphasizes a shared cultural heritage of ancient Chinese thought

Table 1.1 The Scholarship Examined for the Chinese and Anglo-American Traditions

Tradition	The scholarship examined
Chinese tradition	Confucianism (including classic Confucianism in the pre-Qin period, pre-221 BCE), Neo-Confucianism (mainly in Song and Ming Dynasties, 960–1644) and New Confucianism (since the Republican period of China, post 1912), supplemented by Daoism and the Law School, as relevant, especially to higher learning Encounters between Confucianism, liberalism and Marxism-Leninism between the nineteenth and twentieth centuries, as relevant, especially to higher education
	Mixed influence of Confucianism (and Daoism), (neo-)liberalism and Marxism-Leninism in the People's Republic of China (1949–), as relevant, especially to higher education; works on the five key themes in the field of higher education studies
Anglo-American tradition	Scholarship of liberalism in the United Kingdom and the United States (as relevant, especially to higher education): including the work of John Locke, Adam Smith, John Stuart Mill, John Dewey, John Rawls, Amartya Sen; critiques of neoliberalism (as relevant, especially to higher education); works on the five key themes in the field of higher education studies

among many (East) Asian countries (e.g., China, Japan, North and South Korea, and Vietnam) (for the cultural heritage in these countries, see, e.g., S. Lee 2014; Scalapino 1988; Tu 1989).

Early Chinese ideas (especially pre-Qin ideas, pre-221 BCE), in particular Confucianism, spread among numerous East Asian countries mainly during the Tang and Song Dynasties (618–1279) (for the spread of ideas, see, e.g., H. Chang 1997; Zhang et al. 2005). The common tradition has far-reaching influence on those (East) Asian countries. But each of them has adopted its unique way to develop and interpret the ancient Chinese thought in the context of its local traditions, and there is evident diversity among these countries. Nevertheless, even after continuous encounters with, and different strategies of, learning from the West since the eighteenth century, countries influenced by the Chinese tradition still share a certain common cultural heritage. For example, the Sinologist de Bary (1984: 9) argues against the equation of East Asian countries' modernization with Westernization.

In these countries, higher education especially is a field that has demonstrated evident common features, largely influenced by Confucianism. Despite different development trajectories of higher education in these countries, influences from Confucian political and educational cultures have left attributes among their higher education systems. For example, in a comparative study between college students in mainland China, Korea, Japan and Taiwan, Zhang and colleagues (2005) discover the existence of a set of Confucian values shared among the students, including interpersonal harmony, relational hierarchy and traditional conservatism. Furthermore, Marginson (2014b: 91) highlights four common features among East Asian countries that facilitated the take-off of their higher education: 'the comprehensive Chinese state, Confucian education in the home, an effective response to Western modernization, and economic growth sufficient to pay for educational infrastructure and research'.

However, despite the shared heritage, the book does not include the discussion of the higher education of all of the countries influenced by ancient Chinese civilization. The Chinese tradition considered here primarily refers to the mainland Chinese tradition. However, the term 'Chinese tradition' draws attention to the cultural and civilizational domain of the ideas that are discussed here. These ideas are not co-terminal with, or determined by, the modern nation-state of China or its boundaries, or any of the previous definitions of the country in the Imperial era. Like the Anglo-American ideas also under discussion in the book, they have a larger presence than one nation alone and might be capable of broad influence.

In this context, it is important to also consider the time period of the 'Chinese tradition'. The Chinese tradition gradually evolved since at least the Shang Dynasty, around 1600–1046 BCE, and has been influenced by many schools of thought, some of them more than 2,000 years old. For discussions of these Chinese schools of thought and how they have influenced China, see, for example, de Bary and Lufrano (2001) and Zürcher (2007). Connotations of the Chinese tradition have developed and changed over time, and there have been various interpretations of the main or dominant Chinese tradition in different time periods. For discussions of the change of the connotations of the Chinese tradition, see, for example, Bell (2010), and Chang and Kalmanson (2010).

In the pre-Qin period, the Chinese tradition reflected multiple schools of thought, including Confucianism, Daoism and the Law School. These schools of thought have since remained fundamental to the evolution of the Chinese tradition since then. Among them, Confucian ideas, especially those regarding ethical, social and political order, became the roots of Chinese people's moral imagination, guiding the way of governance in Imperial China and shaping social relationships in Chinese society until today (Chan 2013: 2). Confucian thoughts on learning have been a foundational pillar of the Chinese educational culture (T. H. C. Lee 2000). From the West Han Dynasty (206 BCE–25 CE) onwards, when Confucianism became the only official ideology in Imperial China, the term 'Chinese tradition' has become largely associated with Confucianism (R. Yang 2018).

The Chinese tradition in this book mainly considers indigenous Chinese ideas – and especially Confucianism – as the ideological foundation. These ideas continue to be essential in shaping the public (good) of higher education in China. However, the primary focus on Confucianism is also supplemented by Daoism and the Law School. The book also considers the influence of Western knowledge since 1840.

The book does not cover the whole scope of Confucianism, nor does it provide a comprehensive account of it. Instead, it selects high points in the formation of Confucianism that have exerted far-reaching influence on Confucian arguments in relation to higher education. These high points often represent changes concerning how Chinese people regard the state, society, individual and higher education. The main high point is classic Confucianism, or Orthodox Confucianism, in the pre-Qin period. During this period, fundamental Confucian arguments were raised by early Confucian scholars, represented by Confucius (551–479 BCE), Mencius (around 372–289 BCE) and Xunzi (around 316–237 BCE). Classic Confucianism, formed around 2,500 years ago, has been the core basis for interpreting Confucianism throughout history and is still highly relevant to contemporary higher education practice. However, I also pay special attention to important refinements and amendments of classic Confucian arguments made by later scholars, for example, Neo-Confucianism in the Song and Ming Dynasties (960–1644) and New Confucianism in the twentieth century. These discussions of later developments of classic Confucianism also highlight that Confucianism is ever evolving as a school of thought, with an immense capacity to be reconstructed, partly through hybridizing with other schools of thought, to re-present itself in the contemporary world. Nevertheless, the primary emphasis of the book is on classic Confucianism.

In addition, as noted, Confucian discussions are supplemented by consideration of Daoism and the Law School, which emerged at much the same time as classic Confucianism, and were also influential over the course of Imperial Chinese history (for discussions on these schools of thought in Imperial China, see, e.g., Tang 2015). The reasons for this are twofold. First, Confucianism developed itself and experienced changes by learning from other schools of thought, particularly Daoism. Daoism has played a determining role in shaping Chinese epistemology. Examples include the *yin–yang* philosophy (see later). The important Confucian notions *tiandao* (heaven's way) and *rendao* (humanity's way) were developed based on the Daoist concept *dao* (the way) (see further discussion in Chapter 2). Second, while regarding Confucianism as the official ideology, the Law School, though in an opposing position to classic Confucianism in many respects, was adopted by many Imperial Chinese dynasties in order to help them tackle real social and political problems. Examples include the legislation and institutionalization of Confucian moral hierarchy and values (which in classic Confucianism were not seen as compulsory) by the Imperial authority. Supplementing Confucianism with Daoism and the Law School is important in helping to interpret Confucianism, as well as in explaining political, social and educational institutions in both Imperial and contemporary China.

The Chinese-Western encounters since the mid-nineteenth century are also examined. The book particularly highlights the influence of Western liberalism and Marxism-Leninism, and the appearance of modern universities in China. It also considers how the contemporary Chinese higher education system draws on the Confucian heritage, Western liberalism and Marxism-Leninism, and the capitalist influence since the Reform and Opening-up Policy (1978).

1.3.2 The Higher Education-Related Anglo-American Tradition

The book understands the higher education-related Anglo-American tradition as the tradition of liberalism in relation to higher education, concentrating on the limited liberal state and individual liberty (see more about this in Chapter 3). The conceptual exploration of the Anglo-American tradition does not aim to include all of its connected origins and schools of thought. Consideration of the higher education-related Anglo-American tradition only includes theses in liberalism, and this study's conceptual exploration mainly draws on works from liberal scholars. Although both the United Kingdom and the United States have been influenced by many other countries' philosophical ideas, especially those from France and Germany, I mainly examine works in the United Kingdom and the United States.

Scholars sometimes discuss the ancient Chinese ideas of the Spring and Autumn period and the Warring States period when sages such as Confucius, Mencius and Xunzi lived alongside Greek ideas from the classical era when philosophers such as Plato and Aristotle lived (see, e.g., Hartnett 2011). The two groups overlapped in time. Classic Greek philosophy has influenced today's Anglo-American tradition in fundamental ways. The Anglo-American texts that I examine in the book also have roots in classic Greek philosophy. For example, the central value of liberalism – freedom – attracted attention from classic Greek philosophers such as Plato and Aristotle (for the roots of liberalism in classic

Greek philosophy, see, e.g., Manent 1996; Strauss 1959). However, although liberalism draws on classic Greek philosophy, it has departed from classic Greek philosophy and has developed into a new school of thought. Higher education, especially American research universities, gradually developed into contemporary systems from the nineteenth century onwards. Typically, the ideas of von Humboldt (2000)[1] and Newman ([1852] 1996) concerning the university greatly influenced Anglo-American universities today. In addition, the political culture in contemporary Anglo-American societies is also largely shaped by the post-Reformation schools of thought represented by liberalism (see, e.g., Hobhouse 1911/1964 for discussions of the lineage of liberal thought).

Therefore, while I refer back to classic Greek philosophy from time to time, the primary focus is on the work of modern liberal scholars. Specifically, the study's exploration includes works of John Locke, Adam Smith, John Stuart Mill, John Dewey, John Rawls and Amartya Sen. The selected liberal scholars all belong to the post-Reformation period and have contributed greatly to the development of liberalism (see, e.g., Hobhouse, 1911/1964; Ryan 2012). Some of their works are frequently discussed and referenced still today. Arguably, their contentions not only influence scholarly works but have largely shaped aspects of higher education practice. Investigating their works is enlightening in depicting the public (good) in higher education (see also Chapter 11). Further, in order to have a specific emphasis on higher education, I also include contemporary higher education studies, especially those relevant to the public (good) of higher education.

1.4 Exploration, Comparison and Combination of Ideas

Although the book aims to achieve numerous aims, it has just one principal research question containing two interrogate components – *What are the similarities and differences between notions of 'public (good)' in the Chinese and Anglo-American traditions, in relation to higher education? Is there potential for hybridizations, synergies and complementarities between the two traditions?* As will be explained, the book pursues this programme, including scholarship-based exploration, comparison and trans-positional reconstruction through a two-step trans-positional comparative methodology.

---

[1] The specific written year of *Theorie der Bildung des Menschen* by von Humboldt was unclear, around 1793.

1.4.1 Methodological Challenges for Comparison and Combination

Relevant concepts of the public (good) are culturally specific. Unpacking the public (good) in higher education normally requires scholars/researchers to ground their analysis in a certain political and educational culture while taking in relevant aspects that shape the public (good) of higher education, including the relationship between individualized and collective goods, the role of the state, the university–state and university–society relationships, and higher education's missions. This embeddedness in a context, together with the variation between cultures, means that it is difficult to develop a set of interpretations that can work across contexts. The task then becomes to move beyond one specific context, but without losing embeddedness as such, by developing interpretations of conceptions of the public (good) of higher education that can help explain relevant higher education phenomena in more than one context while also facilitating cross-cultural dialogue and understanding.

On the one hand, there is a need to explore the public (good) in higher education in multiple contexts rather than simply borrow concepts developed in Anglo-American contexts. On the other hand, we need to develop a set of interpretations of conceptions, drawing on ideas from more than one context, that may effectively capture the public (good) in higher education on a cross-cultural basis. The two methodological steps mentioned here are linked, as the book devises interpretations of the public (good) in higher education that is common to the contexts of Chinese and Anglo-American traditions.

For this book, a comparative methodology is needed that enables deep embeddedness in the scholarship of both higher education-related Chinese and Anglo-American traditions. The comparative component of the methodology should not privilege one tradition over the other and should contain the potential to derive combined views of the public (good) of higher education from both traditions. This methodology also needs to address the problems of comparing scholarly traditions, including the cross-cultural and lexical challenges.

The comparison of scholarly traditions faces the challenge of finding a common template for cross-cultural comparison that is not guided solely by one scholarly tradition. Addressing this challenge is key in privileging one tradition over the other as little as possible. The fact that the public (good) of higher education is essentially an Anglo-American concept and there only exists approximations of it rather than equivalence in the Chinese tradition (see details in Chapter 8) makes the cross-cultural comparison especially challenging.

Relating to the cross-cultural challenges are lexical challenges. It is difficult for researchers to do comparisons without changing connotations and denotations of concepts after translation. This is especially the case when comparative studies concern nonmaterial traits and require language switches (Osgood 1964). Not all concepts in a language have direct counterparts in another language (Sadiq 2010), and even when direct counterparts in another language can be identified, the original concepts' functions can be different from those of the counterparts. Meanwhile, owing to different cultures underlying the different languages, many concepts in a specific language have unique connotations and denotative uses (Osgood 1964). The uniqueness is lost in the process of translation into another language. Difficulties and problems in translation issues have long been studied by linguists (see, e.g., Lucy 1994; Moindjie 2006). However, they are often overlooked by researchers doing comparative studies. Moreover, when doing comparative studies involving English and another language, in cases when the research outputs are written in English, the other language is often underprivileged.

To the best of my knowledge, there is no existing established comparative methodology that could serve the above needs of the book and effectively tackle its challenges. I have, therefore, developed a novel methodology specific for the book. The methodology developed is a two-step trans-positional comparative methodology, informed by Amartya Sen's idea of 'trans-positional' assessment.

1.4.2 Trans-Positional Assessment

Observations are unavoidably position-based, but scientific reasoning need not, of course, be based on observational information from one specific position only. There is a need for what may be called 'trans-positional' assessment – drawing on but going beyond different positional observations. The constructed 'view from nowhere' would then be based on synthesizing different views from distinct positions (Sen 2002: 467). Sen states that partiality is an outcome of the individual's position from which observations and judgements are made. He seeks for ways to make 'impartial observations'. However, people's observations are determined by their position vis-à-vis the objects of observation, which relies upon sets of parameters that include physical conditions such as locations, and the observer's personal perspectives.

Nagel (1989: 5) argues that objectivity is in the form of invariance with respect to individual observers and their positions. It is a 'view from nowhere'. However, Sen (1993: 127) opposes this argument by stating that this conception could be in tension with observations that cannot escape positionality, especially those in dealing with objectivity of elementary observational claims. According to Sen (1993: 127), objectivity is in fact a view from a 'delineated somewhere' and that different people would have the same observations from similar positions. For example, as Sen notes, people, though with different background knowledge, would all agree that the African continent is located in the South if they stand in the Northern Hemisphere.

However, by taking in more than one position, the scope for objective observation and judgement, in Sen's sense, is enriched. Sen (1993) suggests the device of trans-positional analysis. People's observations depend on their locational positions and their knowledge. Sen (1993) argues that objective inquiry needs to begin with positional observation-based knowledge and then go beyond that to achieve trans-positional objectivity. Trans-positional analysis entails 'drawing on but going beyond different positional observations' without negating the respective observations themselves (Sen 2002: 467). This allows the observer to move beyond cultural relativism without normalizing one particular cultural viewpoint by synthesizing different views from distinct positions (Sen 1993: 130).

Although Sen does not set up a concrete methodology here, his ideas of trans-positional analysis point out a methodological approach for the book. Drawing on Sen's arguments, the book suggests that conducting a trans-positional analysis involves three reasoning procedures. The first procedure is to reject comparison based on benchmarking against one single cultural or contextual position. The aim is to make the comparison 'symmetrical' to the largest extent – that is to 'equally' treat the components being compared to the largest extent. The second procedure is to explore multiple positions separately. In this book, the multiple positions are the higher education-related Chinese and Anglo-American positions. The third procedure is to move beyond the multiple positions and engage in trans-positional assessment and combination. In this book, this means after comparing the two traditions' ideas on the public (good) in higher education, the book develops a trans-positional combination of these ideas. The first reasoning procedure matches and supports the objective in eliminating the privilege of one tradition over the other to the largest extent. The second enables in-depth and separate exploration of each tradition concerning the public (good) in higher education. Notably, the separate exploration should be made by deeply embedding in each tradition and borrowing concepts from the other as little as possible. The third provides an approach for comparing the two traditions, and for developing a set of interpretations of conceptions that draws on both traditions, concerning the public (good) in higher education.

This book is not claiming to reach 'trans-positional objectivity' by doing a trans-positional analysis. The aim is more modest: to develop a set of interpretations of conceptions of the public (good) of higher education that can more effectively explain relevant higher education phenomena across the two contexts – in Sen's words, 'a broader understanding that make[s] sense of the respective (and possibly divergent) positional observations' (Sen 1993: 130). It is also important to acknowledge that there are limitations inevitably caused by my personal 'positions', including my perspectives, that can hinder the attempt to make the comparison 'symmetrical' (see Chapter 11 about methodological reflections).

1.4.3 A Two-Step Trans-Positional Comparative Methodology

The direct employment of the three reasoning procedures in this book is challenging. The starting point of the book is 'the public (good)' in higher education, which has cultural undercurrents, and, moreover, is Anglo-American. Therefore, in part, there is a need to establish a foundation, consisting of cultural and philosophical ideas underlying the public (good) of higher education in both traditions concerning aspects such as the state, society, individual, and individualism and collectivism for further exploration of the public (good) in higher education.

To privilege the liberal Anglo-American tradition as little as possible, it is important to ground in the Chinese tradition in relation to parallel ideas of the public (good) in higher education. 'Parallel ideas' acknowledges that there are no exact equivalents of the Anglo-American concepts of public (good) in the Chinese tradition, though certain Chinese terms overlap with or correlate with heterogeneous Anglo-American concepts. Seemingly, this search for parallel ideas does not make the comparison totally 'symmetrical', as the search still started with the Anglo-American concepts. Nevertheless, I need a starting point for practical reasons. To mitigate the practical limitations, I conducted an in-depth exploration of the Chinese tradition for relevant underlying ideas of the Chinese parallel concepts of the public (good) of higher education. These underlying ideas then became the Chinese starting point for the exploration of the parallel ideas of the public (good) of higher education in the Chinese tradition – the *gong* of higher education (see Chapters 2 and 8).

The two-step trans-positional comparison used in the book is as follows. The first step is Trans-positional Analysis I, designed for explorations of cultural and philosophical ideas underlying the public (good) of higher education in each tradition and a tentative trans-positional assessment based on these ideas. The second step is Trans-positional Analysis II, which builds on Trans-positional Analysis I to explore and make trans-positional exploration of ideas of the public (good) of higher education (or from a Chinese perspective, the *gong* of higher education).

As will be shown in Chapter 4, the outcomes of the tentative trans-positional assessment in Trans-positional Analysis I, especially the lexical basis and the identified five pairs of key terms, form the basis for Trans-positional Analysis II. The lexical basis is designed in response to the possible aforementioned lexical challenges. The five pairs of key terms represent five key themes in examining the public (good) of higher education: (1) *xiushen* (self-cultivation) in the Chinese tradition and *Bildung*, which is used to understand the Anglo-American tradition on individual student development. Both focus on individual development in higher education and connect higher education with the sphere of the individual; (2) *gongping*/equity, each concerning the relationship between higher education and the sphere of society, and particularly emphasizing higher education's role in enhancing social equity; (3) *zhi* (the free will) and liberty, which turn to the relationship between higher education and the sphere of the state, and enable discussion of academic freedom and university autonomy in higher education; (4) *gong*/public and *si*/private, which centre on individualism and collectivism, and explore the resources, and individualized and collective outcomes of higher education; (5) *tianxia weigong* (all under heaven belongs to all/is for all) and global public/common goods, which move to higher education's cross-border activities and collective outcomes at a global level.

Trans-positional Analysis II consists of both comparison and combination. Hybridization and synergy serve as two ways to combine (trans-positional reconstructing) ideas from the two traditions in relation to the five key themes in higher education. Underlying these methods is my epistemological position guided by the *yin–yang* philosophy (see further discussion). This suggests that it is possible to reinterpret and combine two (or more) different and even contrasting ideas/concepts into new explanations of higher education phenomena.

(i) Hybridization takes distinct parts of two (or more) concepts or ideas and brings them together in a 'hybrid' concept or idea. The hybrid is made of parts or all of the original concepts or ideas. In certain hybrids, the origin of the parts can be discerned. In others, the hybrid is distinct from its origins.

(ii) Synergy combines two (or more) separate and distinct concepts or ideas to make them work cooperatively. Unlike hybridization where the two (or more) concepts or ideas stay separate and do not necessarily combine into one new form, synergy worked in parallel with a certain kind of relationship between the concepts. Therefore, the concepts or ideas become more effective than if they worked in a high degree of isolation.

Hybridizations and synergies are made by combining two (or more) concepts or ideas. Some of these ideas, though not all, are not only contrasting but also mutually complementary. I describe combinations of those complementary ideas as 'complementarities' to highlight that the parts being combined are complementary to each other. Therefore, the number of the ways for combination becomes three: hybridization, synergy and complementarity.

1.4.4 My Epistemological Position: Chinese *Yin-Yang* Philosophy

The choice and employment of a methodology is associated with a researcher's epistemological position, the researcher's understanding of how to obtain knowledge that enables the researcher to know the nature of reality. My epistemology is manifested in Chinese *yin-yang* philosophy. It is foundational to the third reasoning procedure of the trans-positional exploration, in a sense that it is possible to make trans-positional reconstruction of (even contrasting) ideas from the two higher education-related traditions. It also implies how the trans-positional reconstruction may work.

Chinese *yin-yang* philosophy is a fundamental way to know the nature of reality in the Chinese tradition. According to *yin-yang* philosophy, the nature of existence is made up of *yin* and *yang*, as the two halves of the whole. Everything in the universe can be explained and understood by *yin* and *yang*. For example, heaven is *yang* while earth is *yin*, sun is *yang* while moon is *yin*, positive is *yang* while negative is *yin*.

> All things stand, facing *yang* and against *yin*. The interaction between *yin* and *yang* creates a state of harmony.[2]

Yin and *yang* need to be used in combination. They are interdependent on one another. 'Ultimately, *yin* and *yang* do not mean anything in themselves at all, being only employed to express a relation; one notion is the opposite of the other, the one is positive, the other negative' (Forke 1925: 214). The interplay between *yin* and *yang* determines the formation and existence of all things. The *yin-yang* progression is in constant rotation following cyclical patterns (see

---

[2] 万物负阴而抱阳，冲气以为和。– Chapter 42, *Daodejing*.

Figure 1.1 The *yin–yang* symbol or *taiji*.

Figure 1.1) – the two concepts exist simultaneously and are in constant dynamic with one another. In Figure 1.1, the black half represents *yin* and the white half *yang*, reflecting the inescapably intertwined duality of all things in existence.

Yin and *yang* are independent, yet they are also in contradiction and opposition. The tension and difference between them allow for interactions whereby dynamic energy is created (Wang 2012: 8). However, although *yin* and *yang* are contrasting, they are at the same time complementary (Allison 1998). In other words, the contrasting and interdependent *yin* and *yang* supplement each other, which is the key to the achievement of harmony and balance between them (Wang 2012: 11). For example, in *Zhouli* (*The Rites of Zhou*), ancient Chinese people argue that in making a wheel, the key is to supplement softness (*yin*) with hardness (*yang*), and vice versa, to achieve the balance between the two. The craft of wheel-making suggests that on certain occasions, people may need to exert effort in order to make the two contradictory sides – *yin* and *yang* – achieve a complementary balance.

> The way of making the hub of wheel must be measured according to *yin-yang*. *Yang* is densely grained and thus is strong; *yin* is loosely grained and thus is soft. Therefore, one uses fire to nourish its *yin*, making it even with its *yang*. Thus, even if the wheel is worn, it will not lose its round form.[3]

---

[3] 凡斩毂之道，必矩其阴阳。阳也者，積理而坚;阴也者，疏理而柔。是故以火养其阴，而齐诸其阳，则 毂虽敝不蕝。 –*Kaogongji, Zhouli.*

Enlightened by Chinese *yin–yang* philosophy, I perceive the ideas of public (good) in higher education in the two higher education-related traditions as potentially complementary, despite their being different or even contrasting. As contrasting concepts may be mutually complementary and completing, there is space for harmony without conformity (*heer butong*) through their combination. In this book, combination is the primary means for trans-positional reconstruction, in order to reach the aim of developing a set of interpretations of conceptions of the public (good) of higher education that can more effectively explain relevant higher education phenomena across the Chinese and Anglo-American contexts.

From time to time, the combination necessitates reinterpretations of the concepts/ideas, and/or using one concept/idea to complete another, in order to reach a complementary balance between *yang* and *yin*. Ideas and concepts from both higher education-related traditions are regarded as heuristic tools to explain higher education phenomena. For example, as will be discussed in Chapter 6, Amartya Sen's idea of equality of freedom to achieve, which emphasizes providing all individuals with a desirable environment for their development while assuming the existence of varying natural talents of individuals, can be complementary to the Confucian idea of equality of potential to achieve, which assumes all individuals' equal natural talents and potential to self-develop. These two seemingly opposite ideas (in the sense of opposite assumptions of individuals' natural talents) are reinterpreted as not antagonistically opposite but mutually complementary. It is thus possible to combine ideas to form a complementarity: equality of potential and freedom to achieve. Indeed, the idea of complementarity is already manifest in certain Chinese concepts such as Confucian individualism and collectivism. Different from the contrasting liberal individualism and collectivism, Confucian individualism and collectivism are mutually complementary and enhancing (for further discussion, see Chapter 8).

1.5 Organization of the Book

The book is set out in three main sections. Part I elaborates on what is meant by the higher education-related Chinese tradition and the higher education-related Anglo-American tradition in the book. Chapters 2 and 3 respectively examine broad cultural and philosophical ideas underlying the public (good) of higher education in the Chinese and the Anglo-American traditions. In particular, these ideas expound the social imaginary of the two traditions, which is fundamental to the further depiction of the public (good) in higher education. Chapter 4 compares Chinese and Anglo-American ideas about the social imaginary, as presented in Chapters 2 and 3, and explains the process of identifying the five key themes. The five key themes comprise five pairs of key terms from the two traditions, which arguably together draw a holistic picture of the public (good) of higher education. It also elaborates on the lexical basis for the comparison in this study. The aim of Chapters 2–4 is to lay the foundation for Part II and Part III.

Part II consists of five chapters, each of which explores one key theme/pair of term identified in Chapter 4. Chapter 5 examines the first key theme in the context of higher education, which focuses on an individual student's personal development: *xiushen* (self-cultivation) in the Chinese tradition and *Bildung*, which is used to unpack student development in the Anglo-American tradition. *Bildung* is used here because of its influence on conceptualizing student cultivation and development in Anglo-American educational philosophies (Siljander and Sutinen 2012).

Chapter 6 examines *gongping* (equity) in the Chinese tradition and equity in the liberal Anglo-American tradition. The emphasis is on social equity and equity in higher education. It argues that despite the consensus on the goodness and desirability of equity, it remains to be explored how and to what extent higher education can contribute to equity. Further, societies do not agree on whether or not the state should intervene in higher education for the sake of equity, to what extent the state may intervene and how effective the state policies may be. Answers to the questions are embedded in interpretations of equity as well as liberty. Divergent interpretations of the two notions in different philosophical traditions largely account for disparity between governments' attitudes towards equity in higher education.

Chapter 7 examines a pair of notions that has been widely discussed but remains highly contentious – *zhi* (the free will) in the Chinese tradition and liberty in the Anglo-American tradition in higher education. Different from other themes that consist of an Anglo-American notion and its nearest approximations in the Chinese language, I use *zhi* instead of the Chinese translation of liberty (*ziyou*) as a key concept to interpret the Chinese liberal tradition. *Zhi* is not the Chinese equivalence of liberty. Besides its different connotations, *zhi* is narrower in scope than liberty. The examination of *zhi* not only reflects different liberal thoughts in the Chinese tradition especially in Confucianism but indicates a wide conceptual distance between the two traditions concerning liberty. Based on the thoughts on *zhi* and liberty in the two traditions, the chapter examines academic freedom and university autonomy in higher education.

Chapter 8 explores the fourth pair of terms in the context of higher education: *gong* (public) and *si* (private) in the Chinese tradition, and the public and private in the Anglo-American tradition. The public and public good of higher education lie at the heart of the book. The chapter unpacks the public/private (good) in two aspects: spheres of social action and value creation. There is also the discussion of the common good in higher education. Following the two aspects, the chapter starts with two separate examinations of the notions of '*gong*/public' and '*si*/private' in each tradition. The public good and the private good of higher education are then investigated, based on the exploration of the two traditions.

Chapter 9 unpacks the notions of 'public/private' at the global level and rethinks the Anglo-American concepts of global public/common goods through the perspective of *tianxia weigong* (all under heaven is for/belongs to all). Arguably, compared to the Anglo-American tradition, the Chinese tradition is more comfortable with anticipating a global ecological imagining, embodied in the idea of *tianxia* (all under heaven). The chapter explores the ideas of *tianxia weigong* and global public/common goods, and examines how the two ideas may contribute to the global dimension of higher education's public/common goods, for example, higher education's role in producing global public/common goods.

Part III turns to the comparison and combination of the two higher education-related traditions surrounding the five key themes/pairs of terms. Chapter 10 is where substantial trans-positional reconstruction is carried out regarding the five key themes in higher education. The comparison reveals both similarities and differences for each theme. The chapter argues that differences often lie in philosophical and cultural undercurrents of ideas, whereas similarities are embodied in more immediate manifestations of these ideas. On the basis of the comparison, the chapter identifies complementarities, hybridizations and synergies. This leads to five trans-positional conclusions concerning of the public (good) of higher education. Chapter 11 concludes the book.

Part I

Cultural and Philosophical Foundations

2

The Higher Education-Related Chinese Tradition

2.1 Introduction

This chapter elaborates on the higher education-related Chinese tradition. It is presented with reference to the three main historical stages of mainland China: Imperial times before the collapse of the Qing Dynasty in 1911, the Chinese-Western encounters between 1840 and 1949, and contemporary China since 1949. There is an overlap between the first and second stages. This is because the Chinese-Western encounters developed before the collapse of the last Chinese Imperial dynasty.

Specific ideas from Chinese traditional thoughts are not always consigned to an exact period. There is no intention to provide a detailed historical account of the evolving Chinese tradition or Confucianism. Rather, the chapter examines primary schools of thought, their higher education-related key concepts and arguments, in conjunction with review of important social, political and higher educational institutions. By doing this, the chapter also reveals the social imaginary of the Chinese tradition. The aim is to interpret traditional thoughts in a way that is relevant to contemporary higher education. In any case, it is not easy to clearly classify arguments according to a time of origin. Presenting the ideas on the basis of a time period classification does not benefit the analysis and may result in misinterpretations.

2.2 The Higher Education-Related Chinese Tradition in Imperial Times

2.2.1 The Whole and Unity

The notions of 'whole' and 'unity' reflect the fundamental anthropocosmic worldview of the Chinese tradition (Tu 1998b: 122). This view highlights a harmonious equilibrium state between human beings and nature (T. Lin and Zhou 1995). This is a state where all things organically belong to a unity – the 'one body'. This view illustrates the Chinese way of viewing the world, state, society, family and individual. As Ying Lu and Jover (2019: 428) argue, this anthropocosmic worldview is one of the Chinese tradition's biggest contributions to a balanced and sustainable development of the world in the twenty-first century.

The 'one body' represents variant things. Essentially, it implies that all things under heaven, despite their multitude, compose one body (D. Zhang 1996: 81). It may also represent collective entities in smaller scales. For example, the family is one body composed of all family members, and society is one organic whole consisting of all social members. Organically composing 'one body' requires all constituent units to have the same end and maintain harmonious mutual relationships.

The idea of 'unity' originated in Daoism, and was later adopted and reinterpreted by Confucianism. It was initially proposed by Hui Shi (around 370–310 BCE) and his friend Zhuangzi (around 369–286 BCE). All under heaven, according to Hui Shi, constitutes a whole body.

> May love flood over the myriad things: heaven and earth are one body.[1]
>
> Heaven and earth are the father and mother of the myriad things. Uniting they form into one body; separating they return to their beginning.[2]

In the Chinese tradition, one essential kind of unity is 'the unity of heaven and humanity' (*tianren heyi*). In the Chinese lexicon, 'humanity' may represent *renlei*, human beings or the core Confucian virtue *ren* that highlights human beings' benevolence and human-heartedness.[3] In the phrase 'the unity of heaven and humanity', 'humanity' is understood as all human beings together as a whole. Similarly, 'heaven', as an essential philosophical notion in the Chinese tradition, also has a twofold meaning. It is 'an objective infinite reality, the "sky"', as well as a symbolic representation of the supreme (D. Zhang 2002: 3). In Imperial times, when the knowledge about the world was limited, Chinese people appealed to heaven for explanations. They understood the world as all

---

[1] 泛爱万物，天地一体也。 –*Tianxia, Zhuangzi*, translated by Edmund Ryden (see Zhang, D. (2002), *Key Concepts in Chinese Philosophy*, trans. E. Ryden, Connecticut: Yale University Press, p. 103).
[2] 天地者，万物之父母也，合则成体，散则成始。–*Dasheng, Zhuangzi*, translated by Edmund Ryden (see *Key Concepts in Chinese Philosophy*, trans. E. Ryden, p. 103).
[3] Because the term 'humanity' has both abstract and concrete meanings (refers to people), in this book, I use 'human beings' instead to refer to people. When the term 'humanity' is used, in most cases, I am only referring to its abstract meaning.

under heaven. Moreover, heaven has its own way (*tiandao*) that has absolute power and regulates the world. To reach the ideal end of 'the unity', people would attempt to grasp the will of heaven and abide by the way of heaven.

> Those who obey the will of heaven, . . . , will surely obtain a reward; those who oppose the will of heaven, . . . , will surely obtain a punishment.[4]

Mirroring the Daoist notion of the way (*dao*), Confucianism employs a pair of concepts: way of heaven (*tiandao*) and way of humanity (*rendao*). The way originally means people's travelling pathways. In the Chinese tradition, it often represents the norm and law that should be respected (Kalton 2010: 198). Thus, the way of heaven is to be respected by all creatures under heaven including human beings. Similarly, the way of humanity is the norm and law governing human beings' daily lives.

In the Chinese tradition, human beings ought to abide by both the way of heaven and the way of humanity. According to Confucianism, the two ways are essentially the same because the way of humanity is originally derived from the way of heaven (D. Zhang 1985: 3–4). However, as the Daoist classics *Daodejing* states, 'the way (*dao*) that can be put into words is not really the way.'[5] It is not possible to articulate the way in a Daoist perspective.

In contrast, Confucianism claims that it is possible to understand the way by staying true to human beings' natural dispositions – that is to understand way of heaven by understanding way of humanity and to understand way of humanity by going back to natural dispositions. It is believed that when human beings behave in accordance with the way of humanity, the way of heaven is simultaneously respected. Such a claim is based on the assertion of the sameness of the way of heaven and the way of humanity. 'The heaven's way is distant; the human way is close. There is no access to the former [unless by accessing the latter].'[6] When both ways are respected, the harmonious unity of heaven and humanity is achieved. This view partly parallels with the idea of equilibrium in the Anglo-American tradition. But the Anglo-American equilibrium is more often discussed in the field of economics and politics (see, e.g., Arrow 1974; Lindbeck and Weibull 1993).

Confucianism regards the realization of 'the unity of heaven and humanity' as a gradual process. It starts from human beings' own dispositions and ends at an

---

4 順天意者，. . . ，必得賞；反天意者，. . . ，必得罰。 –*Tianzhi, Mozi*, translated by Edmund Ryden (see *Key Concepts in Chinese Philosophy*, trans. E. Ryden, p. 48).
5 道可道，非常道。 – *Daodejing*
6 天道远，人道迩，非所及也。–*Zuo's Commentary*, translated by Edmund Ryden (see *Key Concepts in Chinese Philosophy*, trans. E. Ryden, p. 52).

understanding of the way of heaven. Knowledge of both humanity and the world is pursued. Confucianism describes the pursuit of knowledge as the Confucian self-cultivation process (Tu 1998a: 12). Human beings are supposed to be sincere in the process of realizing the unity through self-cultivation (Bol 2008: 48, 231). According to Mencius, 'he who has exhausted all his mental constitution knows his nature; knowing his nature, he knows heaven.'[7]

Certain Greek philosophers, writing at much the same time as Confucius, were also interested in exploring knowledge of human beings. In Plato's eyes, the chief knowledge is 'knowledge of the ends of man and civil society' (Plato and Bloom [1968] 1991: 391). This is because 'justice necessarily and primarily demands a knowledge of what is good for man and the community; otherwise the knowledge and skills of the arts are in the service of authoritative myths' (Plato and Bloom [1968] 1991: 321). Nevertheless, there exist fundamental differences between the ancient Chinese philosophy and classic Greek philosophy. For example, while the Chinese objective in knowing human beings and the world is to realize a harmonious and ordered all under heaven, the Greek aim, as argued by Dewey ([1916] 2011: 152), is 'bringing the mind to a realisation of the supreme purpose of existence as the law of human action, corporate and individual'. In the Chinese tradition, the end is the good of the collective. In the classic Greek tradition, the end is the full development of individuals, although there is also advocacy of the common good. Anglo-American tradition is foundationally influenced by the classic Greek philosophy. Arguably, the divergence between these two different notions of 'the end' leads to a corresponding variation between the Chinese and Anglo-American traditions in other ideas. This is investigated further in Part II of the book.

There is another essential point implied in the sameness of heaven's way and humanity's way – that all human beings equally share the same way. They are born equal in virtue. Every individual has equal potential to grasp the way through self-cultivation, which lays a foundation for the idea of social equity in the Chinese tradition (more is discussed in Chapter 6).

> Heaven and earth give birth to human beings, who are largely identical but with minor differences. The differences lie in human beings' bodies, while their minds are identical; the differences lie in human beings' lust, while their dispositions are the same. It is the indulgence and enjoyment of human bodies that is lust . . . , while men's dispositions lie in their minds including filial piety, fraternity,

---

[7] 尽其心者，知其性也；知其性则知天矣。 –*Jinxin, Mengzi*

loyalty, honesty, benevolence, justice, righteousness, and wisdom. (Qian [2005] 2016: 184)

When the way of humanity is respected by human beings, people continually go back to, and stay true to, their natural dispositions through the process of self-cultivation. When people are self-indulgent they become different. Such differences undermine the 'one body' made up of all human beings. As Qian ([2005] 2016: 184) remarks, 'cultivating virtues makes individuals similar; with filial piety and fraternity, families resemble; royalty and honesty make different communities, countries, and even all under heaven similar.'

The realization of the harmonious unity is illustrated by the nested circles in Figure 2.1. More is discussed in the next sections.

While the way of humanity originates in the way of heaven, there is also the vice versa. Arguably, the Chinese tradition delineates a picture of heaven's will and heaven's way according to Chinese people's interpretations of human nature and the way of humanity. Similarly, while Christians might argue that God created humans in his/her own image, commentators may say that humans made God in their own image.

2.2.2 The Imperial Chinese State: The Civilizational State and the Family State

The idea of unity is embodied in the organization of the Imperial Chinese state. The Imperial Chinese state was part of the ever-expanding series of entities. Different from the modern nation-state, the Imperial Chinese state was a

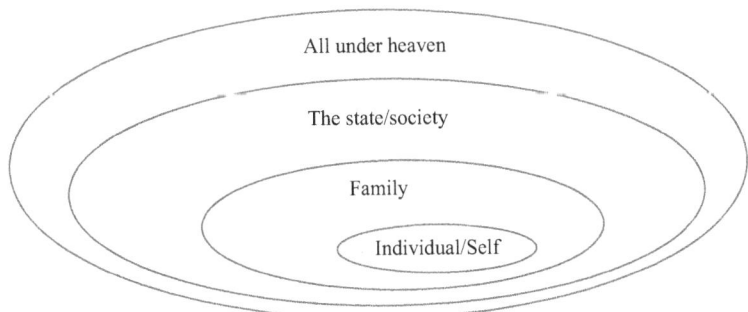

Figure 2.1 The broadening process of the individual in Confucianism. *Source*: C. Huang (2010) and Tu (1985).

'civilizational state'. As A. Y. King (2018: 111) argues, 'ancient China, of course, was a nation, but in a sense very different from the modern "nation-state".'

The term 'civilizational state' has been used by many scholars to refer to the Imperial Chinese state (see, e.g., Jacques 2012; A. Y. King 2018; Levenson 1968; Weiwei Zhang 2012). The civilizational state has two distinctive attributes. First, the longevity of Chinese civilization (Jacques 2012; Xia 2014). Despite the frequent vicissitudes of dynasties, Chinese civilization remains consistent. In this sense, China as a civilizational state lasted for more than two millennia, until the twentieth century (as will be discussed, the turbulence between the mid-nineteenth and mid-twentieth centuries changed the situation and China is now no longer solely immersed in its ancient civilization, but also in Western knowledge) (Xia 2014: 46).

Second, there is a lack of explicit boundaries, reflecting the comprehensiveness of the Imperial Chinese state (Jacques 2012; A. Y. King 2018). When immigrants brought in their different traditions and languages to Imperial China, Chinese civilization embraced these heterogeneous traditions. These traditions were thereby assimilated into the Chinese civilizational order. The key to the embrace of heterogeneity was to reach a mutual understanding, well described as 'value your own value, and that of others. With the shared value, we will share the world peacefully'.[8] However, arguably, the assimilation process resulted in a homogenous Chinese culture united by language, as well as a stagnant political system cemented by homogenous ideas (B. Wang 2017: 8, 19). This final outcome of homogeneity and refusal to change may have undermined the potential for diversity of the Chinese tradition in Imperial times.

In Imperial China, the civilizational state was an organic unity composed of family units. The intrinsic nature of the state was essentially the same as that of the family. Human beings' feelings and attitudes towards the state were an extension of those towards their families. Scholars/researchers call this understanding of the Imperial Chinese state 'the family state' (*jiaguo tonggou*). Using Mencius's words, 'the root of all under heaven is in the state, the root of the state is in the family, and the root of the family is in cultivating oneself.'[9] Family, the state and all under heaven constitute a continuum centring on the self (Jilin Xu 2017: 2).

This continuum is parallel with the Confucian moral system. The system starts with the aim of maintaining a harmonious family by reconciling relationships between individual family members. It ends with maintaining a harmonious all under heaven by reconciling relationships between individual

---

[8] 各美其美，美人之美，美美与共，天下大同。–Fei Xiaotong.
[9] 天下之本在国，国之本在家，家之本在身。–Lilou, Mengzi.

human beings. The realization of harmony requires moral values, including filial piety (*xiao*), fraternity (*ti*), benevolence (*ren*), loyalty (*zhong*) and righteousness (*yi*). In other words, individuals ought to be loyal to their country, love other people and strive for maintaining the justice of the whole state.

Gradually, the Confucian tradition, especially the Confucian moral system, moulded Imperial China into a civilizational state. The state's rule largely relied on Confucian order in local communities, especially the family. Dewey provides an insightful description of this. In Imperial China, the state 'rules but it does not regulate.... Duties are within the family; property is possessed by the family' (Dewey [1927] 2016: 89). Rather than regarding people's identification with the state as a central issue, the Imperial Chinese state expected their approval of the Confucian civilizational order, especially the Confucian moral system (A. Y. King 2018). The state was one entity but not the central one. As the proverbs state: 'Heaven is high and the emperor is far away – it cannot be helped' and 'One with great power [the dragon] cannot defeat a local villain [snake].'[10]

Dynastic vicissitudes were more or less irrelevant to common people. The Chinese people engaged almost exclusively with their family and local communities. Local gentry and kinship systems could survive most turbulent periods, so that ordered grassroots society was often maintained in spite of dynastic vicissitudes. Meanwhile, within the Chinese tradition, the entity of all under heaven was considered more important than the state, at least so before the mid-twentieth century (S. Liang 1990; Jilin Xu 2017: 4). According to Liang (1990: 163), 'in the minds of the Chinese people, what is close to them is family, and what is far from them is *tianxia*. The rest [including the state] they more or less ignore.'[11]

2.2.3 Individuals and Society: Smaller Self (*Xiaowo*) and Larger Self (*Dawo*)

In Imperial China, the unit of political, social and economic life was the family rather than the individual. In general, Chinese 'families' did not refer to nuclear units in Imperial times but to much broader groups of agnates that could number in the hundreds or even thousands (Fukuyama 2011: 97). Individuals were not independent agents in society. The self was regarded as the starting point of the expanding entities (the self, the family, the state and all under heaven). The importance of the individual lay in its identity with

---

[10] 天高皇帝远 & 强龙压不过地头蛇。
[11] 中国人心目中所有者，近则身家，远则天下，此外便多半轻忽的。

the larger entities (Jilin Xu 2017: 5). Correspondingly, there emerged a pair of conceptions: the smaller self (*xiaowo*) and larger self (*dawo*) (K. Cheng and Yang 2015; R. Yang 2011).

The absolute 'self' in the Western sense did not exist in the Chinese tradition (K. Cheng and Yang 2015: 127). In political and social affairs, individuals were tagged as members of the family. The success of an individual would lead to interests of the whole family, and vice versa. The family that one belonged to had great influence on one's career as well as smaller matters. The 'smaller' and 'larger' selves were relative concepts that operated simultaneously at multiple scales (see Figure 2.1 and Table 2.1). The individual was easy to conceptualize as a version of the 'smaller self', and the family could be understood as the 'larger self' that operated around this smaller self. This type of relationship also existed at larger scales. The family unit might be understood as a 'smaller self' in relation to the 'larger self' that is the broader society or the state. Furthermore, the state represented the 'smaller self' in relation to the 'larger self' of all under heaven, or the world in a modern sense. Note that there existed other entities between either two. For example, there were local communities between the family and the state. This is still the case in China today.

2.2.4 Higher Learning in Imperial China

In the Chinese tradition, 'nothing is more honourable than learning.'[12] Literatus, as one social status among the four statuses in Imperial China (literatus, farmer, artisan and merchant), enjoyed the highest status (Elman 2000: 251). Education was a priority in which people should invest resources and effort. Legacies of this value are still tangible among contemporary Chinese people (Marginson 2011c).

The long emphasis on education is a result of Imperial China's residence system as well as its higher learning system (L. Yang 2017). In Imperial China,

Table 2.1 Smaller Self and Larger Self in the Chinese Tradition

Smaller self/Private	Larger self/Public
The individual in family	The family
The family	The state/society
The state/society	All under heaven/the world

---

[12] 万般皆下品，惟有读书高。

people were officially classified into four groups (see earlier discussion),[13] and social mobility between these groups was not easy to achieve (Q. Lu 2007). Many literati served as state officials and had the highest status, followed by farmers. Outstanding farmers could enter the literati. It was only after the Ming Dynasty (1368–1644) that people from the artisan and merchant groups began to have opportunities to enter the literati (Elman 1991, 2000; Q. Lu 2007).

People's rights were defined by their status. Becoming a member of the literati was very appealing as in many dynasties, as only the literati had the right to avoid corvée requirements, including tax, labour contributions and military service. Literati also had high prestige, political power and salary (Elman 2000; Z. Fan 2004). As the prevailing Confucian ideology gradually built direct connections between Confucian scholars and the literati, receiving higher learning and passing the *keju* (the civil service examination) became almost the only way of joining the literati (Elman 1991, 2000).

Families, especially relatively wealthy ones, provided family members with financial and spiritual support in their education. For instance, they established family schools to educate younger members of the family, and provided material and spiritual awards for members who did well in the *keju* (Ouyang 1992; L. Wu 2005). Correspondingly, family members who passed the *keju* were expected to repay the family based on the family's standard criteria (Ouyang 1992; L. Wu 2005). The legacy of education-mediated relationships within the family is still evident in contemporary East Asian countries, embodied in families' large investment in shadow education (Marginson 2011c; Wei Zhang and Bray 2017).

Confucius was himself an educator. On the one hand, Confucius advocates that higher learning should be open to the public. He calls for higher learning opportunities for all people regardless of their family background or social status, as long as one wants to learn and has the ability to learn. As Confucius notes, 'make no social distinctions in teaching (*youjiao wulei*).'[14] This was a pioneering idea at that time. It highlighted Confucius's concerns with equity in higher education. This is discussed in Chapter 6.

On the other hand, higher learning was a way of spreading state-supported values by focusing on students and teaching them to internalize the values (L. Yang 2017: 7). One primary public aim of higher learning was to socialize people to internalize moral principles, thereby supporting the legitimacy of the state. This was good for maintaining social order, especially the state's rule. However, this public function

---

[13] Besides the four divisions, people could also be divided into literati and non-literati (commoners).
[14] See *Analects: Weilinggong*.

of education has led to undesirable results. For example, one outcome that has often been criticized is the suppression of individual autonomy (Chan 2002). This intersects with the homogenization of the Chinese culture, as noted previously.

In his discussion of education's social function in *Democracy and Education*, Dewey, an Anglo-American scholar, develops certain ideas that parallel the Confucian emphasis on society as a community. Dewey views education as 'shaping, forming, molding activity – that is, a shaping into the standard form of social activity' (Dewey [1916] 2011: 10). However, the social function of education in Dewey's theses is fundamentally different to the public function of education in Imperial China. One difference lies in whether education can be used to maintain the legitimacy of the state.

Nevertheless, it should be noted that while Confucianism emphasizes the public role of higher learning, it also stresses the cultivation of the free will (C. Cheng 2004). Confucian higher learning is not only about socializing people and supporting the state but also about developing the self. These aspects will be further explored in Chapters 5 and 7.

2.3 The Chinese-Western Encounters between 1840 and 1949

From the late Ming Dynasty onwards, China's Imperial dynasties adopted a seclusion policy. Being separated from the rest of the world for centuries, China gradually became a closed and conservative state with rigid systems and institutions (Q. Qi 2012: 29, 37). This policy lasted until China was defeated by Britain in the First Opium War (1840–2). Forced to open its door, China hereafter experienced great challenges and changes imposed by the West, Japan and Russia. Due to constant encounters between China and the Western powers, Western knowledge and ideologies became available in China and this triggered the evolution of Chinese ideas (Xie 2018; R. Yang, Xie and Wen 2018).

2.3.1 The Influence Imposed by the West[15]

Learning from the West

The advanced military technology of the West demonstrated its strengths. The awareness of those strengths undermined the Chinese imaginary of China as

---

[15] There was also influence from Japan and Russia. But the book primarily concentrates on that from the Western countries, especially the European countries and the United States.

the Celestial Empire (Lisheng Zhang 2008: 109). Chinese intellectuals started to seriously reflect on China's own traditions and to consider learning from the West. The practise of this awareness was associated with constant struggles. There was fierce resistance from conservatives, who believed in the superiority of Chinese civilization and refused to learn from the West (Q. Qi 2012: 131–3). However, military defeat was decisive in forcing China to accept Western knowledge. Conservative resistance was alleviated but conservatives still insisted on the preservation of Chinese ideology (Q. Qi 2012: 240).

The first attempt to learn from the West was confined to Western technology (G. Zhang 1979). It began after the First Opium War. Slogans were raised including 'Learning advanced technologies from Europeans to fight against them' and 'Chinese studies as essence, Western-learning for practical use'.[16] These slogans soon became the ideological basis of the Self-strengthening Movement (*ziqiang/ yangwu yundong*) (Feng [1897] 2015; Wei and Chen 1998). In this formulation, despite the effort made to learn Western technology, Chinese traditions still enjoyed an essential status. Western values were blocked at the doors. Chinese intellectuals insisted on retaining China's own ideology.

> China's strength lay in preserving rites and righteousness, and the three cardinal guides and the five constant virtues. So these should be the essence. As the West is good at techniques, they should be a supplement, which is certainly nonessential. (Q. Qi 2012: 251)

However, the blockage of Western values was soon broken by the failure of the Self-strengthening Movement, as indicated by China's defeat in the first Sino-Japanese War in 1895. Merely learning technology did not lead to the expected result of national salvation. Chinese intellectuals then turned to Western values and ideologies. It became widely believed that political systems and cultures were key to Western countries' success (X. Huang 2000; Qin 1981). Values like democracy, liberty, equality and individualism were introduced to China via translations of Western classics, including *An Inquiry into the Nature and Causes of the Wealth of Nations* by Adam Smith, *On Liberty* by John Stuart Mill and *The Spirit of Laws* by Montesquieu.

The influence of Western values became apparent in intellectuals' proposals for educational and political reforms (X. Huang 2000; Q. Liang 1989b; Qin 1981). Intellectuals highlighted the importance of educational reform for its capacity to enlighten the populace to give up the 'backward' Chinese civilization (Q. Liang

---

[16] 师夷长技以制夷 & 中学为体，西学为用。

1989a, 1989b) and replaced them by Western traditions. Liang Qichao (1989a: 14) argues that 'the most urgent thing of self-strengthening is to enlighten Chinese people'.[17] The best way to enlighten people was to establish new forms of schools, '[which] required the reformation of the civil service examination'[18] and the addition of Western learning to curricula (Q. Liang 1989a: 21), so that Chinese would learn Western ideologies and values.

Concurrently, there were proposals for political reform to deal with the existing system's maladies, including severe corruption, weakness and the apathy of the state towards its people. For example, Liang Qichao (1989a) attributes Western countries' success to their parliaments. Influenced by the idea of democracy, equality and liberty, intellectuals proposed political reform to turn the Imperial court into a democratic government. The underlying aim was to transform the civilizational state into a modern nation-state.

Influence Posed by the Value of Liberty

Whether Chinese traditions value liberty or not requires detailed explorations and will take place later in this book (see Chapter 7). Briefly, there was an existing idea of liberty, although different from the Western idea, in Confucianism and Daoism. But in reality, Chinese Imperial authority never stopped restraining people's freedom in order to maintain its rule. The introduction of the idea of Western liberty gave the already shaky Qing Court another shock and accelerated its collapse. However, it failed to free individuals from the restraints of collective entities, especially the family.

Holding sovereignty over people and restraining their liberty were deemed by Imperial authority as necessary measurements in order to maintain Confucian order and Imperial rule. Restraints on individuals did originate not only from state authority but also, and more importantly, from the family. It was widely believed that individuals as members of the family ought to follow family rules and prioritize the good of the whole family. Sacrifice of the individual will for the sake of the family good was not only preferred but also often required. This family first principle embodied the primary incompatibility between Chinese traditions and liberalism and individualism. One important appeal of liberalism in the West was to 'enable individuals to picture themselves as being independent of church and government' (Hahm 2006: 479); and while the collapse of the Qing Court made it possible to liberate individuals from the Imperial state, liberation

---

[17] 故言自强于今日，以开民智为第一义。
[18] 学校之立，在变科举。

from the family failed. The family survived as an institution through all the turbulence (Zang 2011a), not only because of deep-rooted tradition but also because of people's deeply felt affections and bonds. The influence of liberal ideas of freedom was primarily confined to intellectuals rather than being expanded to common Chinese people. I shall come back to this in Chapter 7.

Influence Posed by the Value of Equality

Compared to liberty, Western ideas of equality encountered less resistance in China in this turbulent period. Equality was already an intrinsic principle of the Confucian tradition, although Confucian equality, mainly manifested in moral equality, was and is different from the Western idea of equality (see Chapter 6).

When the concept of giving people equal status and rights was introduced from the West to China via the Self-strengthening Movement, this was a massive shock to the existing political order and the ruling emperor's legitimacy. If the masses enjoyed equal status and rights with the emperor, one pillar of the emperor's ruling legitimacy would be broken: the emperor would no longer enjoy the power of guiding the people because he was not the 'son of heaven' and did not enjoy a higher status than the masses. This concept made it possible to overthrow the emperor's rule and establish a democratic system, in which people all enjoyed equal status and political rights.

With the collapse of the Qing Dynasty in 1911, unequal relationships among people were gradually replaced by nominally equal ones. After 1949, equality was officially enforced into policy by the Chinese Communist Party. The introduction of equality in those years of Chinese-Western encounters laid a solid foundation for rebuilding the political order and implementing the Marxist-Leninist collectivism in China. Rather than not being completely compatible with collectivism and potentially generating conflict with authority, as in the case of liberty, equality was more readily accepted by authority and was able to be operationalized as a fundamental principle of the modern political system and of Marxist-Leninist collectivism.

Influence Posed by the Idea of Western Individualism

For Confucianism, 'human beings can only be understood relationally, never as isolates, and are thus best accounted for as the sum of the roles they live, with no remainder or consequence' (Rosemont Jr 2015: 4). This relational and role-bearing individual constitutes the core idea of Confucian individualism. Bodde (1957: 66) summarizes Confucian individualism: 'Confucian "individualism" means the fullest development by the individual of his creative potentialities – not, however, merely for the sake of self-expression but because [they] can thus best fulfil that particular role which is [their] within [their] social nexus.' The responsibilities and constraints that correspond to the roles of individuals are ethical requirements. As Rosemont Jr (2015: 95, 104) states,

> [Individuals] are basically constituted by the roles [they] live in the midst of others . . . constraints on roles are very much like constraints on language. There are many ways to be a good friend or teacher . . . , and it is through the unique way each of us lives these roles that we express our creativity. But there are limits: friends won't betray friends, teachers don't propagandize students. (Rosemont Jr 2015: 95, 104)

Role-bearing Confucian individualism constitutes a foundation of the Confucian order and endows the public good with a superior status in relation to the private good. There is a core incompatibility between liberal individualism and Confucian individualism in relation to how they regard individuals: whether individuals are seen as solitary and free from collective obligations or are seen as role-bearing and belonging to various relational nexuses (see Chapter 8).

When liberal individualism was introduced to China, Chinese families tended to resist its spread, because of the threat to not just the welfare but the existence of the family. Opposition from both the family and Confucian literati weakened the scope for liberal individualism to change China in those years. However, this opposition did not wholly block the widespread influence of Western individualism in China. As Geng (1994: 44) points out, 'the discovery of the "individual" was the most important thing of the New Cultural movement, in which lay the most distinctive difference from the Chinese culture in Imperial times.' In calling for a transition from the old family-based society to an individual-based society, intellectuals argued for the advantages of developing individualities (Hu 1918) such as the individual's role in keeping society vibrant and making continuing progress (D. Chen 1919; S. Wang 1915).

2.3.2 The Establishment of Modern Universities in China

Between the First Opium War and the establishment of the People's Republic of China in 1949, China lacked a strong state able to either uphold the traditional political and social order or build one. A wide array of parties played roles in shaping China's future, including Western colonial and neo-imperial powers.

Against this backdrop, the Chinese people continually sought for ways to realize their national salvation.

Developing higher education was one fundamental way to do this (Xie 2018; R. Yang et al. 2019). Supporting national salvation became the primary principle guiding the establishment of China's modern higher education system. New universities and curricula appeared in place of Imperial higher learning institutions and Confucian classics (see Chapter 2 of Hayhoe 1996). In order to advance the development of national military power, science and technology subjects became core components of higher education. In establishing its own modern universities, China imported Western models.

China abolished the *keju* in 1905. Modern Western knowledge gradually became the content of university curricula. Western ideas of equality became widely spread and influential in higher education. From 1912, previous social classes were abandoned legally in the Republic of China, so that theoretically speaking, all persons, regardless of gender and social backgrounds, had an equal right and opportunity to receive higher education (Y. K. Chu 1933; W. Yang 2011). In the meantime, liberty received emphasis in higher education.

Modern universities emerged in the late Qing Dynasty. The first modern Chinese university was *Beiyang Gongxue*, established in 1895, which later became Tianjin University. Until the establishment of the People's Republic of China in 1949, Chinese higher education interacted closely with Western universities. The interaction was made partly through Japanese higher education system, which served as an intermediate agent. Certain Western university models emerged on Chinese soil (Hayhoe 1989). However, due to wars and the disorder, the higher education system was not stable and experienced great change (Xun 2002). In the aftermath of the Qing Dynasty's collapse, the government of the Republic of China became only one among various players in establishing and developing the higher education system (P. Sun 2001; Xun 2002). Diverse bodies were playing important roles, including the governments of colonial powers, Chinese intellectuals and Western missionaries (Hayhoe 1996: 19).

Different players had varied intentions and aims. The Chinese Republican government and Chinese intellectuals attempted to use higher education as a tool to realize national salvation (Xie 2018; R. Yang et al. 2019). There was an enduring attempt to integrate traditional Chinese knowledge and higher learning with those of the West. Japan, during this period, was an important medium for Chinese to know the West. Chinese translations of Western literature largely relied upon corresponding Japanese translations. Many Chinese intellectuals had studied in Japan, such as Sun Yat-sen and Lu Xun. Moreover, the establishment of the *Jingshi Daxuetang*, the predecessor of Peking University, followed Japan's establishment of the University of Tokyo, which inherited the German model of the university (Hayhoe 1996: 18).

Correspondingly, Chinese intellectuals took advantage of the place of universities to engage in knowledge inquiry (K. Zhang 2016). They debated the future of China at universities (J. C. Wang 2012; K. Zhang 2016). Influential intellectuals including Hu Shi (1891–1962), Cai Yuanpei (1868–1940) and Chen Duxiu (1879–1942) were all university faculty. They not only used their knowledge and expertise to educate students and influence the organization of the university but also undertook the public responsibilities of public intellectuals in serving the nation. Some of their intellectual contributions have left lasting legacies in the political, social and higher education systems. Chen Duxiu was among the founding fathers of the Chinese Communist Party. He contributed intellectually to the introduction and spread of Marxism-Leninism in China. Cai Yuanpei was once president of Peking University and founded the tradition of free academic inquiry of the university.

However, the intentions of the colonial powers were more diversified. Some colonial powers, such as Germany, had economic interests. Some others cared more about their 'soft influence' in China, including the United States (Hayhoe 1996: 18–19). The colonial powers implemented different policies that led to a range of types of universities. Tsinghua University benefited from the American Boxer Indemnity fund and was initially founded as a language school preparing students to study in the United States. It later became a flagship university in China. American-trained intellectuals played important roles in developing the university (Hayhoe 1996: 19; Xie 2018). The university was built largely according to the American model of the university. In contrast, given the German emphasis on economic returns, most universities supported by the German government centred on engineering education, paralleling the German *Technische Hochschule* (Hayhoe 1996: 19). In contrast with Britain's great economic and military influence in China, the British model of the university had very limited influence. Hayhoe (1996: 17) attributes this to the low educational level of English missionaries in China, compared to their American counterparts. This also indicated the importance of Western missionaries in developing Chinese universities at that time. For example, Shanxi University, founded in 1901 with the support of the British Boxer Indemnity fund, was established with the help of an English baptist missionary (A. Li 2014).

One indication of the diversity and disorder of the years prior to 1949, and in contrast with the Imperial period and the post-1949 period, was the absence of a comprehensive power that regulated the higher education system (C. Xu 2013; K. Zhang 2016). Authority imposed limited restrictions on universities, facilitating the various experimentations in transplanting Western university models in China. The Chinese higher education system became a hybridity of different ideas and approaches.

2.4 Contemporary China since 1949

2.4.1 New China in the Mao Era

The wars and revolutionary movements between the mid-nineteenth and mid-twentieth centuries largely undermined the old Chinese civilizational order but did not establish a new order in its place. With the aim of realizing national salvation and bringing order back to China, individuals debated about the new civilizational order and how it could be established (X. Huang 2000).

There were two dominant streams of thought that contended during and after the New Culture movement commenced in 1915. One stream of thought proposed a path guided by liberalism. The other was inspired by the Russian October Revolution and favoured Marxism-Leninism. Ardent debates between the two groups lasted until 1949 when the Communist Party's army defeated the forces of Kuo Min Tang (see, e.g., Hu 1918; D. Li 1919). In 1949, Marxism-Leninism became the official ideology of mainland China.

Arguably, the element of collectivism that was shared between Confucianism and Marxism-Leninism was one of the primary reasons for the success of Marxism-Leninism in China (see, e.g., Chapter 1 of A. Y. King 2018). Influenced in their own formation by Confucian collectivism, many Chinese intellectuals were not interested in Western-style individual freedom. Marxist-Leninist collectivism was closer to their understanding – 'Western liberalism with validity based on individualistic reason was considered by radical intellectuals not as powerful a candidate for a total change as Marxism which couched its validity in collectivist reason' (Fu 1974: 84).

The Marxism-Leninism that the Chinese Communist Party implemented was neither authentic Marxism nor Leninism, but the Chineseized Marxism-Leninism, represented by Maoism. The notion of Chineseized Marxism-Leninism was initially proposed by Mao Zedong (2004: 539) in 1938. It inherited from both Marxism-Leninism and the Chinese traditions especially, Confucianism.

> The Chineseisation of Marxism – that is to say, making certain that in all its manifestations it is imbued with Chinese characteristics, using it according to Chinese peculiarities – becomes a problem that must be understood and solved by the whole Party without delay. (Mao 2004: 539)
>
> As a Chinese Marxist, Mao has inherited willy-nilly the philosophical and moral legacy of the Confucian tradition, in which is deeply rooted in the basic pattern of ethic-social norms (*li*) governing everyday living in traditional China. (Fu 1974: 357)

Maoist collectivism, including altruism and group-centred tendencies, reflected a Confucian heritage, one that is other-concerned. But the primary collectives changed from the family to the communist collective (see following discussion). In the Mao era, the party officially sought to reduce the influence of Confucian practices among the Chinese people. This approach became radical during the ten-year Cultural Revolution. Slogans initiated in the New Culture movement were revived, such as 'Down with Confucianism'.[19] After the 'radical ten years', more rational means were employed by the Chinese Communist Party to restrain Confucian influence.

The party also tried to demolish the kinship-based local communities and social control in Chinese grassroots society (X. Guo 2012: 7; C. Liu 2011: 63). A critical method was to dissolve the Confucian-style family and redistribute individuals into new forms of communist groupings (Hsü 1983: 655–6). The objective was to replace the Confucian expanding entities with communist ones. Policies on land reforms and agricultural collectivization greatly accelerated the weakening of families (Y.-m. Lin 2011: 145–6). They also enhanced the status of the new form of communist collectives.

The transition from family-centred collectivism to state-centred collectivism indicated the transformation of the Chinese state from a civilizational state to a nation-state with a strong potency in grassroots society (see also Chapter 8). State-building was a central task in this period, which to a large extent followed a Leninist party system (Marginson 2018f). The Chinese Communist Party, which regarded itself as representing the state as well as the people's collective will (Marginson and Yang 2021), played an essential and leading role in this process.

---

[19] 打倒孔家店。

The party organization penetrated its power and influence into the most local of levels in Chinese society, mainly through people's commune in rural areas and work units in urban areas. People's communes attempted to realize the all-round development of the rural area (e.g., farming, fishery, animal husbandry and industry) and integrate workers, farmers and even soldiers into one entity. Work units in cities played similar roles (X. Guo 2012). Each work unit was like a small but self-sufficient society containing institutions that people's daily life required, such as housing, clinic, school and shops. The people's commune and the work unit enabled the Chinese Communist Party to further control Chinese grassroots society. They exerted economic and political control over their constituents – for example, they were in charge of approving or disapproving the members' applications for migration (Lv 1997).

In the tension between the state and kinship-based society, the state had the upper hand. The old kinship-based society broke up and partly turned into a party organization-based society. Gradually, state and society became conflated in practice (Fewsmith 1999: 70).

2.4.2 The Capitalist Influence since 1978

Since the Reform and Opening-up Policy (1978), there has been unprecedented capitalist influence in Chinese society (Y. Chu and So 2010; Nonini 2008). This was implemented in the liberalization of the Chinese economy and de-collectivization of communist work collectives (Kipnis 2007; J. Lee and Zhu 2006; C. Liu 2011). In this period, China also adopted a strategy of globalization and internationalization, engaging with the rest of the world.

China and the Chinese Communist Party lay at a crossroads in the aftermath of Mao's death in 1976. There were ardent debates on whether to continue Mao's ideas and policies of political mobilization or adopt a new developmental approach (Hsü 1983: 778–80). When Deng Xiaoping gained power, his aim was to rejuvenate the Chinese economy while maintaining the political and social order (Vogel 2011: 250). He adopted three main approaches to reform: abandoning the class struggle, reforming the economy, and opening China to the world (X. Guo 2012; Marginson 2018f; Y. Zheng 2010). Individuals were granted a certain extent of decision-making autonomy, for example, in relation to geographic mobility and personal enrichment, to assist in liberalizing the economy (S. Zhao 1993). As a result, individuals started to gain greater independence from collective entities, in some cases becoming disembedded from collective entities. I shall return to this in Chapter 8.

Meanwhile, numerous social organizations, such as guilds and local communities, emerged in the growing space between the state and the family. These social organizations can be understood as nodes of civil society in China and buffers between the state and family/individual. Seemingly, the conflation of state and society in the Mao era started to change. The appearance of various social organizations and the disembedding of the individual sphere were both associated with the fostering of private enrichment, encouraged by the party, which saw that enrichment as a tool for economic and scientific development (Marginson 2018f; Marginson and Yang 2021).

Despite the economic liberalization and opening up, the bottom line was maintaining control by the party. It was believed that continuous economic development would help sustain the ruling party's legitimacy, but it was necessary to take measures that would achieve a balance between retaining party control and encouraging self-organization (see Chapter 8 of Vogel 2011). The Chinese people also tended to highly value the making of profits. Although the Chinese state insisted that the collective good should take primacy, the idea of private good started to gain influence, and the importance of the collective good was weakened. Amid the overwhelming influence of capitalist mentality, individualism gradually gained greater legitimacy to guide people's behaviours. Hence, Chinese people became increasingly individualistic, further facilitating the disembedding of the individual. More is discussed in Chapter 9.

The Chinese state had never evolved along European/American lines of a division of formal powers and the limited liberal state. Instead, it drew on the Leninist party-state system and the Chinese tradition of the comprehensive state, while bringing the local authority's initiative into full play (Marginson and Yang 2020b: 15). In other words, the aim of the reforms was to inspire the local authority's subjective initiative while maintaining central control. This formula carries inner tensions, and during Deng Xiaoping's time and after there were oscillations between tightening central control and devolution inside the state system (see Chapter 8 of Vogel 2011). Such oscillations also happened to higher education (see later).

Deng's approach was to encourage toleration of local initiative on most occasions, unless the party's control was in question (see Chapters 8 and 14 of Vogel 2011). For example, expanding inequality was accepted as long as the economy as a whole developed. As Deng's slogan stated, 'let some get rich first to push others to become rich later.'[20] The private ownership alien to Marxism

---

[20] 先富带动后富。

became legally recognized and protected in China as that benefited economic development. In higher education, the general trend was devolution. Regarding science and technology as an engine of China's modernization, Deng attempted to provide an environment that was conducive to scientific research.

> Deng also responded to the continuing complaints of scientists that their professional work should be directed by someone familiar with the content. . . . Aware that intellectuals were upset that they had to spend so much time engaged in physical labor and political education, Deng established a new rule that at least five-sixths of the scientists' work week was to be spent on basic research. (Vogel 2011: 208)

However, devolution to the researchers was primarily limited to science and often did not include the humanities and social sciences (Xie 2018). There were oscillations between highly strict, and loose, control on humanities and social sciences. The university, like many other fields, enjoyed 'a ten-year of flourishing art and literature' in the 1980s. There were active social discussions and movements in universities including those in pursuit of the Western style of democracy (Hayhoe 1996: 111–7). However, when the party felt the growing challenge to its control, it reacted immediately and toughly to tighten its control over the university as well as society. Since then, oscillations between tightening and loosening control over the university have become an attribute of Chinese higher education, with the bottom line always being to retain control by the party (Mok 2013; Zha 2010).

2.4.3 The Contemporary Chinese Higher Education System

Diverse traditions and influences, including those of Imperial Chinese civilization and Western knowledge, have been woven together into the contemporary Chinese higher education system.

Chinese higher education entered into a new era after the establishment of the People's Republic of China in 1949. It began to be supervised and supported by the new Communist government. A unified system of Chinese higher education gradually appeared, on the basis of a reorganization of universities led by the party (Hayhoe 2016; Hayhoe et al. 2012). Arguably, post 1949, Chinese universities began with the Soviet model and subsequently moved to the American model (F. Huang 2017). Before the political break between the Soviet Union and China in the late 1950s, China entirely transplanted the Soviet higher education system onto China's soil. The reorganization of universities in 1952 led to three types of institution: comprehensive universities, single specialty institutions, and polytechnic institutions (Xie 2018: 117). Besides universities, there were also separate research institutes, the Chinese Academy of Sciences and the Chinese Academy of Social Sciences. Research institutes still play important roles in China's higher education system today and have added the function of teaching and student cultivation to those of research and scholarship.

The period of the 'radical ten years' (1966–1976) was a time of political disorder and turbulence. But the full damage of the radical period in Chinese higher education really lasted for two decades, from 1957 to 1977 (Xie 2018: 120–1). Universities stopped functioning properly with regard to teaching and research. Rather, they were constantly engaged in political movements under the guidance of the party. When Deng Xiaoping stated that science should be considered 'to be the most crucial of the four modernizations, the one that would drive the other three (industry, agriculture and national defence)' (Vogel 2011: 197), Chinese science and higher education had to start over again. Since then, Chinese higher education adopted a strategy of internationalization and learning from American and European university models (F. Huang 2017).

The structure of the contemporary Chinese higher education system gradually emerged after 1978. Higher education in China has experienced huge growth in the three decades after 1989, in both overall scale and research capacity (Marginson 2018f). China has become a competent player in the global higher education system. According to the UNESCO data (2018), the gross enrolment rate in China was 51 per cent in 2018, compared to 5 per cent in 1996. The number of mainland Chinese universities listed in the top 500 universities of the Academic Ranking of World Universities rose from 8 in 2003 to 72 in 2020.

The taking off of China's higher education in the last three decades (Marginson 2011c) has been accompanied by not only rapid massification but also the privatization, marketization and governmental deregulation of higher education, even while the government has sustained its massive and growing financial input (Y. Cheng and Wang 2012; Mok 2013). Since the late 1990s, the Chinese government has concentrated on establishing its own world-class universities (F. Huang 2015; J. Li 2012). Successive policies have been implemented to this end, including the '211' project of 1995, the '985' project of 1998, and the 'Double First-Class' of 2015.

In the Mao era, higher education undertook the public responsibility of contributing to the proletarian revolution and socialist construction. This was the Communist approach to realizing national salvation. In the post-Mao era, in spite of the marketization and privatization of higher education, the emphasis on making higher education's missions consistent with the national missions persists. Higher education still undertakes the responsibility of serving the national strategy of modernization, maintaining social stability and upgrading the economy (S. Guo and Guo 2016). I shall return to this in Chapter 8.

3

The Higher Education-Related Anglo-American Tradition

3.1 Introduction

This chapter provides a summary of Anglo-American liberal political philosophy in the post-Reformation period, with particular attention to those aspects that underpin conceptions of the public (good) in higher education. It is not intended to provide a systematic and detailed interpretation of Anglo-American liberal political philosophy. Instead, it draws on key works of John Locke, Adam Smith, John Stuart Mill, John Dewey, John Rawls and Amartya Sen so as to discuss ideas most relevant to the public (good) in higher education. All of these thinkers can be regarded as liberal philosophers. Liberalism as a school of philosophy draws these thinkers together despite their disagreement on certain fundamental issues, such as interpretations of the nature of liberty (see 3.2.2 and 3.2.3 for more discussions on this).

3.2 Liberalism and the Key Thinkers

This section attempts to provide a general account of the listed thinkers' positions in the school of liberalism. Specifically, it focuses on the way the thinkers regard 'liberty' as a value in comparison with other values, especially equality – whether they see 'liberty' as more important than 'equality' or not. This is to demonstrate how the key thinkers regard liberty, as well as to reflect their views on aspects related to the public (good) in higher education.

3.2.1 A Brief Introduction to Liberalism

Paradoxically, one of the few areas of agreement between liberal philosophers is that there is little consensus on fundamental issues of liberalism, such as the substance of liberty, and to what extent liberty should be guaranteed (for discussions on liberal thinkers' diverging interpretations of liberty, see, e.g., Hobhouse [1911] 1964). Ryan (2012: 28) argues that 'we are faced with liberalisms rather than liberalism'. For example, while Rawls has a limited take on liberty as political liberty, Sen regards liberty as a comprehensive concept reflecting different aspects of development, including political freedoms and agency.

Nevertheless, the existence of differences does not undermine the fact that liberalism constitutes a school of thought. Liberal philosophers' agreement on the importance of liberty and of protecting liberty has brought them together, even though they give liberty different meanings and varying degrees of importance. Arguably, it is the common insistence on the central importance of liberty that distinguishes the Anglo-American tradition from the Chinese tradition.

In unpacking liberalism, scholars/researchers have pointed to different streams of liberalism such as utilitarianism (for discussions on utilitarianism, see, e.g., Riley 1988), contractarianism (see, e.g., Kliemt 2004) and pragmatism (see, e.g., Anderson 1990). Among the thinkers listed previously, Mill was a representative of utilitarianism, Locke of contractarianism and Dewey of pragmatism. However, the customary identification of these different streams is not based on the different liberal philosophers' interpretations concerning liberty but reflects their tenets concerning other issues. Utilitarianism centres on how to implement the principle of prioritizing the utility when making decisions (Sen and Williams 1982: 3), whereas contractarianism focuses on the origin and legitimacy of political authority or moral norms (see, e.g., Chapter 8 of Locke [1689] 1976). Not all liberal philosophers fit perfectly to these streams. Sen (2006: 70) expresses disagreement with Rawls's view of Adam Smith as a utilitarian.

Some scholars distinguish between classical liberalism and modern liberalism. Classical liberalism is more politically oriented, being centred on protecting individual liberty by limiting the state (Ryan 2012: 23–4). It is also interested in protecting individual property. The virtue of the limited state is often justified by the corresponding social and economic prosperity enabled by it. In these respects, Locke and Smith are classical liberal philosophers. In contrast, modern liberalism goes beyond the political realm and national borders and builds its tenets on a moral basis (Ryan 2012: 25–6). In the eyes of modern liberal philosophers, limited government is essential in order to reduce government coercion. It is also essential because of the importance of liberty in the development of human agency, which is key to innovation (Ryan 2012: 25). To modern liberalism, not just the state but social mores and norms may constitute threats to individual liberty. Further, some modern liberal philosophers, including Sen, may include the global scale in discussing liberty (see 3.3.4). Sen and Mill are paradigmatic modern liberal philosophers.

However, when categorizing liberalism into classical liberalism and modern liberalism, values besides liberty that are highly relevant to the public (good) in higher education and are also important focuses of liberalism are not given the central status. Equality is an essential theme. Many liberal philosophers have substantially written on equality while discussing liberty. The relationship between liberty and equality is often a central concern. Some prioritize liberty over equality (such as Smith, Mill and Rawls), while some others think that both liberty and equality belong to the most important values (such as Locke, Dewey and Sen). Their attitudes towards the relationship between liberty and equality are arguably key to understanding certain crucial aspects of the public (good) in higher education. For example, whether to insist on equality of opportunity or equality of outcome in higher education practice and to what extent should the state intervene in higher education to promote equality. There is also the important question of whether equality and liberty are mutually contradictory or reciprocal with each other, where again, the key thinkers differ. In order to unpack liberalism in relation to the public (good) in higher education, this section unravels the relationship between liberty and the values represented by equality.

3.2.2 Liberty (At Least Some Liberties) Takes Primacy over Equality

Some liberal philosophers state clearly that liberty should take precedence over equality, while others imply their preference for liberty by choosing not to substantially discuss equality or to not prioritize the importance of equality.

Adam Smith on Liberty and Equality

In his scholarship, Smith seeks to demonstrate the feasibility of free individuals spontaneously forming civil society without government intervention. In *The Theory of Moral Sentiments*, Smith ([1790] 2010: 18) argues that the possibility of having self-regulated civil society is rooted in human beings' natural sympathy, from which sociability develops. The decentralized actions of millions of people lead to the emergent bottom-up order of civil society. Sympathy enables individuals to be spectators of other people's situations and feelings. Impartial spectators, anyone who does not have any relation with the person nor the action, are expected to give impartial judgement based on their sensibility and mutual understanding with the person being observed. The person being observed tries their best to win impartial spectators' approbation. The process of winning impartial spectators' approval helps individuals to adjust their behaviours and sentiments, and will 'generate sufficient social and moral order for the perpetuation of sociability' (Lomonaco 1999: 396). At the individual level, people have mirrored encounters with others every day as an essential part of their social life. The aggregation of this individual level phenomenon leads to the social feedback system of civil society, encouraging good actions and punishes bad behaviours. Hence, there is no need for governmental coercion to establish or maintain civil society (Fleischacker 2013: 10).

However, according to Smith, the social feedback system did not appear until the emergence of commercial society (Boyd 2013: 456). Smith ([1827] 2000: 37) argues that a proper commercial society grows from the situation where 'every [hu]man lives by exchanging, or becomes in some measure a merchant'. In this society, individuals 'stand at all times in need of the cooperation and assistance of great multitudes, while his whole life is scarce sufficient to gain friendship of a few persons' (A. Smith [1827] 2000: 26).

Prosperity comes out of the willingness to trade with people that one does not know. The growing range of exchange enables people from far away to connect. This makes social behaviours in commercial society more complex than in previous societies where for most of the time, only acquaintances were involved. Smith states that commercial and market interactions gradually lead to the development of bourgeois social virtues including honesty, prudence and propriety (see Part I, Section IV, of A. Smith, [1790] 2010). Commercial society is not only about exchange and trade but is a network of manners and morals (Lomonaco 1999: 402). Even though individuals may strive for their own interest, they still have concerns with others' situations and seek to maintain a world of justice. Moreover, the advent of the market also leads to the establishment of a legal system regulating individual rights and obligations. With the installation of a system of law, the order of the market and society are further protected (Boyd 2013: 447–8).

Smith ([1827] 2000: 363) further argues that there is neither need nor rationale for the state to intervene in people's self-regulated civil society, except for three necessary duties – military defence, maintaining social justice and providing public service. The three duties are articulated in 3.3.2. Notably, Smith does not explicitly call for the state to promote equality.

Smith advocates equality but is not deeply concerned with it. In *The Wealth of Nations*, Smith appeals for the state to treat all citizens equally, in accordance with the norms of the legal system, and rejects slavery and opposes the idea of blaming poverty on poor people's lack of virtues. The rejection belongs to his theses on human equality in moral philosophy. Smith points out that human beings are equal in terms of their capacity for virtue and intelligence: 'The difference of natural talents in different men is, in reality, much less than we are aware of' (A. Smith [1827] 2000: 28–9). This moral equality partly parallels with Confucian moral equality (see more discussion on this in Chapter 6). However, Smith does not expressly defend equality of political rights nor call for promoting socio-economic equality. Instead, he sees socio-economic inequality as inevitable in commercial society and argues only for a minimal state redistributive programme (Fleischacker 2013). Equality is in a subordinate position in Smith's theses.

In higher education, Smith's thoughts on liberty and equality may be interpreted as protecting higher education from state intervention, and defending academic freedom and institutional autonomy. Meanwhile, Smith's proposition that humans have equality of natural talents can have important implications for higher education.

John Stuart Mill on Liberty and Equality

John Stuart Mill works explicitly and substantially on both liberty and equality. To Mill, liberty and equality (or at least some equalities) are desirable because they are necessary and conducive to utility as happiness.

In *On Liberty*, Mill examines the reasons why liberty is essential and how to protect individuals' liberty. He explains that liberty contains two elements. The first element is freedom of thought, discussion and action, restrained by the principle of self-protection. These three freedoms should be treated differently (see further). The second element is room for individuals to develop their individuality and mental intelligence. This is to give individuals authentic liberty. The two types of liberty are essential because: (1) individual liberty is a principle of realizing human happiness, and (2) continuing social progress requires individual liberty.

Liberty for Mill does not involve only the limited state but also a limited society. This is a big step forward from previous philosophers including John Locke and Adam Smith. John Locke primarily focuses on potential tyranny from governments and only draws boundaries around the state (this is elaborated in 3.2.3). Adam Smith tends to ignore the existence of potential social control. Mill, however, sees this social control, to a certain extent, as a side-effect of the development and maturation of democratic society. Mill ([1859] 2015: 9) states that 'there is considerable jealousy of direct interference, by the legislative or the executive power', but the dangers of the tyranny of the majority, and social control, are easily ignored by people.

Hence, Mill addresses how to 'make the fitting adjustment between individual independence and social control' (Mill [1859] 2015: 9). He argues that the self-protection principle is 'the sole end for which [hu]mankind are warranted, individually or collectively, in interfering with the liberty of action of any of their number' (Mill [1859] 2015: 14). In other words, individuals shall enjoy absolute liberty as long as no one else is involved or influenced without one's consent. He then presents three regions of liberty, refers back to the two types of liberty and examines the regions in correspondence with the self-protection principle. The three regions include 'the inward domain of consciousness demanding liberty of conscience', 'liberty of tastes and pursuits' and liberty of 'combination among individuals' (Mill [1859] 2015: 14–15).

The 'inward domain of consciousness' emphasizes individuals' spiritual liberty including freedom of opinion, feeling and sentiment on all aspects. Conscious liberty should be absolute.

> There is no medium between perfect freedom of expressing opinions, and absolute despotism. Whenever you invest the rulers of the country with any power to suppress opinion, you invest them with all power ... there is no country in which the power of suppressing opinions has ever, in practice, been ... unrestraint. (Mill [1825] 1996: 6–7)

However, the freedom of expressing opinions and publishing may concern others. It should strictly follow the principle of self-protection and should never harm others. The second region 'liberty of tastes and pursuits' stresses individuals' development of their own character and planning for their own lives. The key is to do 'as we like' as long as the consequences do not 'harm [others], even though they should think our conduct foolish, perverse, or wrong' (Mill [1859] 2015: 19). Mill notes that it is important for individuals to stick to their own character even though it may conflict with social customs, norms and the masses. The liberty of 'combination among individuals' enables people to unite freely as long as the purpose of their union does not result in harm to others.

Mill especially emphasizes liberty of thought and discussion, which is the source of personal happiness and social progress. This is consistent with the idea that the key to liberty does not lie in passive personal freedom but individuals' ability in developing their unique individuality. Only with liberty of thought and discussion could people fight against tyranny or corruption, approach the truth and maintain social diversity. These liberties are necessary for promoting human happiness and social progress. Otherwise, people are trapped in a situation of compelled silence. Gradually, they lose the spirit of caring about public affairs and become apathetic to tyranny and corruption. This undermines the quality and quantity of people's happiness, and blocks the progress of society.

Although liberty does not take formal primacy over utility in Mill's writings, it is arguably more important to him than equality. Nevertheless, in Mill's work, the relationship between liberty and equality is not necessarily conflicting. Some scholars/researchers argue that Mill regards equality and liberty as complementary rather than conflicting (Donner, 1998; Morales, 1996). For example, Morales (1996: 97, 107, 167) argues that the seeming conflict between liberty and equality is in fact that between liberty and power. The development of individuality and human excellence may lead to individuals who desire to treat other people as equals. In other words, without coercion from power (either political or social power), individuals will have the freedom to develop their character and individuality. This freedom may lead to their awareness of, and desire for, equality. Hence, the perfect equality, articulated in *The Subjection of Women* by Mill, 'is closely intertwined with liberty understood as a human excellence' (Donner 1998: 339). This is potentially very important in considering what higher education may achieve in the process of students' developing human excellence. More discussion is provided in Chapter 5.

However, Mill's direct advocacy of equality is narrow, being primarily confined to equality of men and women. Mill does not see genuine differences in capacity between men and women. He is concerned that political inequality between men and women can result in political and social repression of women, hindering their development of individuality and mentality.

> The principle which regulates the existing social relations between the two sexes – the legal subordination of one sex to the other – is wrong in itself, and now one of the chief hindrances to human improvement; and it ought to be replaced by a principle of perfect equality, admitting no power or privilege on the one side, or disability on the other. (Mill [1869] 1996: 261)

However, Mill does not develop the idea of sex equality between men and women into the idea of equality of all human beings. Nevertheless, Mill's point concerning the reciprocal relationship between equality and liberty can provide valuable insights into the public (good) in higher education, especially with regard to academic freedom and institutional autonomy of the university, as well as insights into how to develop students' character and individuality.

John Rawls on Liberty and Equality

John Rawls worked substantially on liberty and equality, attempting to address two central questions: (1) how to guarantee citizens' free and equal status, and (2) how to attain a stable and just society. It can be argued that Rawls stresses both liberty and equality. He asserts that all individuals are born equal and free. However, he explicitly prefers liberty – although only some liberties, basic liberties – rather than equality. Nevertheless, he acknowledges that to some extent liberty and equality are intertwined. For example, all individuals equally share basic liberties. Rawls's basic liberties take precedence over social-economic equality but not over equality of basic liberties.

It is necessary to start unpacking Rawls's theses on liberty and equality by introducing the notions of the 'original position' and the 'veil of ignorance'. Parallel to Locke's idea that all human beings are free and equal by nature, Rawls highlights that 'the parties in the original position are equal' and free to make reasonable decisions (Rawls [1971] 2005: 20). Under the condition of the 'veil of ignorance', persons in original positions do not know to which society or generation they belong, but they have general information about human society. They are supposed to make decisions in the original position. Decisions should be reasonable considering what they anticipate for their societies and thus abide by two principles:

> First, each person is to have an equal right to the most extensive scheme of equal basic liberties compatible with a similar scheme of liberties for others. Second, social and economic inequalities are to be arranged so that they are both (a) reasonably expected to be to everyone's advantage, and (b) attached to positions and offices open to all. (Rawls [1971] 2005: 61)

The aim of the two principles, according to Rawls, is to assign rights and duties, and distribute social and economic advantages. The two principles are in lexical order: the second principle should be subject to the first. Equal basic liberties of all human beings should have absolute weight in regard to social and economic goods. In terms of the second principle, Rawls refers to its two components as fair equality of opportunity and the difference principle. The two components of the second principle are to govern the distribution of social and economic advantages, and to address social and economic inequalities. Particularly, the existence of social and economic inequalities could only be justified when they are 'to the greatest benefit of the least advantaged, and attached to offices and positions open to all under conditions of fair equality of opportunity' (Rawls [1971] 2005: 83).

Rawls divides liberty into two categories – basic liberties and legal liberties – and gives them differing statuses. The former category is the essential one. This division enables Rawls to explore further what the intrinsic nature of different liberties is and how to respond specifically to different liberties with ways of protecting them. More importantly, this makes it possible to balance diverse needs of, and relieve tensions between, liberty and equality. For instance, in utilitarianism, equality among individuals might be compromised because utilitarianism is guided by an idea of liberty that stresses the importance of providing individuals with freedom to develop their individuality. Rawls's conceptions of liberty inherit the liberal tradition and commit to protecting individuals' basic liberties. On the other hand, his conceptions highlight the importance of equality and set up a baseline of inequalities which human beings naturally acquire (e.g., social classes, disabilities) and which should not become restraints to their development and self-fulfilment.

Rawls's basic liberties primarily refer to political liberty – individuals' equal right to vote on political occasions and their eligibility to run for public office. They also include 'freedom of speech and assembly; liberty of conscience and freedom of thought; freedom of the person along with the right to hold (personal) property; and freedom from arbitrary arrest and seizures as defined by the concept of the rule of law' (Rawls [1971] 2005: 61). These basic liberties largely overlap with Locke's idea of rights and Mill's conception of liberty. However, what distinguishes Rawls is his argument that all persons in society enjoy equal basic liberties regardless of their background and personal wealth, and everyone has the liberty to vote with equal weight.

Rawls gives particular emphasis to liberty of conscience and freedom of thought. The liberty of conscience that persons exercise in the original position protects them from being suppressed by any dominant religions or moral doctrines. Liberty of conscience requires toleration and concerns about common interests as well. It is limited by 'the common interest in public order and security' (Rawls [1971] 2005: 212). However, this does not permit the government's suppression of liberty of conscience because the government does not have the right or authority to do so. Rather, this limitation of liberty of conscience is only for the sake of protecting persons' equal moral and religious liberty. Meanwhile, liberty of conscience and freedom of thought are beneficial to individuals and society because they are important to the development of persons' moral powers. This strongly resonates with Mill's statement about the value of protecting freedom of thought. It also echoes Confucian individualism that stresses helping persons to better fulfil their roles in communities.

Beyond basic liberties, other liberties are decided not by parties in the original position under the condition of the veil of ignorance but by members of society at the legislative stage, in light of the two principles of justice. It is possible to have various stipulations of legal liberties and rights in different societies according to their constitutional provisions. For example, one form of legal liberty and right specified in Rawls's theory is the ownership of property.

The second principle concentrates more on equality. The core of Rawls's idea of equality lies in his special attention to persons' abilities and aspirations and disadvantaged persons. He aims to guarantee individuals with similar abilities and aspirations equal opportunity, and compensate those disadvantaged who are victims merely because of their 'bad luck' in 'natural gambling'. Fair equality of opportunity requires that 'those who have the same level of talent and ability and the same willingness to use those gifts should have the same prospects of success regardless of their social class of origin, the class into which they are born and develop until the age of reason' (Rawls [1971] 2005: 44). However, Rawls does not take a position regarding all persons as being born equally gifted as Confucianism does. Rawls argues that some persons are naturally more advantaged and gifted.

Rawls's theses on liberty and equality, especially fair equality of opportunity, have been influential in higher education practice. The theses are highly relevant to debates about whether to implement equality of opportunity or equality of result as a guiding principle in higher education. Meanwhile, Rawls's attitudes of individuals' differentiated natural gifts, which are in line with his advocacy of fair equality of opportunity, are also embodied in higher education practice. There is more discussion of these aspects in Chapters 5 and 6.

3.2.3 Liberty Is One of Many Important Values

There are also liberal philosophers who regard liberty as one of many important values and do not prioritize liberty over equality. This does not mean that liberty does not enjoy a central status in these philosophers' theses but highlights that there are many other values besides liberty, including equality, that should also be insisted on.

John Locke on Liberty and Equality

Liberty and equality are often discussed jointly in the work of John Locke. Arguably, it was the aim of protecting liberty and equality of people that largely guided the development of Locke's political theory. Similar to other classical liberal philosophers, Locke explores liberty and equality in the political realm and primarily focuses on establishing a limited state.

Locke was one of the forefathers of social contractarianism, arguing that individuals' consent is decisive to the legitimacy of the state. It is the people's consent that gives justification for the transfer of power from separate individuals to the state. 'Men are by nature all free, equal, and independent, no one can be put out of this estate, and subjected to the political power of another, without his own consent' (Locke [1689] 1976: 49). In order to explore the origin and legitimacy of the state, Locke raises and attempts to answer two important questions: (1) how can individuals unite to form a community – a civil society; and (2) how to form a government that should prevent the state power from becoming arbitrary, so that an individual cannot be forced to comply with the will of another individual.[1]

Arguably, the process of answering the two questions is also a process of looking for ways to protect individuals' political liberty and equality. Locke ([1689] 1976: 4) argues that in the process of transforming the state of nature to civil society, individuals with equal 'moral autonomy' and 'perfect freedom' are drawn into a unified community. Locke sees the state of nature as 'a state of perfect *freedom* [for human beings] to order their actions and dispose of their possessions and persons as they think fit . . . without asking leave, or depending upon the will of any other man', and a state of *equality*, 'wherein all the power and jurisdiction is reciprocal, no one having more than another' (Locke [1689] 1976: 4, italics added).

Nevertheless, the state of nature is not always an ideal situation, as people serving as their own judges can bring about challenges. Human beings' self-love can make them partial to themselves and their friends when facing controversy. Their 'ill-nature, passion, and revenge' can 'carry men too far in punishing others, and hence nothing but confusion and disorder will follow' (Locke [1689] 1976: 8).

Locke suggests that it is necessary to change the natural state to a more closely connected community with a common judge. Given that the main problem for

---

[1] Without discussing sex equality in detail, I shall discuss Locke's idea in the contemporary context and assume the term 'men' refers to the whole of humanity.

the state of nature lies in human beings' partiality of judgement, the best remedy is to establish a common judge with authority. As Locke sees it, transformation from the state of nature to civil society rests on ownership of the power to punish. In civil society, the power to seek one's own preservation is limited by the law, and the power to punish is transferred to the government. This leads to the answer of the second question, by discussing how the governments use the power including the legislative power and the executive power, to punish. More details of Locke's ideas on the state are discussed in 3.3.2.

It is clear that for Locke, liberty and equality, primarily in the sense of political liberty and equality, are enjoyed by all individuals naturally and should be protected in any circumstance, unless individuals willingly consent to give them up. The central problem he tries to solve is how to reconcile freedom and authority. But the connotations of his political liberty and equality are abstract and ambiguous. There is no explicit articulation of the constituents of liberty and equality or the relationship between liberty and equality. Different interpretations can be drawn from Locke. But it may still be fair to argue that Locke's equality mainly refers to equality of political liberty, which resonates with Rawls's equal basic liberties. However, Locke did provide a way of viewing the relationship between two values – they are often intertwined and both of them are important and should be protected. As a classical liberal thinker, Locke's views on liberty and equality primarily shed light on the relationship between the state and the university in higher education. The relationship is again associated with the limited liberal state idea.

John Dewey on Liberty and Equality

Dewey's ideas on liberty and equality are implied in his discussions about democracy. He does not concentrate much on the relationship between liberty and equality – for example, the question of which one is primary – but views both of these values as irreplaceable in a democratic society.

In a lecture in China, Dewey states that democracy is about more than a polity involving 'popular election of officials, [and] short terms of office and frequent elections' (Dewey [1927] 2016: 130). It also refers to a broader economic, social and political environment that requires a consensus on certain issues in society. The social idea of democracy primarily focuses on people's engagement in communities and their communal life. According to Dewey, a prerequisite of a democratic society is having individuals, who understand, accept and employ democratic ideas, and actively participate in democratic activities. While the essential purpose of being an individual is to continuously develop individuality, the purpose of being members of communities is to have a clear consciousness of communal life. This points to the relation between liberty and equality (see later).

Arguably, in Anglo-American societies, there are long-standing tensions between individuals and human associations. While the Anglo-American tradition recognizes the constant danger that human associations can repress individuals (see, e.g., the previous discussion by Mill), it deliberately ignores individuals' needs for, and engagement with, associations. Although Dewey inherits the Anglo-American liberal idea concerning individualism and freedom, he moves forward in mitigating the existing tensions. Dewey avers that individuals are not isolated entities, and it would be 'a great mistake ... to regard the isolated individual possessed of inherent rights "by nature" apart from associations' (Dewey [1927] 2016: 132). In Dewey's eyes, atomic individualism has gradually become a means whereby the better-off accounted for and justified expanding social inequalities.

> [The old atomic individualism is] really engaged in justifying the activities of a new form of concentrated [economic power, which] . . . has consistently and persistently denied effective freedom to the economically underpowered and underprivileged. (Dewey [1935] 1987: 136)

In addition, according to Dewey, the fact that human beings are born as social creatures is self-evident. Protecting individuals from repressions by communities does not require isolating individuals from communities. True individualism is 'a product of the relaxation of the grip of the authority of custom and traditions as standards of belief' (Dewey [1916] 2011: 167). Dewey discusses liberty and equality in correspondence with the community and human beings' communal life. The development of individuality and mentality, and ability to develop and resist external repressions constitute the essence of liberty. But Dewey argues that the idea of liberty is not to grant individuals 'independence of social ties' nor unlimited freedom regardless of communities. In contrast, it is 'the power to be an individualised self making a distinctive contribution and enjoying in its own way the fruits of association', as well as to secure 'release and fulfilment of personal potentialities which [take] place only in rich and manifold association with others' (Dewey [1927] 2016: 177).

To Dewey, equality is never about 'mathematical or physical equivalence in virtue of which any one element may be substituted for another' (Dewey

[1927] 2016: 177). Unlike liberty which human beings should naturally possess, equality is 'a fruit of the community'. It is led by human beings' living communal lives. In particular,

> [equality] denotes the unhampered share with which each member of the community has in the consequences of the associated action. It is equitable because it is measured only by need and capacity to utilize, not by extraneous factors which deprive one in order that another may take and have. . . . Equality does not signify that kind of mathematical or physical equivalence in virtue of which any one element may be substituted for another. It denotes effective regard for whatever is distinctive and unique in each, irrespective of physical and psychological inequalities. It is not a natural possession but is a fruit of the community when its action is directed by its character as a community. (Dewey [1927] 2016: 177)

Both liberty and equality are important to Dewey but for different reasons. Liberty, especially freedom of speech, is an essential aspect of a democratic society. It should be protected. This claim is closely relevant to academic freedom in higher education. Nevertheless, equality is not a value naturally possessed. It is the potential result of community and democracy. Society needs to work on the mitigation of inequality, including in higher education. But Dewey does not advocate absolute equality. He states that inequality could be acceptable at a moderate level, so that people with capacity could effectively utilize resources.

Amartya Sen on Liberty and Equality

Liberty, which is more often referred to as freedom by Amartya Sen, is a central tenet of his theses. Sen's *Development as Freedom* argues that the expansion of individual freedom is an ultimate aim in itself. 'Development can be seen, it is argued here, as a process of expanding the real freedoms that people enjoy' (Sen 1999: 3). For Sen, development is not only about a rise in human beings' financial income or technological advance, as they do not necessarily lead to an advance in people's overall welfare. Sen also argues that the removal of unfreedoms is at the heart of enabling people to live better lives, though that objective is hard to define.

He does not prioritize freedom in an absolute sense. Sen uses the concept of the information base to illustrate the importance of values besides freedom. This is 'the information that is needed for making judgements using that approach and – no less important – the information that is "excluded" from a direct evaluative role in their approach' (Sen 1999: 56). If certain information is excluded from the informational basis, this would demonstrate insensitivity to that information and result in a biased view.

Libertarianism, which centres on, and prioritizes, liberty and rights, seems to be acceptable if the intention is to protect and enhance individual freedom. However, Sen questions libertarianism, given the terrible results it can lead to. He notes libertarianism's insensitivity to many other vital aspects of human life, such as poverty (Sen 1999: 67). As Sen indicates, a gigantic famine can coexist even when people's rights and liberty are not violated. Similarly, Sen criticizes the insensitivity of utilitarianism to equality. He argues that classic utilitarianism has no concern with principles besides the Principle of Utility, such as equality in the distributional process of utilities. Its information base, only consisting of utilitarian principles, is highly exclusive.

Meanwhile, Sen disagrees with Rawls for what Rawls calls 'the priority of liberty'. In Sen's eyes, freedoms are decisively important, but they cannot be the only content of the information base. Many other concerns such as health care, economic needs and basic education, which are listed as primary goods rather than basic liberties by Rawls, should also be included. Nevertheless, Sen highlights an important idea that Rawlsian theory of justice conveys – the need for a special treatment of individual freedom. Indeed, Sen acknowledges that Rawls has stimulated him to pay particular attention to freedom, not only for its instrumental benefits but for its intrinsic value.

Specifically, Sen argues that there are two reasons why freedom should be valued. One is the instrumental interests made possible by the enhancement of freedom, which is already well recognized. For example, economic development requires free agency. This also has resonance in Mill's advocacy for liberty, in which liberty is necessary and conducive to social progress. The other reason that freedom should be valued is that it is the primary end of development. To support this idea, Sen states that the denial of political freedoms and rights to people would result in the loss of 'important freedoms in leading their lives' and deny them the 'opportunity to take part in crucial decisions regarding public affairs' (Sen 1999: 16). As the denial of these rights restricts human lives socially and politically, such deprivation is repressive, even if there are no other consequential negative effects. This reasoning refutes the argument that individual freedom can be sacrificed to stimulate economic growth. In Sen's eyes, individual freedom should not be sacrificed for instrumental benefit, even if it is so sacrificed, no corresponding interests will emerge.

Therefore, Sen claims that the information basis should be as comprehensive as possible to avoid the problem of information exclusion. To understand freedom in a comprehensive way enables freedom to become a comprehensive information base. To protect and expand individuals' 'comprehensive freedom' is to develop their 'capability'. Sen's arguments on capability are explored in 3.3.1.

> A person's 'capability' refers to the alternative combinations of functionings that are feasible for her to achieve. Capability is thus a kind of freedom: the substantive freedom to achieve alternative functioning combinations (or, less formally put, the freedom to achieve various lifestyles). (Sen 1999: 75)

In sum, Sen defines freedom in a comprehensive way that primarily concentrates on the development of individual capability. His freedom goes beyond the political realm and includes a wide range of values. Expansion of freedom can lead to many desired results. Nevertheless, the comprehensive information base should consider other issues as well. Equality is one of them. Moving beyond equality of opportunity, Sen raises the idea of equality of freedom to achieve that enables individuals to develop their capability and thus expand their freedom. This is discussed further in Chapter 6.

3.3 The Key Thinkers on Spheres of Social Action

The individual (arguably family is included in the individual sphere in the Anglo-American tradition), the state, civil society, the market and the world can be understood as different spheres of social action. Discussions on spheres of social action have the potential to unpack important topics concerning the public (good) in higher education. For example, what public goods can the university produce for different spheres of social action, and the relationship between the university and spheres of social action. This section aims to examine the arguments of the listed liberal philosophers in relation to the spheres of social action. However, the discussion of the sphere of the market is included in Chapter 8.

Despite varying interpretations of each sphere, as will be shown in this section, it is generally agreed that in the liberal imaginary, civil society and the market are not commanded by a comprehensive state but remain at least partly independent (see Figure 3.1). This embodies the idea of the division of powers in the Anglo-American social imaginary. The individual and family are highly autonomous and partly overlap with the three collective spheres. The autonomy of individual and family is protected by the idea of individual freedom. There is

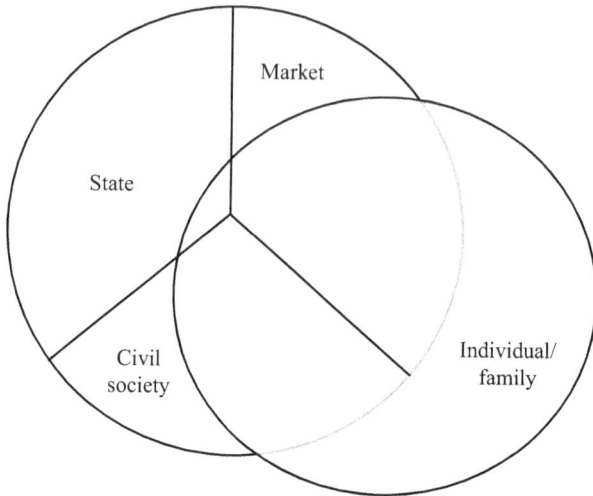

Figure 3.1 Anglo-American spheres of social action. *Source*: Marginson and Yang (2021).

an underlying zero-sum assumption concerning the scope of the liberal spheres: the enlargement of one sphere may lead to a reduction of another. For example, an expansion of the state sphere can result in a reduction of the sphere of civil society. Essential to liberalism is the need to restrain the scope of the state and protect the individual sphere against potential intrusion from the other, especially state and civil society.

3.3.1 Individual: The Development of Individuals

In relation to the development of individuals, four aspects deserve examination – individual freedom, self-respect and mutual respect of individuals, the public spirit of individuals and the capability of individuals. Individual freedom was discussed in 3.2. The other three themes are discussed in this section. These three themes are crucial to the discussion of the public (good) in higher education because they help to answer the question of what qualities of students should be cultivated through higher education and how that objective can be realized.

Self-Respect and Mutual Respect of Individuals: John Rawls

Maintaining people's self-respect is a fundamental argument in Rawls's work on justice. Self-respect is essential partly because it makes possible mutual respect between individuals, which is necessary for social cooperation. Also, in the absence of self-respect, mutual resentment may arise. A well-ordered society needs individuals' self-respect.

Rawls first discusses self-respect of individuals when articulating basic liberties and equality. One distinctive rationale for promoting equality among individuals, according to Rawls, is to maintain persons' self-respect. Rawls ([1993] 2004: 181) argues that providing a social base for the attainment of self-respect is a prerequisite for establishing a well-ordered society. Self-respect is essential to limiting persons' envy to an excusable scope because it gives them self-confidence in their own value and in the worth of carrying out their varied interpretations of what the good is. A lack of self-respect could lead to humiliation and even resentment, which make social cooperation impossible. 'If the equal basic liberties of some are restricted or denied, social cooperation on the basis of mutual respect is impossible' (Rawls [1993] 2004: 337).

As Rawls sees it, self-respect is not solely based on self-determination. People's self-respect is partly decided by the external social environment. For example, an inequality gap in society that is too large may reduce the self-respect of disadvantaged persons. The key is having *equal* basic liberties rather than merely basic liberties.

Public Spirit of Individuals: John Stuart Mill

Mill particularly emphasizes public spirit when discussing the government. While his theses on the government are introduced in 3.3.2, here I primarily concentrate on the arguments about public spirit. Mill argues that individuals should be willing to actively participate in political affairs. Active participation requires individuals to have public spirit. To participate effectively individuals also ought to be mentally intelligent.

Mill points out that the government can satisfy 'all the exigencies of the social state' only when all individual members of society participate in collective affairs (Mill [1861] 2015: 224). However, as in most cases, individuals are more concerned with their own private affairs, if they are to participate in collective affairs they need a feeling for the general interests. This feeling for the general interests is called 'public spirit' by Mill. An individual is regarded as having 'public spirit' when he or she 'feels himself [or herself] one of the public' so that 'whatever is for their benefit [is] to be for his [or her] benefit' (Mill [1861] 2015: 224). Otherwise, Mill remarks that 'every thought or feeling . . . is absorbed in the individual and the family, the man never thinks of any collective interest, of any objects to be pursued jointly with others' (Mill [1861] 2015: 224). When there is a lack of public spirit, private morality suffers and the 'public is actually extinct' (Mill [1861] 2015: 224).

This willingness to participate in collective affairs plus altruism is the essence of Mill's 'public spirit', which is to be cultivated by political participation (Mill [1861] 2015: 224). Nevertheless, participation in itself is not enough to cultivate public spirit. That spirit should also be cultivated through education, especially moral education. Moral education can take the form of formal education in schools and universities, as well as informal education in people's daily lives. In addition, individuals should have the capacity for participation. This capacity primarily refers to individual members' mental intelligence, the promotion of which must be a primary task of education. This suggests an important role for universities, requiring them to consider how to cultivate public spirit of their students, including the necessary capacity that individuals require.

> [Education should provide] peculiar training of a citizen, the practical part of political education of a free people, taking them out of the narrow circle of personal and family selfishness and accustoming them to the comprehension of joint interests, the management of joint concerns – habituating them to act from public or semi-public motives and guide their conduct by aims which unite instead of isolating them from one another. (Mill [1859] 2015: 106)

Capability of Individuals: Amartya Sen

There are two necessities of capability, according to Sen: having alternative choices and being able to make and exercise alternative choices. These two aspects are not only about negative freedom but positive freedom. Not being repressed by external powers is not enough. Having the capability to know what they want and work for what they want is key. Education should prepare people for such a capability.

Sen argues that the capability perspective is able to overcome the problem of information exclusion. One merit of the capability perspective is that it can cover a wide range of concerns that are involved in individuals' pursuit of their own ends. People's having capability requires them to have substantial freedom, to have real opportunities to make decisions, to obtain certain primary goods that are necessary for their pursuits, and to have the ability to take advantage of existing opportunities and goods to pursue their objectives.

> [The capability perspective enjoys] a breadth and sensitivity that give it a very extensive reach, allowing evaluative attention to be paid to a variety of important concerns, some of which are ignored, one way or another, in the alternative

approaches. This extensive reach is possible because the freedoms of persons can be judged through explicit reference to outcomes and processes that they have reason to value and seek. (Sen 1999: 86)

The capability perspective centres on the development of human agency that enables individuals to make decisions based on several available options. Not only should alternate options be made available, individuals should be able to understand options, to choose from options, and to conduct their decisions.

Human capability does not appear out of nowhere. Education plays an important role in capability enhancement. This is suggestive of how higher education may be organized.

3.3.2 The State: The Ideal Form and Responsibility

The state is a central concern of liberal philosophers. For them the state is potentially too powerful, with momentous influence on other spheres of social action and on the degree of liberty exercised in other spheres. As noted, a starting question of classical liberalism is how to establish a limited state. This section mostly considers three aspects of the state: its ideal form and responsibility. In this process, the boundary of the state is discussed, an issue of paramount importance in relation to the public (good) in higher education.

The Ideal Form of the Government: Locke, Mill and Dewey

To Locke, the primary aim of having the ideal form of government is to prevent state power from becoming arbitrary, so that individuals' equal rights and liberty could be guaranteed. He appeals to an elective government, in relation to a commonwealth consisting of independent communities. Locke then explores the distribution and use of power in the commonwealth. He discusses two kinds of power: the legislative power and the executive power. The legislative power is the supreme power of making laws for society, the first and fundamental positive law of all commonwealths, the placing of which determines the form of government. The executive power is that of executing those laws. Although the legislative power is the supreme power, Locke still sets up four terms of limitation for its use:

> First, it is not nor can it possibly be absolutely arbitrary over the lives and fortunes of the people.... Secondly, the legislative, or supreme authority, cannot assume to itself a power to rule by extemporary arbitrary decrees, but is bound to dispense justice and decide the rights of the subject by promulgating standing laws, and authorized judges.... Thirdly, the supreme power cannot take from

any man any part of his property without his own consent. . . . Fourthly, the legislative cannot transfer the power of making laws to any other hands; for it being but a delegated power from the people, they who have it cannot pass it over to others. (Locke [1689] 1976: 68–73)

These limitations apply to both the legislative power and the state. In other words, the states' functions should be limited so that individuals' rights, lives and property are never injured. Locke states that this aim can be achieved by separating the legislative power and executive power.

The primary aim Mill attempts to achieve in delineating the form of government is also to prevent the government from being arbitrary while still enabling the government to promote social progress. Because social progress is dynamic and always under change, 'the proper functions of government are not a fixed thing' (Mill [1861] 2015: 191). There should be mechanisms for adjusting the government in specific situations. In the meantime, individual liberty should always be protected.

Mill sees representative government as the ideal form of government because it enables every member of society to be involved in community affairs. Further, Mill draws attention to two elements of a good government. The first is the virtues and mental intelligence of individual members of society. The second is the quality of the government as a machine – 'the degree in which it is adapted to take advantage of the amount of good qualities which may at any time exist, and make them instrumental to the right purposes' (Mill [1861] 2015: 200). The two elements lead to two criteria of a good government: 'how far it promotes the good arrangement of the affairs of society by means of the existing faculties, moral, intellectual, and active of its various members; and what is its effect in improving or deteriorating those faculties?' (Mill [1861] 2015: 214).

However, Dewey disagrees with the idea of a universal ideal form of the government. For him many existing theories concerning the state are problematic. The defect of theories may lay in their 'travel[ing] in a verbal circle . . . , [and] merely reduplicate[ing] in a so-called causal force the effects to be accounted for' (Dewey [1927] 2016: 64). Instead, he proposes to start from investigating human associations and uncovering the distinctive attributes of people when forming communities. According to Dewey, the state is necessary to society because the effects of the behaviours of individuals and groups are not always limited to those who engaged in the behaviour. When a behaviour influence people who are not involved in the conduct of the behaviour – Dewey calls such influence 'public' – there is a need for a public machine, the state, to regulate that behaviour (I return to this in Chapter 8). Further, Dewey remarks that because communities and countries possess a unique history and environment, there does not exist one single form of the desirable state. Even in the same nation, the state form could differ in different periods.

The Responsibility of the State: Locke and Smith

In Locke's opinion, the state's primary responsibility is to overcome the disorder and inconvenience of the state of nature and guarantee a peaceful and secure society for people in which their lives and property are protected. Responsibilities of the state highlighted by Locke include the protection of individuals' rights and the attainment of social equality. In Locke's theses, there also exists a large overlap between the state's responsibilities and the concept of the public good. Locke mentions the concept of the public good many times, proposing it as the entire and only pursuit of the state – not only in relation to preserving the public peace by restraining injustice but also by promoting the prosperity of the commonwealth, establishing good discipline and discouraging every sort of vice and impropriety (Locke [1689] 1976: 4).

Smith's take on the responsibility of the state is much narrower. He explicitly acknowledges only three essential responsibilities of the state that cannot be carried out by self-regulated civil society or by the market. The first duty is military defence, aiming at 'protecting the society from the violence and invasion of other independent societies' (A. Smith [1827] 2000: 363). The second duty concerns justice. Smith identifies the second duty as 'protecting every member of the society from injustice or oppression of every other member of it' or 'establishing an exact administration of justice' (A. Smith [1827] 2000: 372). Laws and judiciary allow injustice to be identified, and administrative power can be used to implement punishment. Providing public service is the third duty. This duty is to erect and maintain public institutions and public works that 'may be in the highest degree advantageous to a great society' but 'are, however, of such a nature that the profit could never repay the expense to any individual or small number of individuals, and which it therefore cannot be expected that any individual or small number of individuals should erect or maintain' (A. Smith [1827] 2000: 379). Two categories of public service are listed by Smith: to facilitate the commerce of society and to promote the instruction of the people through education.

3.3.3 Civil Society: The Formation and Values

This subsection examines civil society – a crucial sphere of social action in the Anglo-American tradition. The discussion of civil society here does not consider the economic market, which is examined in Chapter 8 when discussing the public/private.

Civil society is often implicitly understood as a sphere between the individual and state (Kasfir 1998: 3–4). However, there is a variety of ways to define it. Arguably, contemporary understandings of civil society have three primary components: civil society comprises a complex of autonomous institutions; it possesses complex relationships between itself and the state; and there is a general pattern of civil manners (Shils 1991: 4). The three components highlight civil society's role in serving to balance the power of the state and to protect the individual from the state's power. This subsection explores the formation and values of civil society.

The Spontaneous Formation of Civil Society: Smith

Adam Smith was among the intellectual forefathers of civil society (Boyd 2013). He discusses civil society primarily from a moral and sentimental perspective.

As noted, Smith argues that it is possible for individuals to self-organize without the government's intervention, which is the cornerstone of civil society. Smith's two books, *The Theory of Moral Sentiments* and *The Wealth of Nations*, reveal two foundational conditions of civil society. One is human beings' natural sympathy, sociability and sense of duty, and the other is the market and commercial society. The two aspects together establish a system of virtue in which altruism and benevolence are valued and result in the establishment of a formalized system of rules and laws. As both aspects were discussed in 3.2.2, I shall not repeat them here.

Social Values of Civil Society: Smith, Mill and Dewey

Smith lists a set of virtues on the basis of natural sympathy to explain how values influence the operation of civil society. In Smith's opinion, the basis for defining this set of virtues is the criterion for moral approval by impartial spectators. Letting people practise these values can enhance the stability of civil society. Here, there are three virtues in Smith's moral philosophy: propriety, prudence and benevolence.

> Virtue consists in the propriety of conduct, or in the suitableness of the affection from which we act to the object which excites it; . . . consists in the judicious pursuit of our own private interest and happiness, or in the proper government and direction of those selfish affections which aim solely at this end; . . . [and] consists in those affections only which aim at the happiness of others, not in those which aim at our own. (A. Smith [1790] 2010: 317–18)

Mill argues that society provides a desirable environment for individuals to develop and progress, and thus individuals in turn owe society for the environment (Mill [1859] 2015: 73). He further proposes an ideal set of values of civil society, including happiness, freedom, individuality, truth and altruism (Mill [1859] 2015: 52–7). There are constant interactions between society and individual members who comprise it. Society influences individuals to internalize its values through its institutions and faculties, and these values are invented and injected into society by individuals.

Dewey looks at how members of society develop social values and how those values can be conveyed through generations. People live in communities and conduct conjoint activities. Moral values 'isolated from communal life are hopeless abstractions' (Dewey [1927] 2016: 176). On the one hand, Dewey argues that there is no simultaneous common consensus on values, beliefs and methods among members of society. The consensus does not exist in organic and physical associations because the members of society are not living communal lives. In human associations, there are no moral connections between members, only joint activities. The common understanding about aims, beliefs, aspirations and knowledge among members make human associations a society. However, the evolution of common values, beliefs and methods rests on human beings' dispositions and deliberations. Only through education can people become mentally mature, able to conduct philosophical discussions and further create, comprehend and accept values, beliefs and methods. On the other hand, when such a consensus is reached, it must be conveyed from older to incoming generations via education. This is a critical prerequisite for the continuation of society. I shall expand on this in Chapter 5.

3.3.4 The World: Transcending the National Border

Among the liberal philosophers considered here, Dewey and Sen explicitly articulate a concept of the world beyond the national boundaries.

Dewey discusses the world in relation to the notion of the public, which can be interpreted as reaching the global scale. When the actions of some countries influence other countries not involved in the original actions, there exist 'public consequences' of those actions. These consequences ought to be examined, and the position of countries not originally involved but influenced by the consequences should be protected. Dewey calls for international organizations to regulate global public consequences. He attributes constant global turbulence to ingrained misunderstandings among nations. 'The atmosphere that makes international troubles inflammable is the product of deep-seated misunderstandings that have their origin in different philosophies of life' (Dewey [1921] 1976: 218). The only way out was to facilitate honest and in-depth mutual understandings between various philosophies.

Sen's emphasis on the importance of a global perspective resonates with Dewey's ideas, but Sen goes further. Sen's approach to the world is based on his idea of 'open impartiality'. According to Sen (2006: 130), open impartiality is to reach disinterested judgements from any fair or impartial spectators, no matter whether they belong to the focal group or not. This is a way of avoiding parochial bias.

In discussing the world, Sen views the nation-state as a focal group. He states that 'a theory of impartiality that is confined exactly within the borders of a sovereign state proceeds along territorial lines that do, of course, have legal significance but may not have similar political or moral perspicuity' (Sen 2006: 130). Sen provides three points to justify this statement. First, the nation-state could not cut convertible bonds among people sharing the same religion, language, gender, political beliefs or profession. These common bonds connect people across countries. People from various countries should do things together if they want to. The second is about possible parochial bias if outside voices are muted when making judgements. The public discussion should involve all existing voices, no matter who they are. This is a 'broadening' of perspectives and ideas, which helps in avoiding parochial bias.

The third point is in line with Dewey's definition of 'the public'. Specifically, the voice from outside a country should be heard because 'the actions of one country can seriously influence lives elsewhere. This is not only through the deliberate use of forceful means (for example, the occupation of Iraq in 2003), but also through less direct influences of trade and commerce' (Sen 2006: 129–30). For Dewey, a matter becomes public when the results of behaviour influence people who are not engaged in the decision-making process of or conduct of that behaviour. However, Sen goes a step further. He does not stop and call the behaviour 'the public', but argues that because of the fact of 'public influence', people excluded previously should be included and their voices heard. Combining the three points, Sen therefore states, 'To conclude this discussion, assessment of justice demands engagement with the "eyes of mankind"' (Sen 2006: 130).

Arguably, viewing the world as an important sphere of social action is crucial in exploring the public (good) of higher education, especially at the global level. With the growing number of internationally mobile people and closer connection among universities across countries, there is a need for more discussions on cross-border higher education activities and global outcomes of higher education. This is a way to overcome the parochial problem by furthering mutual understanding as well as addressing the potential global public consequences. Nevertheless, there are also potential dangers of making idealized cross-national discussions and of creating a 'globally parochial' problem that neglects local considerations. More on this is discussed in Chapter 9.

3.4 Higher Education in the United Kingdom and the United States

Certain attributes of the Anglo-American tradition discussed earlier are imprinted on higher education in the United Kingdom and the United States.

The first attribute is the division of powers that makes the university a public domain in contested separation with other spheres. In the medieval time, the university emerged as an institution with semi-independence from the state and the church. On the one hand, the church hoped to gain support and reinforcement from the university's production of scholarly and scientific knowledge (de Ridder-Symoens and Rüegg 2003: 14). On the other hand, the university secured its privileges, including internal jurisdiction, freedom from duties and levies, and habitation, through the utilization of the dynamic and tension between the church and the state (B. Zhang and Sun, 2004). By moving between the two major players of the time – state and church – the medieval university maintained its partial institutional autonomy and academic freedom (Altbach 2001; Marginson and Yang 2020).

Today, in the United Kingdom and the United States, despite the fact that governments in both countries have reasserted their roles in higher education, for example, by funding allocation and quality assurance, the university's semi-independence, manifested in regulated university autonomy, has survived (Marginson and Yang 2021). The semi-independence of the modern university is codified in the Humboldtian ideal (Rohstock 2012: 166). However, countries differ with regard to where the university is positioned in society. In the UK, policy has attempted to create a narrative that universities are 'private' market corporations. But British universities are de facto not creatures of, or entirely positioned inside, the market (Burrage 2010: 19). In the United States, universities are positioned across the junction between civil society and the market, while the state continues to make a difference in higher education through funding provision (Marginson and Yang 2020: 262).

The second attribute is liberal individualism, embodied in the dominance of human capital theory in capturing private outcomes of higher education. In human capital theory, the output of education primarily refers to the increase of marginal productivity of labour that determines the enhanced earnings associated with holding a degree (Blundell et al. 1999). To expand this good requires only atomized individuals with economic incentives and free markets in higher education and graduate labour. Following this narrative, higher education is understood primarily as a producer of individualized private goods, and the value of education is largely confined to economic returns of individual investment in higher education. As a result, public expenditure in higher education shrinks and collective goods produced by higher education are downplayed (Marginson and Yang 2021).

The UK and US higher education systems are influential in worldwide higher education. For example, modern universities in many countries partly follow the American research university (Rhoads 2011). Ideas from Anglo-American higher education have shaped influential narratives about academic freedom and university autonomy in higher education, and about the outcomes of higher education, with effects in higher education literature, policy and practice across the world. In addition, the US and UK higher education systems play significant roles in the global research system[2] and are the most popular destinations for international higher education students.[3]

---

[2] See https://www.nsf.gov/statistics/2018/nsb20181/report/sections/overview/research-publications (accessed on 7 September 2020).
[3] See https://data.oecd.org/students/international-student-mobility.htm (accessed on 7 September 2020).

4

A New Common Template for Comparison
The Five Key Themes

4.1 Introduction

Building on Chapters 2 and 3, this chapter compares the social imaginaries between the two traditions. As explained earlier, this book understands the social imaginary as the assemblage of important spheres of social action, including the individual, society, the state and the world. The social imaginary concentrates on connotations of the spheres of social action and the relationship between those spheres. It then relates this comparison to the discussion of the public (good) of higher education, which further leads to five themes that point to important aspects of the public (good) of higher education. I argue that the five themes together draw a holistic picture of the public (good) of higher education in the two traditions. The chapter also introduces a lexical basis, comprising English interpretations of certain Chinese terms and Chinese interpretations of certain English terms. These Chinese and English terms are included because they are fundamental to understanding either social imaginaries or the public (good) of higher education in the two traditions. The lexical basis serves as the tool to address the language challenges faced by this study in both Trans-positional Analyses I and II (see Chapter 1). It is also the foundation for the lexical-based comparison.

4.2 The Lexical Basis

As discussed in Chapter 1, comparisons of scholarly works often face language challenges. It is difficult to do comparisons without changing connotations and denotations of concepts after translation. Dealing with translation issues properly is a precondition of doing a good comparative study of scholarship. To address

Table 4.1 Moving from Chinese Lexicon to Anglo-American Lexicon

Term in Chinese	Equivalent, approximation or nearest overlap in Anglo-American thought	Discussion of issues of 'fit' and degree of overlap[a]
仁 Ren	'Benevolence', 'human-heartedness' or 'humanity'. An abstract term referring to an essential virtue and is mostly used to describe a person. Confucius defines it as loving others the way people love themselves.[b]	'仁' is a core term in Confucianism that has received elaborations from many Confucian sages. Its descriptions here only reflect Confucius's original explanations.
礼 Li	Confucius defines it as rites, whereas Xunzi expounds it as principles that regulate individuals' behaviours and become crucially necessary because of people's natural depravity.	'礼' is mostly used in Confucius' and Xunzi's explanations. Since the two sages had opposite assumptions regarding human beings' nature (naturally good or depraved), the understandings of '礼' are different – a virtue, or regulation principles.
天 Tian	Heaven; the owner of all; the place where immortals/gods/goddesses live; the natural law.	Besides being the material 'heaven', *tian* is closely related to Chinese people's notions of worship. It also refers to the highest supernatural force.
天下 Tianxia	All under heaven; everything on earth (including human beings, living creatures, natural resources . . .).	'All under heaven' is a direct translation from Chinese. It contains everything and reflects the belief that heaven is above all and controls all.
公 Gong	Public; common; justice; the benefits of all; altruism and selfless spirit; state; social; openly; official; equally divided; male; Duke.	There are no explicit and commonly accepted explanations of *gong* in Chinese, similar to 'public' in English. It has different meanings in varied situations. Its use requires contextualized interpretation.
天下为公 Tianxia weigong	All under heaven is for/belongs to all: people's pursuit of universal love, which includes fairness between others and oneself, so that people are able to overlook specific differences in reality and seek an ideational and abstract equality.	There are no explicit and commonly accepted explanations of *tianxia weigong* (all under heaven is for and belongs to the 'public'). Thus, connotations of *tianxia weigong* require further exploration, as this book attempts to do.

(Continued)

Table 4.1 (Continued) Moving from Chinese Lexicon to Anglo-American Lexicon

Term in Chinese	Equivalent, approximation or nearest overlap in Anglo-American thought	Discussion of issues of 'fit' and degree of overlap[a]
志 Zhi	The free will; individual's independent decision-making power that is absolutely free; the individual's determination in choosing or deciding upon a course of action.	High degree of overlap. The connotations of '志' can be effectively expressed by the English interpretations in the left column.

[a]The 'fit' and 'overlap' are not about the conceptual distance discussed in Chapter 2. They are mere description of the overlap between the lexicon in the first and second columns.

[b]See *Analects*. 'The one who is *Ren*, wishing to be established himself, seeks also to establish others; wishing to be enlarged himself, seeks also to enlarge others; to be able to judge of others by what is nigh in ourselves-this may be called *Ren*' (夫仁者己欲立而立人，己欲达而达人。能近取譬，可谓仁之方也已。).

this language constraint, the book establishes a lexical basis by embedding in relevant scholarship in each tradition.

Tables 4.1 and 4.2 summarize the instrument that has been developed for the lexical basis. Table 4.1 interprets a list of essential Chinese terms into English, while Table 4.2 provides interpretations of certain essential Anglo-American terms in Chinese. Specifically, there are three columns in each table. The first column lists original terms in Chinese or English. The second column gives their equivalent, approximate or nearest overlap in the other tradition of thought. The third column then discusses issues of 'fit' and degree of overlap between the first and second columns.

Understanding key concepts in the two traditions and building a lexical bridge between Chinese and English are crucial to identifying the corresponding positions from which to observe, compare and combine. In this study, the two tables have acted as linguistic bridges between the two traditions.

4.3 A Comparison of Social Imaginaries between the Two Traditions

According to Chapters 2 and 3, the Chinese social imaginary and the Anglo-American social imaginary are highly different. However, to a certain extent, both social imaginaries overlap with each other regarding their basic components, which pertain to the spheres of social action. However, they diverge with regard to the connotations of these spheres and the relationship between them.

Table 4.2 Moving from Anglo-American Lexicon to Chinese Lexicon

Anglo-American term	Equivalent, approximation or nearest overlap in Chinese thought	Discussion of issues of 'fit' and degree of overlap
State	国家：政治上结合在一起的一个主权政府之下的，有固定领土的，由一个或多个民族组成的人民的实体；中央政府。	The direct translation of 'state' in Chinese is *guojia* (国家). But the Chinese interpretation of 'the state', which is more often accepted and used in China, should be understood in relation to the series of nested circles (the self, the family, the state/society, and *tianxia*).
Society	社会：由居住在一起的人们构成的一个有序的集体；由拥有共同传统、组织机构、共同利益而互相联系起来的人群；通过互动而逐渐形成的拥有特定组织形态和关系的团体。	'*Shehui* (社会) is a widely used word translated from 'society', so they have a high degree of overlap. But *shehui* may also be understood in China in relation to the series of nested circles.
Individual	个人：单独一个人，与集体相对应而言；某个特定的人；单一个体。	Though the two terms represent the same meaning, 'individual' reflects the Anglo-American sense of 'individualism' that the Chinese term does not naturally have.
Collective	集体/集体的：代指由多人组成团体的；有集体主义特点的。	High degree of overlap. 'Collective' and 'collectivism' are core Chinese ideas. However, although the collective idea existed in Imperial China, the 'collective' and 'collectivism' as concepts were imported from the Soviet Union in the twentieth century.

Term	Chinese translation	Commentary
Public good(s) Private good(s) The global public good	公共利益；公共物品；国有利益/物品 私人利益；私人物品/利益；商业产品和服务 世界公共物品/利益：在世界层面上可获得的公共物品/利益（经济学） 公益；世界公益	The connotations of the Chinese translation are narrower and refer to the economic or political meaning respectively. There is no clear differentiation between the public/private good (singular) and public/private goods (plural).
The common good The global common good	共同利益；共同福祉；公益；公用资源 世界公益；世界福祉；人类福祉	The connotations of the Chinese translation are narrower and do not reflect underlying ideas conveyed by the '(global) common good', such as diversity and a binding destination highlighted in the UNESCO definition.
Public sphere	公共领域：与公民社会相对应的社会生活内容，围绕公共部门的核心而展开的公共生活形态。 公共领域（哈贝马斯）：一个国家和社会形态之间的公共空间，公民们假设可以在这个空间中自由舆论，不受国家干预；作为民主政治基本条件的公民自由讨论公共事务，参与政治的活动空间。	High degree of overlap. The corresponding Chinese terms of the 'public sphere' are translated from English terms. Chinese terms are thus defined based on English connotations of the 'public sphere'.

4.3.1 The Sphere of the Individual

The comparison of the sphere of the individual between the two traditions can be summarized as the smallest self in the Chinese tradition vis-à-vis the primacy of the individual in the Anglo-American tradition. As Figure 2.1 shows, the self is the smallest entity in the Confucian social imaginary and has the least important status in comparison to other collective spheres. It is the least important in the sense that the interests of the individual can be compromised for the sake of the interests of the collective spheres. This shows a Chinese collectivist tradition. However, at the same time, Confucianism also highlights the cultivation of the self. According to Chapter 3, the development of individuality and the protection of the individual from undesirable interference caused by others take primacy in the Anglo-American tradition. This reflects an individualistic tradition in the Anglo-American tradition. Arguably, despite the two traditions' divergence regarding the status of the sphere of individual, both of them attach importance to the development of the individual.

The divergence between the two traditions and their emphasis on individual development are crucial to the discussion of student development in higher education, and of higher education's individualized and collective outcomes.

4.3.2 The Sphere of Society

The comparison of the sphere of society between the two traditions can be summarized as a society with ambiguous definition and highly overlapping with the state in the Chinese tradition vis-à-vis the idea of civil society in the Anglo-American tradition. It is noteworthy that although in the Anglo-American tradition, the usage of 'society' is broader than civil society and may include the state and the market, in this book, the sphere of society in the Anglo-American tradition refers to the sphere of civil society. The idea of the Anglo-American sense of civil society does not exist in Confucianism, although such idea has been imported from the West in contemporary China. However, the imported idea has not turned Chinese society into a civil society in the Anglo-American sense. In China, society was and is to a large extent overlapping with the state, partly because of the tradition of the comprehensive state (see later). In contrast, as Chapter 3 shows, liberal scholars such as Adam Smith argue that civil society emerges spontaneously from voluntary interactions between individuals. There is no need for external forces to step in to establish or sustain a civil society.

They argue that the state's role in civil society is distant, only providing legal conditions for it but not interfering in it.

These ideas of society enlighten an investigation of how higher education can be influenced by society, for example, pressure from society to compromise (or support) academic freedom and the shaping role of financial contributions from society to higher education. They also inform how higher education can influence society, for example, by turning students into desirable members of a society and contributing to social equity.

4.3.3 The Sphere of the State

The comparison of the sphere of the state between the two traditions can be summarized as the comprehensive state in the Chinese tradition vis-à-vis the limited liberal state in the Anglo-American tradition. The Chinese state is comprehensive, with strong potency in other spheres including the spheres of society. In contrast, liberal scholars agree on the necessity to set a clear boundary of the state, to protect other spheres (e.g., the spheres of individual and civil society) from the state's undesirable intervention. In this sense, the state is 'limited' in the Anglo-American tradition. The state is also 'liberal' in a sense that liberty is an essential value in the Anglo-American tradition.

The difference between the limited liberal state in the Anglo-American tradition and the comprehensive state in the Chinese tradition is fundamental to their varying attitudes towards the relationship between the state and the university, the public financial support for the university and the university's engagement with the state.

4.3.4 The Sphere of the World

The comparison of the sphere of the world between the two traditions can be summarized as the world-as-*tianxia* in the Chinese tradition vis-à-vis the *international* world composed of numerous nation-states in the Anglo-American tradition. In the Anglo-American tradition, the world is understood as an aggregation of nation-states. In contrast, the Chinese *tianxia* is not 'beyond-states'. It imagines the world as all under heaven, encompassing all (see also Table 4.1).

The varying views of the world in the two traditions are enlightening to the discussion of higher education's engagement with the world – how it is connected across countries and how it can contribute to the world.

4.3.5 The Relationship between the Above Spheres

The two traditions differ with regard to the relationship between the above spheres. The relationships are illustrated in Figures 2.1 and 3.1. To briefly compare them here, the relationship in the Anglo-American tradition can be described as the division of powers. The spheres of the state, market and society are independent from one another, while the individual sphere, with the primary status, overlaps with the other three spheres. The relationship in the Chinese tradition can be captured as nested circles (smaller spheres are nested within larger spheres), and larger circles having comprehensive powers towards smaller circles (in practice, the legitimate state, representing the will of heaven, can exercise the comprehensive powers towards other entities, echoing the comprehensive state tradition).

The tenets concerning the relationship between the spheres of social action are enlightening to the position of higher education in the social imaginary – how higher education is connected with each of these spheres.

4.4 Five Key Themes: The New Starting Point for Trans-Positional Analysis II

Higher education interacts with each of the spheres of social action in the social imaginary. The interaction embodies how higher education is influenced by different spheres of social action and how higher education can in turn influence these spheres of social action. By examining the interactions, it is possible to establish a common template for exploring specific ideas of the public (good) of higher education in Trans-positional Analysis II.

For the sphere of individual, higher education interacts with it in at least two ways. First, individual students are important subjects of higher education, which points to the need of discussing student development in higher education. With an aim to embed in both traditions, I use the term *Bildung*[1] in the Anglo-American tradition and *xiushen* (self-cultivation) in the Chinese tradition to capture relevant ideas in each tradition. The two terms are used because they embody each tradition's ideas about individual development and ensures a

---

[1] See Chapter 5 for detailed reasons of using this German term to express the ideas of student development in the Anglo-American tradition.

balance, language-wise, between the two traditions.[2] Second, higher education interacts with the individual with regard to the individual's investment in higher education, and contributes to the social and economic interests of the individual. As will be shown in Chapter 8, these contributions to the interests of the individual interests can also result in contributions to the interests of other spheres (discussed later). These point to the need to discuss higher education's outcomes and resources.

Higher education's interaction with the sphere of society is also manifest in at least two ways. First, higher education receives support from society, pointing to the need to discuss the resources of higher education. Second, higher education contributes to society in various ways, which can be understood as outcomes of higher education. Examples include higher education's contributions to social diversity, solidarity, harmony and equity. Among them, the contributions to social equity have attracted wide attention from higher education scholars and practitioners (see, e.g., Cantwell et al. 2018), but remain contentious regarding how, and to what extent, higher education can enhance social equity. The theme of higher education and social equity deserves specific examination in this book. Thus, I use the term 'equity' in the Anglo-American tradition and *gongping* (equity) in the Chinese tradition to capture this theme, for the similar reasons of choosing *Bildung* and *xiushen* (this works for the selection of other terms too).

The interactions between higher education and the sphere of the state are embodied in three aspects. First, higher education derives significant resources from the state. Second, the ongoing relationship between the state and higher education is shaping both academic freedom and institutional autonomy in higher education. Third, higher education contributes to the state. These three aspects point to the need to discuss higher education's outcomes and resources, and academic freedom and institutional autonomy in higher education. For the discussion of academic freedom and institutional autonomy, I investigate liberty in the Anglo-American tradition and *zhi* (the free will) in the Chinese tradition. In contrast, with the other four themes, that consist of a Anglo-American notion and its nearest equivalence in the Chinese language, I use *zhi* as the key concept of the Chinese tradition in relation to liberty, instead of the more direct Chinese translation of liberty (*ziyou*). *Zhi*, meaning the free will, is central to the Confucian idea of moral autonomy. It is narrower in scope than liberty. The focus on *zhi* not only reflects different liberal thoughts in the Chinese tradition,

---

[2] The detailed connotations of these terms, and why they are able to capture relevant ideas in the two traditions, will be explained in the Introduction section of each of Chapters 5 to 9.

especially in Confucianism, but indicates the wide conceptual distance between the two traditions concerning liberty.

National higher education systems are connected across countries. Higher education also contributes to the good of the world. Thus, there is the need to discuss cross-border activities of higher education and higher education's outcomes at a global level. I shall return to this later.

Until now I have proposed three pairs of terms, representing three key themes in discussing the public (good) of higher education: (1) *Bildung* and *xiushen* for student development in higher education; (2) equity and *gongping* for equity in higher education; (3) liberty and *zhi* for academic freedom and institutional autonomy in higher education. There is still need of a theme to capture higher education's resources and outcomes, and a theme to capture cross-border higher education activities and higher education's global outcomes. I propose the terms 'public' and 'private' in the Anglo-American tradition and '*gong*' (public) and '*si*' (private) in the Chinese tradition for the former theme, and the terms 'global public' and 'common goods' in the Anglo-American tradition and *tianxia weigong* in the Chinese tradition for the later theme.

In sum, five themes have been identified. Each theme is expressed by a pair of terms, consisted of one term from each tradition. I argue that these five themes together draw a holistic picture of the public (good) of higher education, in the sense that they capture higher education's interactions with the four spheres of social action and higher education's position in the social imaginary. These five themes together then become the common template for the exploration of the public (good) of higher education in the two traditions – that is, the new starting point for Trans-positional Analysis II in Part II and Part III.

Part II

The Individual, Society, State and World in Higher Education

5

Student Development in Higher Education
X*iushen* (Self-Cultivation) and *Bildung*

5.1 Introduction

This chapter examines the first key theme in the context of higher education: the Chinese *xiushen*, which is often translated into English as 'self-cultivation', and *Bildung*, originally an idea from Germany, which found its way into the Anglo-American tradition of the theme that parallels *xiushen*. Both concepts centre on the individual's personal development. I start with *xiushen* and *Bildung* as the first examined key theme because student development is a core mission of higher education (e.g., see discussions of 'higher education as self-formation' in Marginson 2014d, 2018d), drawing different aspects of higher education together such as teaching and research. In addition, the ideas of *xiushen* and *Bildung* are enlightening in relation to the exploration of the other four themes.

Bildung is used here because of its influence in Anglo-American educational philosophies in relation to conceptualizing student cultivation and development (Siljander and Sutinen 2012: 1–2). As will be elaborated in 5.3, *Bildung* influenced American pragmatist philosophers including John Dewey. Moreover, through the spread of the idea of 'Humboldtian' university, and the influence of the German university in the development of American research universities, *Bildung*'s idea of student cultivation has become a core idea in modern universities in many countries, including those of the Anglo-American world (Nybom 2003; Östling 2018; Rohstock 2012).

Higher education has long established primary importance to the development of students. In the Chinese tradition, including Confucianism, Daoism and Buddhism, *xiushen* is a life-long process requiring higher learning. In Europe, before the unity of research and teaching was developed in the Humboldtian model of the university in nineteenth-century Germany, teaching was the primary activity of the university and for many the sole activity, in relation to both student cultivation and preparing students for certain professions. In the ideal of the 'Humboldtian' university, although universities also conduct research activities, *Bildung* centres on student formation, which is a core mission of universities (Rohstock 2012). There is also a tradition of student cultivation in British universities that is separate from the *Bildung* idea. Lauwerys (1965) argues that there is a British ideal of 'liberal education' that highlights the development of individual personality with an aim of cultivating 'well-rounded' persons. Furthermore, Newman's propositions demonstrate a milestone in making liberal education the primary content of the university, that is to provide training for university students to gain intellectual powers through apprehending and contemplating truth.

> I have been insisting, . . . first, on the cultivation of the intellectual, as an end which may reasonably be pursued for its own sake; and next on the nature of that cultivation, or what that cultivation consists in. Truth of whatever kind is the proper object of the intellectual; its cultivation then lies in fitting it to apprehend and contemplate truth. . . . Such a union and concert of the intellectual powers, such as enlargement and development, such as comprehensiveness, is necessarily a matter of training. . . . This process of training, . . . is called Liberal Education; . . . this I conceive to be the business of a University. (J. H. Newman [1852] 1996: 108–9)

However, the ideas of *xiushen* and *Bildung* in higher education are facing challenges primarily from the model of higher education as producing human capital and the focus on students' acquisition of competencies and skills (Blundell et al. 1999; Tröhler 2012). In human capital theories, the acquisition of higher education is regarded as an investment by both students and the government (Becker 1993). Students develop their productive capacities such as knowledge, skills, talents and understandings through higher education. These educated attributes generate additional earnings in graduate labour markets. Their individual productive capacities also become assets of society, part of its joint capital (Paulsen and Smart 2001). Thus, both the government and students should invest in higher education. In turn, universities are expected to focus on students' acquisition of skills and competencies in order to optimize the economic returns, and other purposes of higher education are seen as less important or disappear from sight. Higher education becomes defined as largely or solely a preparation for work (Shelton and Yao 2019). The idea of humans becoming humans, highlighted by *Bildung* and *xiushen*, is challenged.

Scholars/researchers have pointed out limitations of using the human capital model to guide higher education practice (see, e.g., Marginson 2019) and have reaffirmed the concepts of *Bildung* and *xiushen*, drawing people's attention to student's individual development rather than the mere acquisition of skills and competencies (see, e.g., Biesta 2002; C. Cheng 2004; Rohstock 2012). Notions with similar ideas are raised and employed in higher education practice. For example, the concept of capability developed by Amartya Sen is used to guide a student's learning (Boni and Walker 2013). Additionally, Marginson (2018d: 1) proposes the statement of 'higher education as self-formation' through partly drawing on the German *Bildung* tradition and the Confucian *xiushen* tradition.

Nevertheless, despite the shared focus on the individual's personal development, *xiushen* and *Bildung* are not the same. They are built on divergent philosophical traditions. Moreover, although the ideas of *xiushen* and *Bildung* may be a solution to the problem of overemphasis on skills acquisition in higher education, how these ideas can be used in relation to student cultivation in higher education remains to be explored.

5.2 The Idea of *Xiushen* in the Chinese Tradition

5.2.1 The Confucian Anthropocosmic Worldview and *Xiushen*

The idea of *xiushen* reflects the Chinese understanding of 'the way of being human in traditional China' (Tu 1979: 238). Drawing on different schools of thought, Confucianism, and Neo-Confucianism in particular, developed the comprehensive idea of *xiushen*, which has been widely practised by Chinese people and has largely shaped the Chinese way of learning and attitudes towards knowledge.

As discussed in Chapter 2, Confucian *xiushen* is developed in terms of the Confucian anthropocosmic worldview, with its expanding entities of the individual, family, society, state and *tianxia* (all under heaven) (see Figure 5.1). The anthropocosmic worldview differs from the dualist worldview in the German idealist tradition, the origin of the *Bildung* idea, in which I is opposed to non-I/other (discussed later) (Kivelä 2012: 60). Confucianism views the world as a harmonized whole and strives for the realization of the unity of heaven and humanity. The realization requires the individual's persistent effort to grasp heaven's way (*tiandao*) through apprehending humanity's way (*rendao*)

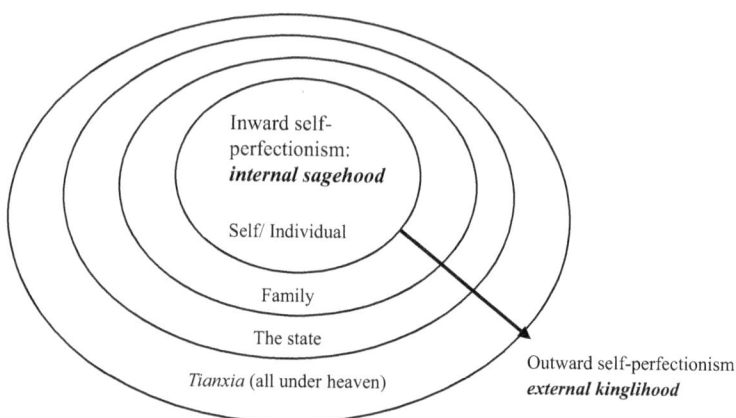

Figure 5.1 The expanding entities and *xiushen*.

(see Chapter 2). In Confucian thought, when everyone grasps humanity's way, the 'Great Harmony' is achieved.

> When the Way prevails, all under heaven is for and belongs to all, in which the selection criteria are wisdom and ability. Mutual confidence is promoted and good neighbourliness is cultivated. Men do not regard as parents only their own parents, nor do they treat as children only their own children.... They despise indolence, yet they do not use their energies for their own interests. In this way selfish scheming are repressed.... This is called the Great Harmony (datong).[1]

The method whereby individuals apprehend humanity's way is *xiushen*. *Xiushen* involves both inward and outward perfectionisms (see Figure 5.1). The effort to stay true to human beings' natural dispositions is the first and fundamental step of inward perfectionism, the aim of which is the achievement of internal sagehood (*neisheng*). The sage not only grasps the humanity's way but cooperates with and follows it (see, e.g., Chapter II. The Continuity of Being: Chinese Visions of Nature of Tu 1985). The process of following and cooperation involves the sage's engagement with the collective spheres, seeking the harmonization of the external world – this is the process of outward perfectionism. The aim of outward perfectionism is to achieve external kinglihood (*waiwang*). Mou (1999: 4) argues that internal sagehood refers to 'the individual's internal self, who is able to willingly and consciously behave and practice as a sage (especially morally speaking), and to develop and achieve his inwardly virtuous personality', while

---

[1] 大道之行也，天下为公 。选贤与能，讲信修睦；故人不独亲其亲，不独子其子…力恶其不出於身也，不必为己…是谓大同。 – *Liyun, Book of Rites*

external kinglihood emphasizes 'the need to act outwardly to reach and influence all under heaven, and develop and practice the Kingcraft'. Internal sagehood and external kinglihood are the realization of a morally virtuous inside together with actively spreading kingcraft outside. Outward and inward perfectionism together lead to 'the ultimate self-transformation of the person as the key to the realization of social and political values' (Tu 1985: 12).

5.2.2 Staying True to Oneself and the Cultivation of Moral Qualities

The quality of staying true to the human beings' own natural dispositions is cultivated through inward self-perfectionism but remains fundamental to both inward and outward perfectionisms. Moral perfectionism, primarily referring to the cultivation of moral qualities, is a thread running through both inward and outward self-perfectionism, aiming at making individuals morally virtuous. The apparent paradox between staying true to oneself and becoming morally virtuous is justified by the argument that human beings are naturally virtuous. To quote Mencius's teachings,

> All people have a heart that cannot stand to see the suffering of others. . . . The sense of concern for others (or sympathy) is the starting point of Humaneness. The feeling of shame and disgust is the starting point of rightness. The sense of humility and deference is the starting point of Propriety and the sense of right and wrong is the starting point of wisdom.[2]

The idea that human beings share the same natural dispositions leads to the further assertion that all human beings have the same potential to realize the Confucian ideal. The statement partly parallels with *Bildung* – Kant claims that human species have natural predispositions and natural abilities for the development and use of reason. In Kant, however, these abilities are not identical in every case (for further discussions on this, see Kivelä 2012). In Confucianism, every human being is equal in natural morality and capacity to self-cultivate. This equality in morality and capacity is now often referred to as the sameness of personhood by scholars (Chan 2002: 298; de Bary 1983: 20). This is further discussed in Chapter 6. Here there is a distinctive difference between Confucian personhood and individuality in liberalism. Liberalism avers the diversity of human individuality and calls for diversified ways of cultivating individuality,

---

[2] 人皆有不忍人之心， . . . . ，恻隐之心、仁之端也。羞恶之心、义之端也。辞让之心、礼之端也。是非之心、智之端也。 – *Gongsun Chou (Part I), Mencius.*

as will be discussed in the next section. In contrast, Confucianism argues that all persons are born with the same personhood and human beings are expected to follow the same process of *xiushen*. The *Book of Rites* describes the process of *xiushen*:

> Men in old times when they wanted to further the cause of enlightenment and civilisation in the world began first by securing good government in their country. When they wanted to secure good government in their country, they began first by putting their family in order. When they wanted to put their family in order, they began first by ordering their conversation aright. When they wanted to put their conversation aright, they began first by putting their minds in a proper and well-ordered condition. When they wanted to put their minds in a proper and well-ordered condition, they began first by getting true ideas. When they wanted to have true ideas, they began first by acquiring knowledge and understanding. The acquirement of knowledge and understanding comes from a systematic study of things.³

However, despite the assumption of the same personhood and the same process of *xiushen*, the results of *xiushen* are different in outcome. In the eyes of the Confucian literati, such differences are derived from individuals' differing agency, their varying personalities including their levels of perseverance, diligence and resilience. For example, 'putting their minds in a proper and well-ordered condition', which may be understood as the establishment of an individual's agency, is an early and fundamental step of *xiushen*. This step involves individuals coming to a resolution of self-cultivation. I shall now explore the two aspects of *xiushen*: staying true to oneself and the cultivation of moral qualities.

Staying True to Oneself

Many argue that Confucian *xiushen*, which stipulates a template for human development, confines the individual's free and diverse development (see, e.g., Hahm 2006). For Confucianism, sameness of personhood added to the same pathway of *xiushen* would ideally lead to the same destination: internal sagehood and external kinglihood. Differently, for *Bildung*, the existence of diverse individuality and unlimited possible pathways makes the destination potentially highly diverse.

---

³ 古之欲明明德于天下者，先治其国；欲治其国者，先齐其家；欲齐其家者，先修其身；欲修其身者，先正其心；欲正其心者，先诚其意；欲诚其意者，先致其知，致知在格物。格物而后知至，知至而后意诚，意诚而后心正，心正而后身修，身修而后家齐，家齐而后国治，国治而后天下平。–*The Method of Higher Education, Book of Rites* (Translated by *Hongming Gu*).

Nevertheless, the development of individual's moral autonomy, and in particular the cultivation of the free will, is not limited by such confinement. *Xiushen* centres on providing room for an individual to develop free will and expand moral autonomy, which is an endless inward process of expanding one's moral autonomy to reach the status of authentic *zide* – staying true to oneself (de Bary 1983: 22; Kim 2008: 394; see also Chapter 7). As Confucius states,

> At fifteen, I set my heart on learning; at thirty I stood firm; at forty I was never in two minds; at fifty I understood the Decree of Heaven; at sixty my ear was attuned for the reception of truth; at seventy I stay true to myself without overstepping the line.[4]

According to Confucianism, inward perfectionism requires higher learning, especially the learning of the Confucian classics. The intention of learning the classics is not to blindly follow the teachings but to voluntarily and actively make critical reflections on, and reinterpretations of, the teachings. Reinterpretation is a process of repossessing the Way (de Bary 1983: 19; Tu 1994: 1138). Then *zide* is achieved. The person's mind is attuned to the way. In this manner, people exercise free will. As will be elaborated in Chapter 7, this idea of free will embodies the Confucian tradition of liberty.

In addition, underlying the emphasis on perseverance and diligence is another difference between the Anglo-American tradition and the Chinese tradition. The Anglo-American tradition attaches great importance to the determining role of the external environment in individual development (see, e.g., Chapter I of Dewey [1916] 2011). In contrast, according to Confucianism, every person has the same potential and capacity to self-cultivate, and the outcome of *xiushen* entirely relies on human beings' own efforts. *Xiushen* is a highly individualized process, independent from external resources and environment. It is a personal journey.

However, many scholars/researchers have criticized Confucianism's setting aside of the environment and making it irrelevant to the individual's *xiushen* (Chan 2013: 79). Arguably, echoing Rawls's idea of 'callous meritocratic society', deliberate neglect of the influence of the external environment conceals the fact that social inequity does make a difference in *xiushen*. In Imperial China, the individual's journey in *xiushen* often required at least basic living and academic support (L. Yang 2017: 14). The tendency to overlook this reality is associated

---

[4] 子曰：吾十有五而志于学，三十而立，四十而不惑，五十而知天命，六十而耳顺，七十而从心所欲，不逾矩。– *Weizheng, Analects*.

with the meritocratic nature of Confucianism. These issues are further discussed in Chapter 6.

The Cultivation of Moral Qualities

Despite neglecting the external environment, an essential feature of Confucian perfectionism is the interaction between the individual and social embeddedness. Here *xiushen* stresses the cultivation of morality and virtue, embodied in human relationships. A typical example is the 'five constant virtues (*wuchang*)' in Confucianism – benevolence and humanity (*ren*), righteousness and rite (*yi*), propriety (*li*), wisdom (*zhi*) and integrity (*xin*). All of the five virtues centre on human relationships. Confucian literati assume that when all individuals behave according to the Five Constant Virtues, human relationships are in harmony and the social order spontaneously emerges.

Confucian learning is about learning knowledge and, more importantly, about learning to be a human, which is comprised by inward and outward perfectionisms. An essential aspect of learning to be a human is to deal with social relations in a harmonious way. In this sense, outward perfectionism attempts to make individuals useful to society. Their usefulness lies in their efforts in harmonizing all under heaven, harmonizing their relationships with others and governing both their family and the state. This emphasis on the usefulness reflects the pragmatic aspect of Confucianism (see Chapter 8).

5.2.3 The Interaction between Individual and Community throughout *Xiushen*

According to Tu (2013: 335), outward perfectionism, based on inward perfectionism, is a process of harmonizing and balancing the relationship between the self and the successively expanding collective spheres, through the individual's engagement with community and being responsive to the values, rituals and customs shared by the community. The dynamic between the self and the expanding collective spheres not only shapes the social context but also individuals themselves.

The self's engagement with community in outward perfectionism arguably parallels with Dewey's arguments regarding the relationship and dynamic between individual and community. Dewey centres on the individual's involvement in community as a way to develop. In his own words, 'to learn to be human is to develop through the give-and-take of communication an effective sense of being an individually distinctive member of a community'

(Dewey [1927] 2016: 180). However, Dewey and Confucianism diverge on the relationship between individual and community, reflecting fundamental differences between liberalism as an individualistic tradition and Confucianism as an essentially collectivist tradition (see more about this in Chapter 8).

For Dewey and also liberalism, the individual's diversified development is encouraged partly because diversity is itself a good and also instrumentally good to social growth. Although social cohesion is pursued, there is no principle that requires individuals to strictly follow shared customs and values. In contrast, Confucian *xiushen* centres on the preservation and harmonization of the community. An important method of achieving this is to develop individuals that behave in accordance with shared customs, values and rituals (Tan 2017; Tu 1979). Hence there is a separation between free will and free action. These are further explored in Chapter 7.

Inward perfectionism seems to suggest that Confucian *xiushen* is an independent and individualistic process, without requirements in relation to the external environment (I shall demonstrate later that in *Bildung*, there are at least two prerequisites related to the environment). Nevertheless, outward perfectionism does stress the importance of the interaction between the self and other. The self is situated within the social context. On the one hand, outward perfectionism involves social participation and requires individuals to transcend their personal development and interests to promote the creation of the public good, and sacrifice the private good if necessary (Chapter 8 discusses this).

It is important to recognize that for Confucianism the social context is not static. According to Bellah (1976: 118), the social context 'is not a fixed entity, but a dynamic interaction involving a rich and ever-changing texture of human-relatedness woven by the constant participation of other significant dyadic relationships'. Even though individuals ought to follow social customs and mores, social customs and mores are constantly changed and updated by individuals. The harmonization of all under heaven is de facto inviting individual's ongoing engagement with, and alteration of, the external environment and human relations.

On the other hand, human relatedness also contributes to individual's *xiushen*. Both inward and outward perfectionisms involve cultivation in the social settings. For example, the internalization of Confucian teachings, as the approach to inward perfectionism, requires guidance from teachers. The Neo-Confucian master Cheng Yi states, 'who learns must look for teacher's help, with cautiousness and rigour.'[5]

---

[5] 学者必求师，从师不可不谨也。

Therefore, despite Confucian literati's efforts to theorize *xiushen* in an individualized way, *xiushen* is embedded in actual social settings and relies on the external environment. As demonstrated by the Anglo-American tradition (see later) and numerous empirical studies (see, e.g., Boudon 1974; Y. Liu 2016; Luo et al. 2018), the external environment does make a difference in the individual's development. Thus, the deliberate individualization of *xiushen* by Confucian literati may need to be taken with caution when applying *xiushen* to student cultivation in contemporary higher education.

5.3 The Idea of *Bildung* in the Anglo-American Tradition

Bildung has become a key concept in relation to student development in Anglo-American societies. As Løvlie, Mortensen and Nordenbo (2003: viii) assert, 'there is no doubt that the idea of *Bildung* has been of crucial importance to the development of education, most obviously in Germany and parts of northern Europe but also indirectly throughout the Western world'. Between the late nineteenth and early twentieth centuries, there was frequent exchange of ideas between American and European philosophers, through which the German *Bildung* idea was introduced to, and became well accepted in, America (Kivelä, Siljander, and Sutinen 2012: 7). A book edited by Siljander et al. (2012) closely examines the influence of the *Bildung* idea in American pragmatism. It concludes that *Bildung* influenced many American pragmatists including John Dewey.

> In essence, Dewey's most important contribution, Democracy and Education, is basically a theory of Bildung – particularly in those areas where he writes about the role of interests, self-discipline and a curriculum of 'humanistic and naturalistic studies'. (Retter 2012: 287)

Despite this pattern of influence, there exists no lexical equivalent to *Bildung* in English, only approximations (Siljander and Sutinen 2012: 2). Possible English translations include self-cultivation, self-formation and self-development. These translations embrace the core of *Bildung* – that is the cultivation of individual's inner self to become an integrated whole (Biesta 2002; von Humboldt 2000). However, no translation is able to entirely grasp the idea of *Bildung* (Siljander and Sutinen 2012: 2), partly because *Bildung* itself may be interpreted in a range of ways.

I shall examine the idea of *Bildung* in the German tradition before moving to the Anglo-American tradition's take on it. Examination of the German *Bildung* tradition inevitably involves scholarly works in the German language. The works of Wilhelm von Humboldt are essential to the investigation of both the ideas of *Bildung* and the 'Humboldtian University'. Nevertheless, examining von Humboldt's original texts creates certain problems: to the best of my knowledge, there is no published English collection of his works, and only few passages concerning *Bildung* and higher education have been translated into English.

> The corpus of [von] Humboldt's writings consists of a wide spectrum of diverse types and genres of texts of which only a small portion was ever published during his lifetime. Until this day all editions of his works have remained incomplete. His texts consist of philosophical reflections, fragments, studies of varying types and length, notes, diaries, as well as entire treatises and monographs. (Mueller-Vollmer and Messling 2017: 20)

Therefore, while acknowledging the potential limitations, it is necessary to make use of secondary materials, in scholarly works written in English.

5.3.1 The Idea of *Bildung*

Schwenk (1996) points out two historical traditions of the modern concept of *Bildung*: the *cultura animi* (spiritual cultivation/refining of the soul) idea from antique Hellenism and the Christian doctrine of *Imago Dei* (God's image) (Siljander and Sutinen 2012: 3). Since the Enlightenment, *Bildung* became associated with the expansion of individual's rational autonomy through the cultivation of reasoning (Kivelä 2012). According to Siljander and Sutinen (2012: 3–4), regardless of different interpretations, *Bildung* comprises at least two meanings: (1) 'a creative process in which a person, through his or her own actions, shapes and "develops" himself or herself', and (2) 'a person's "improvement"'.

The Dualistic Worldview

Underpinning the concept of *Bildung* is a dualistic worldview (Wills 2017: 317), which epistemologically understands the world through an opposed duality: I and non-I (von Humboldt 2000). According to German thinkers, including Kant, Fichte and von Humboldt, it is through the interplay between I and the other that 'I' further develops and perfects himself/herself (Kivelä 2012; Wills 2017). The ultimate aim is for I to become a rational autonomous individual in social settings. The duality of I and non-I reflects a long-lasting tension between individual and community. Arguably, there are at least two kinds of alienation embodying this tension: first, there is 'alienation from the present self, the letting go of immediate desires and egotistic interests in order to allow for an immersion into the world'; and second, there is 'alienation from the world in order to return home to the self' (Schumann 2019: 491).

A distinctive example of the tension is the contradiction between the freedom of I and limitations on I. In this case, an important aim of *Bildung* is to expand the freedom of I while harmonizing the relationship between I and non-I, through their interplay. The aim is for individuals to become rational autonomous beings and achieve the harmony between I and non-I. Fichte states,

> Human being's highest drive is the drive toward identity, toward complete harmony with itself, and – as a means for staying constantly in harmony with itself – toward the harmony of all external things with his own necessary concepts of them. . . . All of these concepts found within the I should have an expression or counterpart in the not-I. This is specific character of man's drive. (cited from Kivelä 2012: 70)

To empower the individual's process of self-perfection throughout his/her interplay with the other, in *Bildung* there are certain requirements of the non-I, in the form of the external environment. Von Humboldt mentions two prerequisites of the environment:

> The true purpose of [the human] – not that which changing inclinations prescribe but that which the eternally unchanging reason enjoins – is the highest and most harmonious Bildung of his powers to a whole. Freedom is the first and essential condition for this Bildung. Besides freedom the development of human powers requires one other thing, which is closely associated with freedom, a great manifoldness of situations. Even a free and highly independent person, when restricted to monotonous situations, cannot develop fully. (cited from Konrad 2012: 110)

These two prerequisites of *Bildung* resonate with Mill's ([1859] 2015: 64) two prerequisites for the development of individuality: 'freedom and variety of situation' and 'individual vigor and manifold diversity, which combine themselves in originality'. Arguably, in the *Bildung* tradition as well as in liberalism, negative freedom is a requirement of an individual's personal development including the expansion of positive freedom. This argument is enlightening to the relationship between institutional autonomy (mainly referring to negative freedom) and academic freedom (centring on positive freedom) in higher education. More is discussed in Chapter 7.

Bildung as Socially Nested Self-Formation

Bildung is an intellectual as well as moral endeavour that concerns an individual's holistic development and how such development may contribute to the achievement of a vision of better society (C. A. Taylor 2017).

Bildung is an intellectual endeavour to develop the individual's reasoning ability. According to Kant ([1784] 1963: 2–3), the aim is to release people from 'self-incurred tutelage'. Freedom is realized through the development and exercise of one's own reasoning, in the process of *Bildung*. *Bildung* is also a moral endeavour. It happens in social settings and expects individual development to be conducive to social cohesion. In Kant's views, ideally, the individual's development of reasoning, especially public reasoning, leads to social harmony. Here public reasoning highlights the contextualization of reasoning in social and historical settings. There is a strong social dimension to public reasoning. It signifies the individual's social responsibility to independently employ his/her reasoning in relation to 'public' issues, and critically express opinions (Kivelä 2012: 65). In this way, the public use of reasoning contributes to the betterment of society, as long as individuals have the freedom of and possess the capacity to exercise that public reasoning.

5.3.2 The Anglo-American Tradition's Take of *Bildung*

Drawing on the idea of *Bildung*, either directly or indirectly, many liberal thinkers developed their own tenets about individual development in the modern context. Here I mainly focus on Dewey's idea of growth/education and Sen's concept of capability.

Dewey's Idea of Growth/Education

Dewey's idea of growth as education centres on the individual's personal growth. According to Dewey, the Anglo-American tradition is obsessed with the lasting danger of the potential repression of individuals by forms of human associations. He argues that because of this obsession, there is neglect of the individual's need for, and engagement with, associations (see Chapters 3 and 8). For Dewey, finding ways to mitigate the existing tensions is essential.

According to Dewey ([1916] 2011: 6), individuals develop and grow through the interplay between themselves and community, echoing *Bildung*'s idea of the interplay between I and non-I. But the relationship between individual and community in Dewey's sense is less contradictory than that imagined between

I and non-I. For example, Dewey argues that freedom is not a condition of 'independence of social ties' nor can there be unlimited freedom regardless of communities. Rather, freedom is 'the power to be an individualized self making a distinctive contribution and enjoying in its own way the fruits of association', as well as securing 'release and fulfilment of personal potentialities which take place only in rich and manifold association with others' (Dewey [1927] 2016: 180). This reflects Dewey's assumption of a reciprocal relationship between individual and community. Freedom to cultivate and manifoldness, as an environmental prerequisite of individual development, is again emphasized.

> Education offers a vantage ground from which to penetrate to the human, as distinct from the technical, significance of philosophic discussions. . . . The educational point of view enables one to envisage the philosophic problems where they arise and thrive, where they are at home, and where acceptance or rejection makes a difference in practice. (Dewey [1916] 2011: 178)

In Dewey's conceptualization, education is essential to individual growth. It is more than a matter of conveying knowledge or training skills. It is a process of individual formation. Through education, individuals become members of democratic society, echoing the socially nested *Bildung* and the outward self-perfectionism of *xiushen*. Nevertheless, individuals do not spontaneously become members of a community. The public spirit of individuals is key. It is also fundamental to democracy. Dewey ([1927] 2016: 178) argues that communal life is moral and 'emotionally, intellectually, consciously sustained'. The realization of a democratic society rests on members' consciousness of, and devotion to, communal lives.

When a consensus is achieved, it needs to be passed from older to incoming generations. This is essential to the continuance of society. The growth of human beings is not merely physical growing up but should involve the passage of 'habits of doing, thinking, and feeling from the older to the younger'. 'Education, and education alone, spans the gap' between generations (Dewey [1916] 2011: 6). For Dewey, education itself is an end. There is no one template for educating individuals. Nor are there stepladders or milestones. The content and way of education is determined by the attributes of the individual student. The argument is distinct from Confucian *xiushen*.

Dewey sees the environment as playing an essential role in an individual's growth through education, which is in contrast to *xiushen* as a highly individualized process. 'The formation of mind is wholly a matter of the presentation of the proper educational materials' (Dewey [1916] 2011: 41).

Dewey also acknowledges that the environment can impose 'dictations' on individuals and influence the process of education. He warns that education may become a coercive approach to controlling younger individuals. 'Social control of individuals rests upon the instinctive tendency of individuals to imitate or copy the actions of others' (Dewey [1916] 2011: 22). Common understandings, unless being available for continual evolution and renewal, may turn into the traditional repression of individuals. When social and political powers realize how repression can help to sustain themselves, they may utilize education as an accomplice of social and political control. It is necessary to find ways to overcome this possibility. Dewey's solution is to develop people's individuality and mentality, so that they can make their own judgements, based on experience. When that happens, those individuals become rational, autonomous and desirable members of society. They are not only able to contribute to democracy but also able to protect themselves from social and political repression. Such individuals possess both negative freedom and positive freedom.

Accordingly, education needs to be organized in a way to support each student's growth in accordance with his/her own personality. The teacher needs to adjust pedagogy and content as required. Such a process of adjustment is scarcely feasible when teachers face many students and is possible only in small-scale elite schools, where the families of students mostly have abundant social, economic and cultural capital. Social inequality makes a difference. This difference is more salient in informal education, which almost entirely depends on family and local community.

Sen's Concept of Capability

As discussed in Chapter 3, according to Sen, the development of the individual is a process of the expansion of freedom – the enhancement of capability. Being free from external interference, as negative freedom would suggest, is not enough. Having the capability to know what one wants, and work for those objectives, is the key. These two aspects again resonate with the two environmental prerequisites of *Bildung*.

Sen underscores the importance of the environment in individual development. He argues that individual freedom, to a large extent, relies on social arrangements. As Sen (1999: 31) notes, 'individual freedom is quintessentially a social product.' In addition to *Bildung*'s two prerequisites of the environment, the capability concept includes one further prerequisite: being able to support the individual's development. Sen moves a step forward from *Bildung*'s prevention of environment-generated limitations of the individual's formation, negative freedom, to make the environment supportive of the individual's formation, thus highlighting positive freedom. This suggests provision that develops individual agency. Sen suggests a number of means whereby the capacity of people to reason and make choices is augmented, including good health care, opportunities for public debate and education. He provides a simple but illuminating example. If the same opportunity is provided to two people, one of whom is well-educated while the other is not, there is a much higher possibility that the well-educated person will know how to turn the opportunity of what she/he wants than is the case with her/his fellow citizen.

5.4 *Xiushen* and *Bildung* in Higher Education

In this section, I attempt to demonstrate that higher education plays a crucial role in *xiushen* and *Bildung* (here the notion of *Bildung* embraces both the German *Bildung* idea and its take-up in the Anglo-American tradition). *Xiushen* and *Bildung* in turn shed light on how higher education can support student development.

When students enter higher education, they are expected to have already become self-responsible adults about to commence their last phase of preparation before being fully immersed in society, unless they are mature students who come back to higher education after being immersed in society for some time. As such, they need freedom to develop their capability and decide their own pathways throughout higher education. In higher education, students begin to undertake a closer engagement with society, beyond their family and local community, which widens and deepens the socially nested aspect of their development. In addition, according to both *xiushen* and *Bildung*, in higher education knowledge plays an important role in the development of students and the expansion of their autonomy. Higher education's emphasis on research activity and the combination of teaching and research enable at least some students to become involved in knowledge creation. The knowledge aspect is highlighted by Marginson (2018d: 12). He argues that academic instructors and students' immersion in knowledge enable and facilitate students' self-transformation. These aspects – the adult status of students, their social engagement and their immersion in knowledge – make higher education especially important and effective to *xiushen* and *Bildung*.

The modern university is not an ivory tower but itself a sphere that closely interacts with other collective spheres including state and society. According to *xiushen*, the individual's outward perfectionism, which parallels socially nested formation in *Bildung*, involves the individual's undertaking socially nested responsibilities and contributing to the collective good. In higher education, as an important sphere of individual *xiushen/Bildung*, individuals cultivate their sense of communal life and faith in conjoint communicative experiences and acquire a sense of responsibility for collective entities. For Dewey ([1916] 2011: 47), students need to equip themselves with skills, knowledge and attitudes to become desired members of society and use their powers for social ends. The outward implications of *xiushen* and *Bildung* imply the need for moral education in China and moral or citizenship education in the United States and the United Kingdom. Moral education is incorporated in the 'Humboldtian' university, which encompasses 'belief in the possibility of moral education through knowledge' (Ash 2006).

As noted in 5.2 and 5.3, there exists a tension in both (either acknowledged or not) the Anglo-American tradition and the Chinese tradition between individual and collective entities. Arguably, a core mission of moral education and citizenship education is the mitigation of that tension. But the two traditions endorse differing approaches to mitigation. In the Chinese tradition, where the individual is positioned as a nested part of collective spheres, the tension between the individual and collective is evaded. This is often criticized by Chinese scholars (C. Huang and Jiang 2005b: xi). Confucian individualism provides a pathway to integrate individual and collective interests by emphasizing the fulfilment of one's duties in collective spheres (A. Y. King 2018) (see Chapter 2). However, there is the lasting problem of how to protect individuals from external interference (C. Huang and Jiang 2005b: xiii). In contrast, the Anglo-American tradition directly recognizes the tension between individual and community and attempts to solve the problem by prioritizing the interests of the individual. Liberal individualism, therefore, faces an ongoing danger of turning into atomic individualism (Dewey [1916] 2011: 52–7). These two approaches seem to be mutually complementary and may well benefit from learning from each other. I investigate this in Chapter 10.

In relation to knowledge, there is a certain overlap between the two traditions. For *xiushen*, 'getting to the truth' and 'acquiring knowledge and understanding' are more than the mere acquisition of knowledge as such. 'Getting to the truth' requires the ability to understand and use knowledge to think, to discover and to create new knowledge. *Bildung* conceives of realizing individual development through the acquisition and transcendence of knowledge. For Taylor (2017: 422), '*Bildung* combines knowledge and feelings or sentiments and requires an education imbibing the arts and sciences that made us human, that formed and cultivated us as human beings.' The immersion in knowledge, according to Horlacher (2012), is important not only to the multiplication of one's store of information but to the cultivation of one's agency.

The expansion of autonomy, primarily in the form of moral autonomy, is at the core of both *xiushen* and *Bildung*. Human agency and the free will require a base of knowledge, but also extend beyond this. Horlacher (2012: 142) asserts that one's own lack of free agency is 'the result of a lack of insight, and knowledge cannot compensate for that'. The ability to problem-solve, as well as critical and independent thinking, is essential. Sen (1999) notes that the development of capability requires the multiplication of individual's information base and the training in independent and critical thinking. Nevertheless, though knowledge acquisition alone is not enough, the cultivation of abilities benefits from immersion in knowledge. The individual's desire to become knowledgeable in itself is important, indicating an agential will 'not dependent on blind powers, semblances of ideas, obsolete concepts, outworn opinions, and illusions' (Horkheimer [1972] 1981: 160).

Another crucial condition higher education provides for students to cultivate and become 'humans' is the room for them to explore and decide. In Sen's sense, this refers to the room for individuals to choose from alternatives. Higher education is a facilitator of students' becoming (Marginson 2014d, 2018d; Tran 2016). Universities are often arranged in a way to assist the individual student in planning his/her own development. For example, students normally choose which major to study, and even within a certain field or discipline, there may be scope to decide what to learn, provided fundamental courses are included. There may also be opportunities to change majors. In addition, an important task of academic tutors is to inspire and facilitate the student's autonomous learning through guidance and by exposing students to knowledge (Marginson 2018d).

Giving students room to choose and self-cultivate is particularly important in international higher education. Numerous studies have demonstrated that there can be a much faster pace of the student's 'becoming' or capability development when she/he studies in another country (see, e.g., Montgomery 2010; Tran 2016). This happens when individuals have both the necessity and the space to self-cultivate and decide. According to Marginson (2018d), this accelerated learning also illustrates the process of the student's development as 'self-formation' rather than 'other-formation'.

An individual's own agency and the provision of space for individual agency to evolve and perform are crucial to *xiushen/Bildung*. Both individuals and the environment are essential in *xiushen/Bildung*, which embraces both 'self-cultivation' and 'other-cultivation'. Neither the Chinese attribution of all learning entirely on the individual's personal effort, nor the Anglo-American emphasis on environmental conditions, are sufficient in themselves to explain and sustain the development of individuals. The two may need to be combined to better account for individual development.

Further, *xiushen* and *Bildung* concern an individual's becoming 'a human'. They represent the holistic formation of the human being, a process that is not measurable.

> *Bildung* is not measurable, and it is at the same time a process and its result; it is not knowledge or competency, but an inward transformation of the soul with the result of a *Persoenlichkeit*. The *Persoenlichkeit* as the result of *Bildung* is the self-sufficient mature and harmonious person. (Tröhler 2012: 172–3)

However, as mentioned earlier, ideas of *xiushen* and *Bildung* in higher education are facing challenge from the model of human capital that is supported by neoliberal ideas and systems, including focus on the acquisition of measured skills and competencies, and measured 'employability', at the expense of ideas about broader development (Rieckmann 2012). Neoliberal influence is manifest in the marketization of higher education, whereby it is modelled in terms of inter-institutional competition and individual/family investment. On the one hand, competition is encouraged – universities and students are competing for resources and positions, resulting in the need for measurement of performance, which focuses only on elements such as skills that are open to calibration. As Biesta (2009) indicates, gradually items that are measurable de facto become the end of education. In the commodification of teaching and learning, individual development becomes underemphasized (Ranson 2003; Sayer 2011). On the other hand, students are often regarded as 'consumers' of a higher education understood in terms of economic and social instrumentalism. The student's satisfaction and their later rewards associated with higher education dominate the narrative of higher education (C. A. Taylor 2017). Such narratives arguably impede the individual's development of agency by weakening the focus on autonomy.

When individual interests and satisfaction become primary considerations, broader development is neglected and the influence of socially nested *xiushen* and *Bildung* is attenuated. Higher education loses much of its essential functions and responsibilities, including its support for the process of student becoming, the cultivation of student agency and the preparation of students as desired members of society. Yet, these functions are pivotal not only to the self-development and social development of persons but to the harmony and progress of society.

6

Equity in Higher Education
Gongping and Equity

6.1 Introduction

This chapter examines *gongping* in the Chinese tradition and, correspondingly, social equity in the Anglo-American tradition. The emphasis is on the social aspect of *gongping* and equity in general and then in higher education. *Gongping* in Chinese is not identical with social equity in English, but there is a large extent of overlap.

In the Anglo-American tradition, the notion of equity is often discussed in combination with equality. Equality and equity are philologically connected, similar in phonetics, and there is overlap between their connotations. Discussion of them also gives rise to confusion. Equity and equality are often examined in relation to distribution (Deutsch 1975). While some scholars/researchers use the two terms interchangeably (Lerner 1974), Secada (1989) argues that they are not synonymous. According to Espinoza (2007), equality mainly reflects equivalence and sameness between individuals, whereas equity as a notion invites ethical judgement dependent on the idea of justice and fairness. In other words, equity is subjective whereas equality is objective. The book focuses on equity, with an emphasis on the philosophical and cultural embeddedness of the equity concept.

According to Cantwell et al. (2018), in higher education, equality emphasizes the comparability of quality between individuals and is arguably context-independent. In contrast, equity is custom-bound and varies in different philosophical traditions (Marginson 2018a; McCowan 2016). Connotations of social equity may change in different contexts and even in different times of the same context. Such changes often reflect a divergent emphasis on different aspects of equality – as raised in the question of 'equality of what?' (Sen 1992: ix). For example, in the Anglo-American tradition, social equity stresses equality of opportunity in access to higher education. In Nordic countries, social equity not only embraces equality of opportunity in higher education access but highlights equality of social outcomes from higher education.

In the Chinese language, several concepts are used to describe ideas related to equity, including *gongping* and *pingdeng*. H. Chen and Xiong (2011) elaborate on connotations of these two concepts in Chinese. *Gongping* means addressing things fairly and reasonably, whereas *pingdeng* emphasizes equal status and equal treatment (H. Chen and Xiong 2011). As in Espinoza (2007), H. Chen and Xiong (2011) point out that *pingdeng* tends to imply objective facts or fixed comparable quality without ethical judgements.

The Chinese concept of *gongping* is a combination of two characters: *gong* and *ping*. *Gong* can be understood as a Chinese equivalent of public or fairness, while the relevant connotation of *ping* in Chinese is fair and equal. When combined together, *gongping* becomes a public value, embracing fairness and justice and inviting ethical judgement. *Pingdeng* is a combination of *ping* and *deng*, both of which may refer to objective equivalence and sameness. However, as *ping* has the meaning of 'fair', some may argue that *pingdeng* can also be normative and subjective. Indeed, *gongping* and *pingdeng* are sometimes used in a mixed way in the Chinese literature. There is thus room for researchers to define them accordingly. Despite the ambiguity, it is still possible to argue that *gongping* is the Chinese equivalent of equity and *pingdeng* the equivalent of equality. In line with the purpose of this chapter, I use *gongping* to indicate a particular focus on the philosophical and cultural embeddedness of the concept.

I will not distinguish in detail the relevant nuances of *gongping* and equity, from those of *pingdeng* and equality. *Gongping* and equity are discussed more broadly in order to unpack the philosophical and cultural ideas underpinning them.

Despite the existence of cultural differences, most societies agree on the goodness and desirability of equity. Equity was 'not only among the foremost revolutionary demands in eighteenth-century Europe and America, but there has also been an extraordinary consensus on its importance in the post-Enlightenment world', argues Sen (2006: 291). The notion of equity is essential in higher education, reflecting a crucial collective good of higher education, which is that of enhancing social equity (Pasque 2010: 43). Higher education accepts members of society (access to higher education), and after a few years of education and training, sends them to society, or more narrowly the labour market, with credentials, better knowledge and skills, and stronger agency (higher educational outcomes). As such, there are two important transitions occurring: transitions from secondary education to higher education and from higher education to the labour market. According to Marginson (2018a: 153–4), these two transitions are points where higher education closely interacts with the social structure and issues of social equity are brought to the fore. However, there is the question of how and to what extent higher education can contribute to social equity (Marginson 2011a).

Societies use various approaches in their attempts to enhance social equity in and through higher education. It is assumed that with a more equal higher education system, there is a more equal society (Marginson 2018a; McCowan 2016). In many societies, the state bears the main responsibility for enhancing higher education equity as well as social equity. Equity policies in higher education include building a 'flat' higher education system, thereby working to equalize outcomes and provide students from low socio-economic groups with opportunities for upward mobility (Marginson 2018e). Nevertheless, there is no consensus among societies on whether or not the state should intervene in higher education for the sake of social equity, to what extent the state may intervene and how effective the state policies can be. Answers to these questions are embedded in interpretations of both equity and liberty. Divergent interpretations of the two notions in different philosophical traditions largely account for disparities between different governments' attitudes towards equity in higher education. I shall come back to this point later. Therefore, uncovering equity in higher education can be facilitated by examining the connotations of social equity in particular national-cultural contexts. This approach sheds light on not only how higher education interacts with social equity but how equity can be enhanced in higher education.

6.2 Equity in the Anglo-American Tradition

As demonstrated in Chapter 3, considerable disagreement exists surrounding attitudes towards, and connotations of, social equity in the Anglo-American tradition. But there is a general commitment to it (Tawney 1938). For liberal scholars, although social equity in a sense of absolute equality can hardly be achieved, 'movements shall be carried forward year by year . . . because the important thing, however, is not that [social equity] should be completely attained, but that it should be sincerely sought' (Tawney 1938: 31, 38).

As indicated, social equity may be understood in terms of different types of equality, such as equality of civil rights and status, equality of outcome or equality of opportunity. According to Sen (1992: 1), the diversity of social equity stems from two factors: 'the basic heterogeneity of human beings, and the multiplicity of variables in terms of which equality can be judged.' Different schools of thought hold varying standpoints about connotations of social equity and social arrangements that are designed to enhance social equity, including arrangements in higher education. There are differences both between and within traditions.

The differences concerning social equity are closely associated with its different philosophical rationales (6.2.1). From the philosophical rationales, I derive three constitutes of social equity in the Anglo-American tradition (6.2.2). These are democracy, social justice and social order. In relation to social justice, I refer to social/background justice rather than procedural justice (for discussions of the two kinds of justice, see, e.g., Jacobs 2013). In other words, I mainly consider what may be regarded as fair in a broad picture of society.

6.2.1 Philosophical Rationales for Social Equity

The Rationale of Democracy

Democracy is a primary rationale for social equity in the Anglo-American tradition. A democratic society requires the elimination of political privilege (Tawney 1938: xvii). Further, in the Anglo-American tradition, liberal equality is essential because it is a condition of universal individual freedom, the master concept of liberalism. In other words, every individual has equal political and civil rights and status, regardless of race, gender or other identities (Rawls [1971] 2005: 195). With equal rights and status, individuals are provided with equal access to participation in public affairs (Rawls [1971] 2005: 228).

The rationale of democracy distinguishes the Anglo-American from the Chinese tradition. Despite the agreement between the two traditions on equality of rights and status, their rationales for that agreement vary. In the Chinese tradition, the pursuit of equality of rights and status emerged in the late nineteenth century, under Western influence, and, as was noted in Chapter 2, it has been strongly supported by Marxism-Leninism. The Chinese version of equality of rights and status was not driven by democracy as it is understood in the Anglo-American tradition. I shall return to this issue in 6.3.

Rationale of Social Justice

The second rationale is social justice. According to Rawls ([1971] 2005: 250), social justice stipulates at least two kinds of equality – equality of basic liberties, and social and economic equality. Equality of basic liberties in Rawls's theory to a large extent overlaps with equality of political and civil rights and status as required by democracy.

In addition, many liberal scholars, including Rawls ([1971] 2005: 73), argue that people are born with varying natural capacities and talents – some are more advantaged and gifted than others. As previously discussed, and as further explored in the next section, this is in contrast with the Confucian assertion of equality in natural morality and capacity. Equality of opportunity is designed to stop the monopoly of resources by advantaged individuals, so that individual talent and aspiration become the primary determinants of social outcomes. Equal opportunity in receiving education and training is essential in providing an equal chance for individuals 'to leave the less fortunate behind in the personal quest for influence and social position' (Rawls [1971] 2005: 107).

The intention of providing equal access to education is to enable every capable individual to acquire social and cultural knowledge and skills, the basis of their further pursuit of advantages and interests. This argument has largely shaped the organization of higher education in the twentieth century. According to Marginson (2018a: 152), in the 1950s and especially in the 1960s, the organization of higher education moved progressively closer to ensuring that all able individuals would have equal opportunity of receiving higher education. Higher education became a possible way for able students from low socio-economic background to realize upward social mobility. Higher education practice in this sense was regarded as moving towards social equity and social justice. However, notions of educability have shifted. Rawls's assumption that natural talents (and hence deserving opportunity) are distributed unequally has been challenged by the idea that potentially all persons are educable in higher education (Marginson 2018a: 152), which has resonance with Confucian notions of essential moral equality. For many, universal social inclusion is now a primary goal (Marginson 2018c: 27).

Societies do not always enable capable individuals to develop and display their talent. One primary constraint is prior social and economic inequality, especially inequality in individuals' family backgrounds (Boudon 1974; Shavit 2007). Studies demonstrate that upper- and middle-class families are often effective in securing more and better opportunities for their children (see, e.g., Ball 2003).

In addition, even in an ideal society that meets the requirements of fair equality of opportunity, if it is agreed that individuals had varied talent and capacity, those who were more gifted and had stronger aspirations would normally have abundant available opportunities. It would be reasonable to anticipate their later success in education, career and in gaining social goods. In the end, they would form the 'better-off' group. Even though there were equal opportunities for all, those who were less gifted might not be able to acquire similar abilities and skills through education and training. They might thus lack subsequent opportunities and remain as underprivileged individuals lacking self-respect. Equality of opportunity itself might then become an excuse for 'better-off' people to justify the expansion of inequalities. Therefore, *sensu stricto* following the principle of fair equality of opportunity may only lead to 'a callous meritocratic society', as Rawls ([1971] 2005: 100) calls it, one without social justice. This limitation in the idea of fair equality of opportunity suggests problems that can arise in higher education. For example, Bowen and colleagues (2005) argue that competition for higher education places based on the idea of equality of opportunity, especially elite higher education places, is partly accountable for the increasing inequity in higher education access, resulting in negative influence on social equity.

To address these limitations, Rawls states that social justice should also embrace the principle of difference – the fair distribution of wealth and income. This principle requires society to compensate disadvantaged people. The distribution should lean towards the interests of those who are worse off, even though this would reduce efficiency and the total accumulation of goods. Here, Rawls refutes the utilitarian idea that society should pursue the largest accumulative interests regardless of any individual's loss of interests. As he states, 'while the distribution of wealth and income need not be equal, it must be to everyone's advantage' (Rawls [1971] 2005: 61).

Arguably, collective spheres, especially the state, play an essential role here. If it is possible to attain equality of opportunity through social and institutional agency then fair distribution of wealth and income depends on the state and its instruments of wage regulation, taxation policies and public funding. In higher education, universities might be able to collectively work on equal opportunity in university access, without the state's intervention, but state policy is often crucial in this respect.

There is a need to distinguish between theoretical discussions and their policy manifestations. Arguably, the rationales of democracy and social justice are generally agreed inside and outside Anglo-American societies. For example, Nordic countries pursue social equity by guaranteeing equal civil rights and status, equality of opportunity and fairness and equality of distribution. However, the policy manifestations significantly vary between Nordic and Anglo-American contexts. The difference is largely due to varied understandings of the role of the state. Anglo-American societies have adopted a version of the limited liberal state which can be called the 'neoliberal state' (Harvey 2005: 7). A neoliberal state is expected to prioritize the status of the market and foster competition. In this policy framework, it is believed that the state should step in only when there is market failure – to 'underwrite those vital public goods which the market fails to produce' (D. S. King 1987: 86). The idea is to make the state 'the guarantor rather than the invader of individual liberty' (Hayek 1960: 140). Correspondingly, neoliberal state's policies concerning social equity centre on competition and minimal state intervention (Turner 2008). It is assumed that with a minimal state, order in liberal society will emerge spontaneously.

In contrast, Nordic societies take a social democratic approach. Social democracy, which is closely associated with the idea of the welfare state, describes a society 'where the state acts to regulate the economy in the general interest, provides welfare services outside of it and attempts to alter the distribution of income and wealth in the name of social justice' (Craig 1998: 827). A guiding principle of the social democratic state is social justice, including social equity. Competition is not particularly emphasized. State intervention is seen as necessary to moderate social inequity, including equality of outcomes.

Neoliberalism fiercely refutes standpoints held by social democracy. It claims that equity only refers to equality before the law and excludes equality of outcome. According to Turner (2008: 150), neoliberalism sees state-driven income redistribution, guided by social democratic ideas of equality of outcome and social justice, as a mistake, and a subtraction from individual liberty. Compared to the liberal thinkers discussed in Chapter 3, such as Rawls and Sen, neoliberal scholars are less interested in moderating tendencies to economic inequality.

> Neo-liberals argue that the fundamental conceptual error of social justice has been the most significant motor of welfare state development in the Western world.... For neo-liberals, equality is 'formal equality' or equality before the law, which is the only form of equality that is compatible with individual freedom. (Turner 2008: 150–1)

Policy manifestations markedly differ between the Nordic and the neo-Anglo-American contexts, with implications for equity in higher education. In Anglo-American higher education, competition is endorsed, and fostered, leading to systems with vertical stratification that is steep compared to continental European systems and characterized by isomorphism of institutional mission and type (Shavit 2007). Nordic higher education systems are binary, non-competitive and relatively 'flat', largely because institutional equality of status and resources is promoted by state intervention (Cantwell and Marginson 2018; Shavit 2007). Chinese higher education has both neoliberal and social democratic features. For example, competition and stratification are encouraged, while there is a high degree of state intervention and moderate fees. However, the rationales for and the underpinning theoretical roots of these attributes are different in the Chinese context, as will be discussed in 6.3.

There is a primary divergence between neoliberalism and social democracy in their understanding of the relationship between equity and liberty. Chapter 3 discussed the debate in the Anglo-American tradition on whether to prioritize liberty over equity and whether equity and liberty are mutually reciprocal or not. Without repeating that discussion, I note that Sen has been able to integrate equity and liberty by identifying the distinction between *equality of achievement* and *equality of freedom to achieve*. Social equality of achievement is another way of expressing social equality of outcomes. As a liberal, Sen does not insist on equality of achievement, the goal of social democracy. However, he argues for the decisive importance of equality of freedom to achieve, as an aspect of social justice. In Sen's eyes, Rawls's principle of difference is not sufficient to deal with the problem of a callous meritocratic society (Sen 1999: 291). According to Sen, social justice requires *equality of freedom to achieve* not *equality of opportunity*. Equality of freedom to achieve is associated with the concept of capability. It stands for equality of individuals' development of substantial freedom. Equality of opportunity is a more limited notion.

> The capability perspective differs from various concepts of 'equality of opportunities' which have been championed for a long time. In a very basic sense, a person's capability to achieve does indeed stand for the opportunity to pursue his or her objectives. But the concept of 'equality of opportunities' is standardly used in the policy literature in more restrictive ways, defined in terms of the equal availability of some particular means, or with reference to equal applicability (or equal non-applicability) of some specific barriers or constraints. (Sen 1992: 7)

Sen highlights the development of *all* individuals' substantial freedom. Social arrangements need to genuinely pursue equality of the individual's substantial freedom. Paralleling with the negative and positive freedoms of Berlin (1969), Sen (1985) identifies three components of human capability and substantial freedom – agency freedom, freedom as power (akin to positive freedom) and freedom as control (akin to negative freedom). Equality of freedom to achieve requires the provision of external equal opportunities, means and resources for *all* individuals to develop their capability especially their agency freedom (Sen 1999: 74–5). In comparison, equality of opportunity provides equal rights only for individuals with similar capacity and talent.

This has implications for equity in higher education. The assumption that higher education is meant to educate only able individuals is replaced by the assumption that every individual is educable and equity in higher education involves the promotion of all individuals' equality of freedom to achieve. I shall come back to this in 6.4.

The Rationale of Social Order

Social equity contributes to social order in the Anglo-American tradition. Rawls ([1971] 2005: 545) argues that social equity helps to maintain social order by ensuring a moderate level of social inequity. For the goal of social order, social equity is a *good* rather than the necessity it constitutes for the goals of democracy and social justice.

As Chapter 3 has shown, for Rawls ([1971] 2005: 545), one prerequisite of a well-ordered society is the provision of a social base for the attainment of individual self-respect. Self-respect ensures that individual envy does not become troublesome. It gives individuals self-confidence in their value and in the worth of carrying out what they believe to be good.

> In a well-ordered society then self-respect is secured by the public affirmation of the status of equal citizenship for all; the distribution of material means is left to take care of itself in accordance with the idea of pure procedural justice. Of course doing this assumes the requisite background institutions which narrow the range of inequalities so that excusable envy does not arise. (Rawls [1971] 2005: 545)

Societies need to ensure a moderate level of social and economic inequality, and in certain respects the social arrangements must favour disadvantaged people. State intervention may be necessary to achieve these outcomes.

6.2.2 Constitutes of Social Equity

Following discussions in 6.2.1, the answer to Sen's question 'equality of what?' is that social equity has at least three constitutes: political and civil equality; social and economic equality, including fair equality of opportunity and fair distribution of wealth and income; and equality of freedom to achieve. These three constitutes are important in the development of a combination between the two traditions in relation to *gongping*/equity, as will be discussed further in Chapter 10.

Political and civil equality. Democracy and social justice require every individual to have equal political and civil right status. Such equality is not only fundamental to the operation of any democratic system but also essential to a just society.

Social and economic equality. Social justice regards social and economic equality as a right. According to Rawls, the attainment of social and economic equality requires fair equality of opportunity and the fair distribution of wealth and income. Social and economic equality is also a good, beneficial to the maintenance of social order. Here *equality of opportunity* is included in the idea of social and economic equality.

Equality of freedom to achieve. According to Sen, social justice can be attained when there is equality of freedom to achieve. The key is to provide equal means, opportunities and resources for every individual to develop their substantial freedom. The emphasis is on correcting the external environment. However, Sen's idea of achieving equality of freedom is not the dominant or mainstream liberal view.

6.3 *Gongping* in the Chinese Tradition

The rationale for *gongping* in the Chinese tradition largely lies in the second and third rationales in the Anglo-American tradition: social justice and social order. The rationale based on democracy is less important. Social order is the most pivotal rationale. Social justice is seen as both good in itself and desirable for social order.

6.3.1 *Gongping* in Confucianism

Confucian Moral System

There is no consensus among scholars on whether Confucianism appeals to equity or not. One criticism of Confucianism highlights that Confucianism 'merely pays lip service to the idea of [equity] while in fact, it promotes elitism and meritocracy' (Nuyen 2001: 61). Many argue that Confucian inequity is embodied in the three Cardinal Principles that establishes a hierarchical system: 'ruler guides subject', 'father guides son' and 'husband guides wife' (C. Li 2012).

Nuyen (2001) claims that it is the notion of *li* (rite) that reinforces an unequal hierarchy.

This highlights the need to distinguish between theoretical discussions and policy manifestations. The three Cardinal Principles first appeared in China in the Han Dynasty (206 BCE–220 CE). They were articulated by an important Confucian literati, Dong Zhongshu (179–104 BCE), who developed an ideological and political framework to uphold Han rule. The principles were not pure theoretical contentions but were essentially politically oriented. Dong's articulation of the principles drew on, but arguably also distorted, pre-Qin classical Confucianism (F. Zhou 1961).

Classical Confucianism asserts two core principles in dealing with interpersonal relations: affection for one's kin (*qinqin*), and respect and exaltation of the worthy, who are able and virtuous (*zunxian/shangxian*). *Qinqin* highlights people's natural affection for their parents and kin, and calls for the extension of such affection to others. Classical Confucians believe that this affection would foster public virtues. *Qinqin* partly converges with Adam Smith's idea that natural sympathy and affection are the cornerstone of the evolution of a spontaneous social order. *Zunxian* embodies admiration for virtuous and able people, who should be assigned political power and official positions by those already in power, so as to make effective use of their ability and virtue in governance. Arguably, *qinqin* and *zunxian* are two important components of classical Confucian social justice. I shall come back to this later.

Classical Confucian teachings do not prescribe politically unequal status among human beings. However, the moral principles of *qinqin* and *zunxian* were reinterpreted by Dong Zhongshu to establish a morally and politically hierarchical system in society. According to F. Zhou (1961), Dong absorbed ideas of hierarchy from the Legal School and changed the classical Confucian relationships based on 'affection' and 'respect and exaltation' to strict superior and inferior status, in both the ethical and political senses. He also resorted to heaven and *yin–yang* cosmology to justify the hierarchical system (R. Yang 2018). Dong's inequality was no longer based on an individual's acquired ability or virtue, as in classical Confucianism. Arguably, it was not until Dong that the Confucian *li* (rite) started to engage with strict political inequality and hierarchy.

As noted, classical Confucianism believes that if everyone follows the Confucian virtues, such as filial piety, the social order would spontaneously emerge. In the original Confucian universe, there is no need for strict hierarchy, although classical Confucianism does call for a moral system in which individuals hold different positions based on their virtue and ability. Nevertheless, in order to help uphold the dynastic rule, the Imperial Chinese authority, confirmed by Confucian literati's theoretical justification, used its coercive power to support a strict hierarchical system (F. Zhou 1961), as in the case of Dong Zhongshu's Cardinal principles. The Imperial authority particularly valued the first of the three Cardinal Principles – 'ruler guides subject' – in maintaining the political order (Nuyen 2001). Hence, the moral system was gradually turned into a part of official regulation.

Confucian Moral Equality

Confucianism asserts equality of people's natural talent and capability, which is an essential component of Confucian moral equality. As mentioned, the moral system assumes that individuals will take different roles in society. *Zunxian* is an essential principle to determine the individual's roles. The assignment of roles is solely concerned with a person's ability and virtue, which are to be developed through self-cultivation. While becoming a sage may no longer be the only aim for individuals today, equality of the potential to self-cultivate means that it is equally possible for every individual to work towards the achievement of their understanding of what is good, undertake important social roles, and become worthy of respect (C. Li 2012; Niu 2011; Nuyen 2001). It is an individual's perseverance and diligence that makes the difference (see Chapter 5 on *xiushen*).

Zunxian is an important component of social justice, requiring society to centre on an individual's ability and virtue. When the assignment of social roles considers the individual's capacity and character, rather than one's family background or identity, that system of assignment can be said to be in line with social justice. Many would also argue that Confucian *zunxian* is meritocratic in nature (Y. Liu 2016: 190–1). Indeed, the meritocratic idea largely shaped the Chinese social and political system in Imperial times. For example, as noted, there was a general commitment in higher learning in Chinese society, and the selection of governmental officials was primarily merit-based.

Confucian social equity does not expect absolute equality among individuals in terms of social roles and positions. It accepts a certain level of inequality derived from individuals' varied achievement in self-cultivation. However, self-cultivation is within reach of every individual, and upward mobility is possible, though not always easy.

The Rationale of Social Order Including Social Justice

The priority in Confucianism is order and harmony (Tu 1998a). Arguably, social justice is desirable and pursued above all because of its instrumental importance to the social order. For example, to assign individuals who are able and virtuous to positions as governmental officials is to achieve a better governed society and hence one more likely to be harmonious and prosperous. Further, Confucian social equity manages social and economic inequality on the basis of the social harmony and order. Notwithstanding its acceptance of inequality of social positions and roles, Confucian social equity values equal distribution of social and economic goods. This partly converges with Rawls's argument which concerns maintaining a moderate level of economic inequality so as to sustain the individual's self-respect and, therefore, the social order. Confucius goes further in suggesting an even distribution of goods:

> I have heard it said that those who preside over states or family domains do not worry that they will have too few goods, they worry that distribution of goods may be uneven; they do not worry about poverty, they worry they will not bring peace. When distribution is even there is no poverty; when there is harmony there is no underpopulation; when there is peace there is no danger the ruler will topple.[1]

6.3.2 *Gongping* in Contemporary China

With the collapse of the Qing Dynasty (1636–1912), official regulations supporting inequality of status and rights lapsed. Unequal relationships among people were gradually replaced by the equal ones. The former inequality between father and son gradually turned back into the classical Confucian virtue of filial piety to parents. After 1949, equality of political and civil rights and status was officially enforced in policy. The Chinese Communist Party government regards such equality as fundamental to the legitimacy of the political system (B. Guo 2003). Under the influence of Marxism-Leninism, the idea of absolute equality, including social and economic equality, also became important in China, particularly in the Mao era.

In contemporary China, connotations of social equity have become a mixture of Chinese and Western ideas. While the traditional equality of natural abilities and virtues is still accepted, understandings of political and civil equality, and the acceptance of a moderate level of social and economic inequality, have been largely moulded by Anglo-American arguments. K. Jia (2007) argues that for the sake of social equity, the state should maintain a moderate level of economic inequality through redistribution and at least provide all individuals with equal

---

[1] 丘也闻有国有家者，不患寡而患不均，不患贫而患不安。盖均无贫，和无寡，安无倾。 – *Jishi, Analects*.

access to basic education and health care. Since 1978, the Marxist-Leninist notion of absolute equality practised in the Mao era has been replaced by Deng Xiaoping's encouragement of entrepreneurship, which inevitably generates economic unevenness and inequality (B. Guo 2003). Meanwhile, equality of opportunity has become an influential argument, including in higher education (Dongping Yang 2006), a sign of the influence of Western thinking.

6.3.3 Constitutes of *Gongping*

Derived from both Confucian ideas of *gongping* and Western ideas of social equity, there are at least four constitutes of *gongping* in the modern Chinese tradition: political and civil equality, social and economic equality, equality of opportunity and equality of potential to self-cultivate. To a large extent, these overlap with the three constitutes in the Anglo-American tradition, forming a foundation for further comparison and combination between the two traditions, as will be explored in Chapter 10.

Political and civil equality. Equality of political and civil rights and status was introduced to the Chinese tradition after the mid-nineteenth century. In contemporary China, this form of equality has become essential to social equity, key to the legitimacy of the Chinese political and social system, and essential to the maintenance of social order.

Social and economic equality. Social and economic equality is crucial to the maintenance of social order, including social justice. Although Confucius personally argues for the even distribution of wealth, a moderate level of social and economic inequality has been justified by the meritocratic tradition both historically and today.

Equality of opportunity. Equality of opportunity reflects Western influence but echoes the meritocratic tradition in China. Such equality, especially in higher education (see studies on the Chinese college entrance examination, e.g., Y. Liu 2013), has become an important embodiment of social justice, key to maintaining the social order.

Equality of potential to self-cultivate. Confucian moral equality is the philosophical foundation of equality of potential to self-cultivate. Confucianism assumes that every individual has equal potential to self-cultivate and become a sage. The key determinant of this process is not the external environment (such as opportunity, resources and means) but the individual's personal efforts and character, which include determination, diligence, perseverance and resilience.

6.4 *Gongping*/Equity and Higher Education

6.4.1 Participation and Equity

Social equity is manifest in both access to higher education and the outcomes of higher education. This does not mean other aspects, such as students' higher education experience (see, e.g., J. Jin and Ball 2019), are irrelevant; it means that the two transitions connect higher education outcomes to background inequalities and unequal careers. In this chapter, higher education equity has primarily referred to *equity of access to higher education* and *equity of higher education's social outcomes*.

Marginson (2018a: 152) states that there are two dimensions of social and economic equality: 'the extent to which social positions are equal or unequal in relation to each other – the degree of social stratification of wealth, power, and status', and 'the probability of inter-generational upward mobility, measured in terms of income, occupational status, educational level, or other social indicators.' The first dimension points to a potential relationship between the social structure and higher education structure. The second suggests the potential impact of higher education in changing social structure, though not all social mobility is transformative.

Social structure plays an essential role in influencing both equity of access to higher education and its social outcomes. Reflecting on Smith's point ([1827] 2000) concerning the universal desire of people to better their condition, Marginson (2018c: 27) argues that parents want to lift their children above themselves in terms of their achievements and social standing or at least maintain an upper middle-class position. This drives investment in their children's education, including private school and university fees and private tutoring (Bray 1999; Wei Zhang and Bray 2017). Inequality of family resources and status is inevitable. Although many societies claim to select higher education students primarily on merit, so as to provide equality of opportunity, family inequality largely excludes students from low socio-economic backgrounds from elite higher education and makes such students under-represented across all of higher education.

Equality of educational opportunity means that students with similar capacity and aspirations, regardless of their family backgrounds, should have an equal probability of receiving similar higher education opportunities. This embodies a meritocratic assumption. The meritocratic idea, unmodified, may generate larger inequalities and a callous meritocratic society. The already accumulated advantages of upper middle families help to place their children in better educational locations, advantaging them in the contest for elite universities (Marginson 2018a). This is repeatedly confirmed by empirical studies. Luo et al. (2018) point out that majority of students of Chinese elite universities are from well-off families. Although more disadvantaged students are now included in higher education, most of them are enrolled in the second- or third-tier higher education institutions in China. The same accumulating advantages may lead to better outcomes for socially advantaged families at the graduate stage. Family social and economic capitals are often decisive in translating higher education credentials into social outcomes (McCowan 2016). These accumulating advantages, much discussed in social science, are also called the 'Matthew effects' (Walberg and Tsai 1983).

Equity of access to higher education is an essential component of social equity (Goastellec and Välimaa 2019). The collective spheres, especially the state, should promote equity of access to higher education (Goastellec and Välimaa 2019). Studies and experience show that policy intervention can make a difference (Cantwell and Marginson 2018; Marginson 2018a).

In general, there are two main ways to promote equity of access – widening overall social participation in higher education and adjusting the structure of participation within higher education (Yu and Ertl 2010). The two strategies are 'to advance "inclusion"' and 'to advance "fairness"' (Marginson 2011a: 23). Financial support for students from poorer families is necessary, regardless of whether a society attempts to advance inclusion or to advance fairness.

The advance of inclusion is supported by the worldwide trend of the massification of higher education (Trow [1973] 2010). In expanding the overall size of the system of higher education, the number of students from previously under-presented social groups can expand. When higher education becomes universal, it becomes a right for every individual, consistent with the idea of social equity as an aspect of democracy (Trow [1976] 2010: 152). An increasing number of societies now have high participation systems of higher education, meaning more than 50 per cent of the youth cohort enrols (Cantwell, Marginson and Smolentseva 2018). Nevertheless, studies have repeatedly shown that the advancement of inclusion does not necessarily promote greater equity of access in the sense of the access for poorer families to the elite institutions (see, e.g., Marginson 2018a; Schendel and McCowan 2016). The most positive outcome of the global trend to massification is the advancement of equity between countries on the global scale. This is discussed further in Chapter 9.

6.4.2 Family Background and Systemic Stratification

The reason for the failure of growth to establish greater equity in access to elite institutions is the interactive relationship between family inequality and the vertical stratification of the higher education system. According to Triventi (2013: 48–9),

> stratification of higher education refers to the degree of variation in selectivity, quality/prestige and labour market value of different courses, fields of study and institutions. All else being equal, the higher is the stratification of higher education, the more important is the role of social background in the occupational attainment process. (Triventi 2013: 48–9)

Higher education institutions compete for limited resources and reputation, the process of which is zero-sum in nature (Marginson 1997: 43). The steeper the stratification of a higher education system, the larger the gap in value between the credentials of elite and mass institutions. Elite institutions receive abundant resources, enjoy high reputations and award credentials with relatively high value in the labour market, but only take up a very small proportion of the overall higher education system. There is a strong motivation to build and sustain world-class universities in all of the United States, United Kingdom and China (Altbach and Balán 2007). Fierce competition plus world-class universities, fostered by government, leads to steep vertical stratification (Cantwell and Marginson 2018: 120).

Education is a positional good. Higher education credentials serve as an important sorting instrument in the labour market and a means of assigning social positions. Non-elite institutions undertake the main responsibility for higher education. Higher education expansion primarily involves these institutions. Most systems are characterized by a vertical hierarchy and an elite/mass bifurcation (Cantwell and Marginson 2018: 126). Students from previously excluded social groups are mostly found in mass institutions, not elite institutions, reproducing inequality inside higher education (see, e.g., Blanden and Machin 2004; Luo et al. 2018).

Further, there is a deepening divide between those inside higher education and those still left outside. Horlacher (2012: 141) describes the formation of two new classes: 'Although through ... education a possible route opened up to emancipation in the sense of surmounting the obstacle of class privilege, at the same time a new social difference, ... [between] an "educated" class and an "uneducated" class, ... was created.'

6.4.3 Advancing Social Equity

In contrast with simply relying on aggregate expansion, a more effective way of promoting equity in access to higher education is to benchmark the social mix in higher education against the social structure. Countries implement various policies targeting specific groups of students. In China, extra points are added to the scores of ethnic minority students in the *gaokao*, the Chinese college entrance examination. Some elite Chinese universities employ a Self-improvement Plan designed to recruit students from low socio-economic backgrounds (Li et al. 2016). In the UK, contextual data is collected by some universities at the point of college admission. The University of Oxford is running a one-year foundational course for disadvantaged students (O'Sullivan et al. 2019). In the United States, some universities are particularly focused on boosting the number of minority students they recruit, though the discrimination towards certain groups of students remains (for discussion of this, see, e.g., Karabel 2006).

The rationale for these policies is no longer merely equality of opportunity with a meritocratic component. There is a twofold rationale. First, receiving higher education is seen as a right that should be shared by all individuals, a right embedded in ideas of social justice and democracy in the Anglo-American tradition, and ideas of social order, including social justice, in the Chinese tradition. In Anglo-America, Rawls's principle of extra care for disadvantaged students is apparent. In China, receiving higher education is seen as an important way of realizing upward social mobility (K. Cheng and Yang 2015). Enabling students from disadvantaged groups to receive higher education, especially elite higher education, is a key aspect of the justice of Chinese higher education system and arguably of the justice of the Chinese social system (Luo et al. 2018). Fair access to higher education, a principle embedded in Chinese *gaokao*, has been important in maintaining the social order in China.

Nevertheless, the *gaokao* in China has been challenged for its effects in promoting equity. It is the subject of fierce debate (Wang Li 2008; H. Wang 2011). Critiques of the *gaokao* often focus on three aspects. First, there is regional inequality of higher education access based on *gaokao* scores, as universities including elite universities often recruit a higher proportion of the overall student body from well-developed regions (Y. Liu 2015). Second, the *gaokao* considers only academic scores and overlooks students' real capacity (Q. Jia and Ericson 2017). Q. Jia and Ericson (2017) suggest the development of a mixed admission system combining the *gaokao* with evaluations of students' capacities that are not demonstrated in *gaokao* scores. Third, family inequality makes a great difference to the outcomes of the examination. In recent years, there has been a decrease in the proportion of entrants to Chinese elite universities who come from families with a low socio-economic status (H. Li et al. 2015). Nevertheless, it is still generally believed that *gaokao* is necessary to maintain minimal equity of access to higher education. Yi Lu and Yu (2014) argue that *gaokao* at least provides disadvantaged students with a way to receive (elite) higher education and to realize upward social mobility. To replace *gaokao* with other selection processes, such as those used in the United States, may actually reduce social equity of access to higher education in China (Yi et al. 2015).

A distinctive argument of the Anglo-American tradition, though one it shares with the Chinese tradition, is that higher education can enhance equality of life chances (Schendel and McCowan 2016). Labaree (2016) and Shavit (2007) note that higher education is a gatekeeper to professions that provide a middle-class level of income and to positions of civil leadership. Despite all its limitations as an equalizing instrument, higher education is seen as a primary way for students from low socio-economic backgrounds to realize upward social mobility, making equity of access to higher education a crucial consideration of social justice. Perhaps this is why higher education's effect in enhancing social equity through enabling upward social mobility is often exaggerated by researchers (Marginson 2011a). There are many other more effective and direct ways to enhance social equity that do not involve higher education, including changes to government taxing and spending, and to the wages and salaries attached to occupations (see, e.g., Marginson 2011a, 2018e).

However, while family inequality can hardly be eliminated, the foregoing analysis suggests that institutional stratification can be modified by policy. As discussed, not all higher education systems are stratified in the same pattern.

6.4.4 Self-Formation as Equity

Equality of opportunity emphasizes students' achievements before entering higher education. Some students, limited by family social and cultural capital, cannot access high quality basic and secondary education. They are uncompetitive at the point of admission to higher education. This may not mean they are less likely to succeed in or after higher education. If every person is seen as equally educable, the focus moves from their prior academic achievements to their potential.

As noted, Confucianism understands human beings as born with common and equal virtue and capacity. Motivations, perseverance, diligence and attitudes determine the differences in lifetime outcomes. The quality of higher education also depends on student self-development and the qualities that students apply to that central task. One critique of higher education in China is that families and students are overwhelmingly focused on the *gaokao* and university selection, and students are less motivated to learn and improve after entering university. Arguably, this limits the quality of higher education and the extent and intensity of student self-formation. Moreover, the role of higher education in preparing students to become members of a society is also important (Jarvis 2002); and the future potential of students as civil actors is not captured by academic attainment (McCowan 2016). This suggests that in the process of admission to higher education, it would be beneficial to take into account attitudes, aspirations and motivations. In addition, ongoing financial support can be crucial for students from low socio-economic families who are admitted to higher education. When all of these elements are taken into account, the unequalizing influence of students' social and cultural capitals can be modified.

It may seem that there are potential dangers in assuming that all human beings are born with equal virtues and capacities – dangers of homogenizing higher education. However, the Confucian assumption of equality in virtue and capacity does not dictate the content of higher education. Given the variation in the motivations and interests of individuals, their formation will vary. The important point is that all should be seen as holding the potential to achieve what they wish of themselves. We might call this equality of agent formation in higher education.

The parallel Anglo-American process is the formation of democratic agency, embodying equal rights to resources and to the self-creation of capability. This process sets out to enhance individual freedom and develop individuality. Sen's concept of capability captures both. Correspondingly, equality of agent formation, alongside other aspects of equality, is seen as essential for capability development because the environment is important in the process. This does not mean that everyone receives the same higher education. Higher education should be both tailored and self-tailored to the interests of each person.

7

Academic Freedom and University Autonomy
Zhi (the Free Will) and Liberty

7.1 Introduction

This chapter examines a pair of notions that are widely discussed but highly contentious both in themselves and in relation to each other – *zhi* (the free will) in the Chinese tradition and liberty in the Anglo-American tradition. *Zhi* is used, instead of the Chinese translation of liberty (*ziyou*), to discuss the Confucian idea of moral autonomy. More details about *zhi* and Confucian autonomy are provided in 7.2.2.

Despite the disagreement on the connotations and importance of liberty, worldwide scholars/researchers often benchmark practice, including that in higher education, against Anglo-American norms (Tierney and Zha 2014); and they readily criticize other traditions such as the Chinese for their neglect of liberty (see, e.g., J. Chen and Zhong 2000; Howland 2005). In higher education, two essential terms are derived from the idea of liberty – 'academic freedom' and 'university autonomy'. Different views about liberty have resulted in varied strategies of academic freedom and university autonomy in different countries. Efforts to implement universalized norms concerning liberty in higher education systems fail (Zha and Hayhoe 2014; Zha and Shen 2018). While some scholars/researchers see liberty as a transcendental value (Tierney and Lanford 2014), many others acknowledge the need to take cultural variation into consideration (Marginson 2014a).

7.2 The Liberal Tradition in Confucianism: *Zhi* and Moral Autonomy

Scholars/researchers debate whether in the Chinese tradition liberty is absent (see, e.g., Chan 2002; Hahm 2006). Hahm (2006) argues that the concept of liberty is not only absent from but alien to Confucianism. In contrast, de Bary (1983) and Chan (2002) see liberty as an intrinsic Chinese concept and as part of Confucianism. In this section, I argue that there is indeed a liberal tradition in Confucianism, centring on moral autonomy and largely embodied in the concept of *zhi* (the free will) and certain moral qualities.

Some scholars/researchers directly benchmark Confucianism against liberalism. Using this method, Hahm (2006) finds that there was no Chinese equivalence of the Western concept of liberty before the notion was introduced into China from the West in the nineteenth century. Chinese intellectuals struggled with it and eventually adopted *ziyou* as the Chinese translation of liberty (see also Chapter 2). Despite being new, *ziyou* became widely used in Chinese literature for the modern Western concept of liberty. Partly because Confucians did not use or discuss *ziyou*, both *ziyou* and the idea of freedom became widely seen as alien to Confucianism (see C. Li 2014).

Nevertheless, although there is no equivalent of a modern Western idea of liberty in Confucianism, those claiming that the concept is altogether absent have missed the relevance of the Confucian idea of moral autonomy centring on *zhi*, the free will.

7.2.1 Confucian Moral Perfectionism

Confucianism argues that individuals share a common personhood and have equal potential to self-cultivate (see Chapters 5 and 6). This is a process of moral perfectionism, aiming to develop an individual's moral autonomy through Confucian learning. T. H. C. Lee (2000) notes that Confucian learning is for the sake of oneself (*xueyi weiji*). This idea does not mean learning for selfishness or self-interest (de Bary 1983: 22; T. H. C. Lee 2000). Instead, Zhu Xi (1130–1200), a master of Neo-Confucianism, explains 'for the sake of one self' as 'being true to oneself (*zide*)'. It requires individuals to discover and stay true to their natural dispositions. By doing so, individuals are able to derive inner satisfaction and achieve full self-fulfilment. Confucianism, therefore, proposes the idea of *zhi* (the free will).

7.2.2 Moral Autonomy: *Zhi* (the Free Will) and Moral Qualities

The individual's moral autonomy centres on *zhi* and is supplemented by further moral qualities. C. Cheng (2004: 132) argues that *zhi* is 'an independent decision-making power that is absolutely free'. Reflecting on this definition,

C. Li (2014: 906) points out that *zhi* may also refer to human beings' determination and purpose in addition to the free will, as a 'mental faculty by which a person deliberately chooses or decides upon a course of action'.

Self-determination, as one aspect of the free will in Confucianism, is distinctively different from self-determination in the Anglo-American tradition. The latter understands self-determination in terms of the individual's independent decision-making and action (C. Li 2014: 906). The ability to reason is regarded as a condition of exercising self-determination (Deci and Ryan 2004), suggesting a role for individual cultivation, as in *Bildung*. The Anglo-American notion of self-determination is widely employed in different fields. For example, in modern international law, it underwrites the individual's right to freely choose their sovereignty and international political status (Pink 2004). In contrast, Confucian self-determination does not suggest absolute independence of individual action. Confucianism makes a clear distinction between *zhi*/the free will, self-determination as an internal process and the freedom to act. Influenced by the collectivist tradition in China, as will be discussed in Chapter 8, self-determination is seen as subject to determination by the collective spheres, for example, family determination and social determination.

Further, different from the Anglo-American tradition, for which the individual's ability to reason is a condition of their exercising of self-determination, Confucianism does not see moral perfectionism and sagehood as prerequisites for exercising self-determination. The aim of moral perfectionism is not to enhance individual self-determination; self-determination and moral perfectionism are entangled from the very beginning and *lizhi*, meaning setting up a goal or purpose and sharpening one's determination and perseverance are integral to the whole moral perfectionist journey towards sagehood (R. Fan 1997: 309).

The twofold definition of *zhi* suggests free agency and individual personality, in this case achieved through moral perfectionism/self-cultivation. However, while in Western liberalism there is no clear limitation on individual free will, in the Chinese tradition free will and moral autonomy are not absolute. *Certain moral qualities, especially those in relation to serving the collective good, are indispensable to Confucian moral autonomy.* These moral qualities highlight human beings' natural sympathy, reciprocity between people's behaviours, the collective good and the individual's responsibility to serve it. These moral qualities do not come from nowhere but are deeply embedded in people's natural dispositions and embodied in human interactions and social relations. They are to be discovered and strengthened by individuals through moral perfectionism.

The exercise of *zhi* does not contradict these moral qualities. They are reciprocal. As Chapter 5 demonstrates, moral perfectionism requires constant self-refinement to keep individuals attuned to the way (the repossession of the way), which needs the development and establishment of *zhi*.

Cheng Yi (1033–1107) points to an approach to develop and follow *zhi* while staying consistent with Confucian moral qualities, based on Confucian classics. He claims that 'the individual's reinterpretation of [classics] takes precedence over the tradition of commentary attached to the classic... though the text is still important, the individual's understanding of its significance becomes far more so' (de Bary 1983: 19). It is necessary for individuals to reinterpret the text of the classics, for example, as adaptations to the ongoing context. The internalization and reinterpretation of Confucian classics, an essential task, involve the individual's autonomous voluntary endorsement of, and engagement in, creative reinterpretation of the classical teachings. In other words, Confucian moral perfectionism involves understanding, (re)interpreting, internalizing and implementing the tradition, based on critical reflection and free thinking.

The individual's autonomy in thinking and reinterpreting is incorporated in Confucian moral autonomy. However, such autonomy is not absolute. Although there is room for the individual to reinterpret, reinterpretation is based on the original text of the classics. Despite these limits, what matters is the individual's voluntary endorsement of, and reflective engagement in, moral life. According to Chan (2002: 282), individuals are 'morally autonomous if they are in some sense masters of their moral lives'. There are four elements of moral autonomy: 'the voluntary endorsement of morality; a reflective engagement in moral life; morality as self-legislation; and morality as the radical free expression of the individual's will.' Chan states that while Confucianism contains the former two elements, the latter two are absent. Chan's argument confirms the gap in Imperial times between having free will and practising free will.

7.2.3 The Separation of *Zhi* (the Free Will) and Freedom to Act

Confucianism emphasizes moral perfectionism. Free action is restrained. Individual autonomy in an Anglo-American sense is not only concerned with the individual's moral autonomy but emphasizes liberty as a right (Rawls [1971] 2422001: 28). According to Mill's ([1859] 2015: 55) principle of self-protection, individuals can act freely so long as their actions do not harm others. The Confucian *zhi* does not establish personal autonomy. Mill's right of the individual to act as that individual desires, provided others are unharmed, is absent from Confucian moral autonomy (Niu 2011).

Restraints of liberty in Imperial China were embodied in the lack of freedom of expression, discussion and action, as well as the lack of room for individuals to develop their unique individuality and mental intelligence, the means of giving individuals authentic liberty. From time to time, some Confucian literati enjoyed a larger space of freedom to act than was available to the masses, mainly embodied in a privileged freedom to express (see later). Confucianism calls upon individuals to develop moral perfectionism and mental intelligence, yet confines them in practice, subjecting them to the norms of Confucian self-cultivation. Especially after the Song Dynasty (960–1279), people's learning was focused on Confucian classics. Though some Neo-Confucian masters endorsed critical reflection and reinterpretation, the Imperial authority and officials restricted them politically. Strict rules of publication were implemented under the Ming (1368–1644) and Qing (1636–1912) Dynasties, supported by higher learning and the civil service examination as the curricula and examination were also restricted to the officially approved text and commentaries of Confucian classics.

Restraints on individuals did not originate solely from the authority but also, and importantly, from the family. Individuals as members of the family were expected to follow family rules and prioritize family interests, in the form of collective goods. Western liberalism enables 'individuals to picture themselves as being independent of church and government' (Hahm 2006: 479). In China, it was and still is difficult for individuals to picture themselves as independent from family.

Restraining people's freedom to act was seen as necessary to Confucian order and Imperial rule. Nevertheless, Imperial restraint was not solely derived from Confucian tradition nor was Confucianism repressive as such. Neo-Confucian masters encourage freedom of thought, expression and discussion. They argue that these freedoms should be focused on improving the status quo, rather than overturning the existing order, consistent with mutual reciprocity (de Bary 1983: 31; Mullis 2008). Critiques are meant to be framed as constructive suggestions. For example, Confucians believe that good governance depends on the emperor's correctness of mind and mutual trust between emperor and populace. To make the emperor's mind correct, it is best to discuss matters freely in front of the emperor. Any action's 'good and evil implications are brought to light before decisions are made' (de Bary 1983: 39). Discussions are free but expected to be constructive within the principle of reciprocity.

As will be mentioned in Chapter 8, in many Chinese dynasties there was a group of officials named *jianguan* whose job was to make comments and criticisms (S. Cheng 2001). To help the emperors better fulfil their duties, they granted the *jianguan* freedom of expression and protected them from being punished (Q. Chen 2001). When the emperor valued critical opinions, *jianguan*'s freedom of expression was well protected.

7.3 Liberty in the Anglo-American Tradition

This section introduces Anglo-American liberty. Drawing on an assumption of human beings' natural individuality that differs from the Confucianism, the Anglo-American tradition particularly stresses protection of freedom of thought and discussion, for both the free development of persons and the progress of society.

7.3.1 Free Development of Individuality

In contrast to the Confucian assumption of moral equality, liberal thinkers believe in the diversity of individuality and its capacity. Mill ([1859] 2015: 56) argues that letting individuals freely develop their diverse individuality is essential to society. In Mill's eyes, there is no one model of human nature. Human nature is 'a tree, which requires to grow and develop itself on all sides, according to the tendency of the inward forces which make it a living thing' (Mill [1859] 2015: 58). For each individual, before the maturity of personal character, he or she ought to cultivate and develop his/her own individuality, which may not be compatible with the prevailing customs or traditions.

Diversity plays a central role in social progress. Mill attributes the successful development of Europe to its 'remarkable diversity of character and culture'. He notes that 'Europe is...wholly indebted to this plurality of paths for its progressive and many-sided development'. He also argues that China's stasis resulted from its lack of diversity. China was 'decidedly advancing towards the Chinese ideal of making all people alike' (Mill [1859] 2015: 70–1). By controlling the content of education, China successfully pressed the 'best wisdom upon every mind in the community'. By using the civil service examination to recruit governmental officials based on merits, China secured that 'those who have appropriated most of [the best wisdom]...to occupy the posts of honour and power' (Mill [1859] 2015: 70). This, he says, was why China had 'the rare good fortune of having been provided at an early period with a particularly good set of customs'. But these customs had limited China's further progress by suppressing new thoughts and opinions. China was 'stationary . . . and has remained so for thousands of years'.

Although Mill's comments on China overlooks the cultural, religious and ethnic diversity within Imperial China, and the fact that technological and philosophical innovations constantly appeared in Imperial China, he sensibly points to the decisive importance of social diversity, and having an external social environment that supports the free development of diverse individuality, one characterized by freedom, variety of situation and diversity in the form of originality (see also Chapter 5).

7.3.2 Freedom of Thought and Freedom of Discussion

Chapter 3 has noted that, for Mill, freedom of expression should abide by the self-protection principle. In contrast to the Confucian argument that freedom of expression is protected on condition that the expression is out of good will and is constructive, rather than made just for the sake of being critical. Mill's constraint is negative, to avoid harming others. The Confucian arguments are positive, designed to render criticism beneficial to others. Mill's statements about the freedom of expression are consistent with those about freedom of action.

Mill makes the point that truth always benefits from the freedom of thought and discussion. To justify this statement, Mill discusses three possibilities of the content of thought and discussion. If the opinion that is compelled to silence is true, 'to deny this is to assume our infallibility'. If the opinion that is compelled to silence is an error:

> It may, and very commonly does, contain a portion of truth; and since the general or prevailing opinion on any subject is rarely or never the whole truth, it is only by the collision of adverse opinion that the remainder of the truth has any chance of being supplied. (Mill [1859] 2015: 52)

Even if the opinion that is compelled to silence is completely false while the received opinion is totally true; only when the received opinion 'is suffered to be . . . vigorously and earnestly contested, it will, by most of those who receive it, be held in the manner of a prejudice, with little comprehension or feeling of its rational grounds'. 'For the interest of truth and justice', it is vital to guarantee the liberty of thought and discussion as long as 'the manner [is] temperate', and they 'do not pass the bounds of fair discussion' (Mill [1859] 2015: 52). Mill calls this the 'real morality of public discussion' (Mill [1859] 2015: 54).

According to Sen, each society is composed of heterogeneities, including 'personal heterogeneities, environmental diversities, variations in social climate, differences in relational perspectives and distributions within the family' (Sen 1999: 109). In the making of public policies, especially those with broad policy outreach, these heterogeneities should be taken into account. This is not easy. Disadvantaged people, or as Sen describes, poor people, are often underrepresented. It is essential to pay serious attention to heterogeneities in the policy-making process. The best way to do this, argues Sen, is public discussion, and interaction and the involvement of people in the policy-making process. Letting people have public discussions is also a way of supervising government and regulating its behaviours and decisions, and it creates a climate of consultation between different agents, including the individual, community and institution, within society (Sen 1999: 110). One example he provides is that severe famine seldom happens in democratic countries. Those in power in democratic societies are more compelled to respond to people's needs in return for their political support. Authoritarian power is less likely to be sensitive to people's appeals. Public judgement also builds individual capability. Caring about heterogeneities allows individuals the opportunity to enhance substantive freedom – capability.

Only with the freedom of discussion and expression, with 'discussion, criticism, and dissent', can individuals be well informed of all choices and adequately reflect on them (Sen 1999: 153). Further, individuals' contributions to the revision and generation of ideas could happen only through public discussion. 'Not only is the force of public discussion one of the correlates of democracy, with an extensive reach, but its cultivation can also make democracy itself function better' (Sen 1999: 159).

In addition to the above arguments, Rawls ([1971] 2005: 212) claims that freedom of thought and expression are key to the social order. In Rawls's views, the world is composed of individuals with variant cultural backgrounds, religious beliefs and character. Liberty of conscience and freedom of expression protects individuals from possible oppression, hence maintaining the social order (Rawls [1971] 2005: 212).

7.4 Academic Freedom and University Autonomy in Higher Education

An essential question about higher education is whether it is an independent sphere or belongs to other spheres, such as the state. The question is fundamental to academic freedom and institutional autonomy. In different contexts, the answer to this question may differ. As Marginson (2014a: 25) argues, there are at least three factors that may influence the answer – 'variations in state traditions and political cultures, . . . , variations in traditions specific to higher education, . . . , and variations in university-state and university-society relations'. There have been numerous debates about whether academic freedom and institutional autonomy are universal rights or relative terms depending on contexts in higher education (see, e.g., Altbach 2001; Tierney and Lanford 2014; Zha and Hayhoe 2014). In this section, I primarily consider these issues in universities.

The mostly widely accepted understandings of academic freedom and university autonomy worldwide today have been largely shaped by the Anglo-American tradition (Altbach 2001; Tierney and Zha 2014). The modern university, especially the comprehensive research university, evolved from the Humboldtian model in the nineteenth century and was later influenced by the American research university (Marginson 2014a). In the evolution of the modern university, academic freedom and university autonomy were largely taken for granted in Anglo-American countries (Altbach 2001), and were supported by the protection of liberty in liberalism. After the Anglo-American universities become models for universities across the world, discussions about academic freedom and university autonomy were and are often benchmarked against Anglo-American norms (see, e.g., Zha and Hayhoe 2014). Nevertheless, such benchmarking can hardly work effectively and the process is not conducive to mutual understanding and cooperation between universities in different contexts.

Academic freedom and university autonomy in different contexts are rooted in unique traditions (Shao 2015; Tierney and Lanford 2014), which often differ remarkably from each other. For example, as has been discussed, moral autonomy in Confucianism is not absolute and differs from liberal individual autonomy. Confucian academic freedom in the pursuit of knowledge and student cultivation is not identical with that in liberalism. In relation to university autonomy, as will be elaborated in Chapter 8, the state in China is traditionally centralized and comprehensive. The state–university relationship, crucial to this type of university autonomy, is different in China.

Notably, although both academic freedom and university autonomy are related to liberty, they are different. According to Marginson (2014a: 26), scholars/researchers tend to explore academic freedom normatively but investigate university autonomy descriptively. Academic freedom centres on academia as an autonomous community, requiring freedom of academic activity and inquiry (Kassimir 2009). University autonomy highlights the university as an organization and its relationship with state, society and market (Pan 2007; Ren and Li 2013; L. Wang 2010). Although academic freedom and university autonomy intersect, they both require separate examination.

7.4.1 Academic Freedom in Higher Education

Academic freedom is a core mission of the university and should be protected to enable the university to freely carry out its research and teaching (Altbach 2001; Zha and Shen 2018). This is widely understood. But it is also generally agreed that the concept of academic freedom is elusive and lacking in clear definition (Altbach 2001). Tierney and Lanford (2014: 4) define academic freedom as 'the freedom to teach and conduct research without fear or concern or retribution'. This definition seems straightforward. However, it leaves aside key questions such as how to define the scope of teaching and research activities. Moreover, this definition only involves negative freedom. It overlooks the element of positive freedom that can be particularly important in academic practices.

In the medieval European university, teaching was the primary mission. Having two masters, church and state, the university managed to maintain partial autonomy from both, and compared to most social institutions, the university enjoyed a larger degree of freedom of thought and expression. However, academic freedom was not and has never been absolute (Altbach 2001; Marginson 2014a). The content of professors' teaching was often influenced by either state or church. There were cases of professors being sanctioned because of what they taught (Altbach 2001).

In the nineteenth century, the Humboldtian university added research activities on a systematic basis and academic freedom began to embrace freedom of research and inquiry (Marginson 2014a; Tierney and Zha 2014). When Wilhem von Humboldt designed his model university, he made freedom of research and teaching one of its five fundamental pillars (Ash 2006; Rohstock 2012). In von Humboldt's design, universities conduct independent academic activities without state intervention. More importantly, academic freedom involves positive freedom, the first and essential prerequisite of *Bildung* (see Chapter 5). Nevertheless, although academic freedom has become understood as an essential value of the university, first in Germany, then in the United States and later throughout most of the world, it was and has, for the most part, remained restricted to classroom and laboratory. I shall return to this later.

The idea of public sphere imagines the university freely and critically engaging in discussions on social and political issues, while remaining independent of civil society and the state (Calhoun 1993). However, the university's broad engagement with social and political issues has not always been protected, even in Anglo-America (Altbach 2001). An important case is the 'political turmoil' at the University of California in the 1960s (see Chapter 1 of Kerr 2003). Moreover, many would agree that academic freedom does not cover academic activities outside the campus (Kerr 2003).

It remains unclear whether academic freedom should be extended to the full range of social and political issues, and whether it should be limited to classroom and laboratory. Indeed, in the United States, academic freedom in its most recognized legal form is generally limited to classroom and laboratory. The 1940 Statement of Principles on Academic Freedom and Tenure of the American Association of University Professors (AAUP) states that 'teachers are entitled to freedom in the classroom in discussing their subject, but they should be careful not to introduce into their teaching controversial matter that has no relation to their subject.'[1]

If academic freedom only includes the teaching and research activities of the university, faculty and students' broad engagement in social and political issues would not be protected by academic freedom, as such engagement is not essential to either teaching or research. However, one essential mission of the university is educating students. Teaching is not just knowledge transmission. It is a process of personal development including development as social persons who take responsibility for the collective good.

In both Chinese and Anglo-American traditions, critical reflection through *xiushen* and *Bildung* are essential, which requires freedom to engage in social and political classroom discussions. The university is also responsible for cultivating good citizens, an important public good role (Jarvis 2002). Merely mastering disciplinary knowledge does not make a student a good citizen. A good citizen should have the capacity and the public spirit to engage in public issues. In addition, in the Anglo-American tradition, freedom of thought and expression are protected as individual democratic rights.

Although there is no tradition in Confucianism of freedom of thought and expression as a natural right, free expression is encouraged because of its contribution to the public good of prosperity. However, as noted, that freedom is seen as productive only when discussions are constructive and grounded in reciprocity. Some may claim that this requirement is harmful to academic freedom, especially in research. This claim is not untenable. The essence of

---

[1] Retrieved from www.aaup.org (20 August 2020).

freedom lies in the capacity of individuals to critically reflect and exercise judgement. The sole concern of research and inquiry should be with the truth. The Confucian requirement of contributing to the collective good can create dilemmas. However, that Confucian requirement does not impose thoughts on individuals, or bend the truth. Instead, it elevates an important human value often overlooked in higher education: mutual trust. If academia is trusted to be constructive and reciprocal, the potential for dilemma is minimized.

As mentioned, academic freedom and the freedom of thought and expression are vulnerable not only to political authorities but to social customs and norms, and the market. Trow ([1991] 2010: 206) asserts that there is a crisis of mutual trust between higher education and society. The spread of formal requirements for public accountability, the growing competition among universities and researchers for funding, and people's growing scepticism towards intellectuals and experts are embodiments of this decreasing mutual trust between higher education and society (Trow [1991] 2010: 206). The Confucian expectation of constructive academic activities does not mean that each activity must be specifically sanctioned in terms of intentions. Rather, it is premised on mutual trust between the university and other spheres including the state and society. Being constructive is compatible with being critical. When state and society have trust in university activities, believing that university activities are conducive to and produce public goods, they will genuinely protect academic freedom. Moreover, when there is trust, the critical reflections of universities are more influential. With academic freedom and support from state and society, the university is more actively engaged and able to advance the improvement of the status quo through the exercise of criticism.

This ideal situation does not always emerge. Along with the decrease in mutual trust are threats to academic freedom, including in the US and UK universities where academic freedom is under legal protection. In the United States, academic freedom at universities is under the protection of the AAUP for the purpose of guaranteeing academic freedom and job security of university faculty. Despite the institutionalized arrangements to protect academic freedom, it has been pointed out that American universities are facing threats to their academic freedom. For example, Nelson (2010: 53–9) provides a list of threats, including instrumentalization, abuses of the national security state, neoliberal assaults on academic disciplines, unwarranted research oversight and political intolerance.

In the UK, the *Robbins Report* stresses the need to establish a balance between freedom for academic institutions and the institutions' role in serving the country's ends (see the Chapter of Academic freedom and its scope of Committee on Higher Education 1963). According to Pritchard (1998: 103), when the *Robbins Report* was written, 'a climate of trust was still in existence . . . and Robbins had confidence in the good sense of both government and university leaders to sort out any difficulties which might occur.' Nevertheless, scholars/researchers have observed threats to academic freedom in British universities too. For example, Traianou (2015: 39) points out that from the 1980s onwards there have been internal changes within universities in the UK that have 'significantly reduced academic freedom'. This was due to certain changes regarding the external environment, such as the UK government's increasing intervention in university affairs based on the assumption that universities should seek to maximize the (economic) returns of public investment.

In Chinese universities, scholars/researchers have identified problems of academic corruption and plagiarism (Zha 2010). In China, the tradition of the comprehensive state means that it is the state's responsibility to regulate academia and make it trustworthy, in contrast with the Anglo-American tradition that sees academia as an independent community, responsible for sustaining the public trust on its own behalf. As Zha (2010: 18) states, the government 'has now had to become a watchdog for the academic integrity of scholars and universities in China'. With a state that is closely involved in universities' academic activities, there are potential dangers for academic freedom. Yet in China the state supervision is seen by people as an indispensable responsibility, partly because the state functions as a kind of watchful parental figure for other spheres of social actions. All of this confirms that the Anglo-American approach to academic freedom can hardly work in the Chinese context (Marginson 2014a; Zha and Shen 2018).

In China, the best strategy is to develop China's own interpretations of academic freedom drawing on its own traditions. Arguably, the government as a watchdog is a side-effect of the Confucian tradition of mutual trust and reciprocity between higher education, state and society. Only when Chinese universities win the trust of state and society can they enjoy academic freedom in the Anglo-American sense. At the same time, as discussed, Anglo-American universities do not always enjoy authentic academic freedom in the sense of their tradition (Altbach 2001; Ren and Li 2013; Tierney and Zha 2014), and trust is an issue.

Another reason why mutual reciprocity and trust matter in China is the political and social responsibilities that universities exercise. As will be discussed in Chapter 8, in China, knowledge is not pursued for the sake of knowledge itself.

Its practical use is crucial. Inquiry and new knowledge are expected to meet social needs. The pure interests of academics are exercised but are less important. In these circumstances, it is hard to sustain absolute academic freedom. On the other hand, intellectuals are expected to be involved in knowledge application, as in Imperial times when scholar-officials participated in the making and implementation of policy. Rather than following the Anglo-American practice of the independent critic, Chinese professors are mostly interested in proposing suggestions and influencing policies. This is an attractive role. One mission of Chinese universities is that of an influential think tank (Hou 2011; Yuan 2012). This is seen by Chinese people as an important task and it contributes to public trust. All these activities involve the exercise of positive freedom.

Researchers who benchmark Chinese universities against Anglo-American norms of academic freedom often criticize Chinese academia's close engagement in government agendas (see, e.g., Zha and Hayhoe 2014). However, the practical orientation to knowledge does not in itself retard positive academic freedom, and may instead contribute to individual agency and capability. This practical orientation does not coerce, nor does it restrain universities' academic activities. Chinese universities are free to conduct pure inquiry and are well supported in conducting basic research. As Hayhoe (2011: 17) states,

> The term 'academic freedom' (*xueshu ziyou*), which is used to denote a kind of freedom particularly appropriate to the university in the Western context, and which arose from the dominant epistemology of rationalism and dualism in a European context, is not a good fit for China. On the one hand, Chinese scholars enjoy a greater degree of 'intellectual authority' (*sixiang quanwei*) than is common in the West, due to the history of the civil service examinations and the close links contemporary universities have with major state projects. On the other hand, there is a strong tradition of 'intellectual freedom' (*sixiang ziyou*) in China, which is rooted in an epistemology quite different from that of European rationalism. It requires that knowledge be demonstrated first and foremost through action for the public good, also that knowledge be seen as holistic and inter-connected, rather than organized into narrowly defined separate disciplines. (Hayhoe 2011: 17)

7.4.2 University Autonomy in Higher Education

Berdahl, Graham and Piper (1971: 8) define university autonomy as 'the power of a university or college . . . to govern itself without outside controls'. According to this definition, a university should control its own activities on an independent basis. This suggests that university autonomy concerns protecting the university's negative freedom.

Arguably, the difference between academic freedom and university autonomy is insufficiently studied. Many scholars/researchers see university autonomy as the institutional aspect of academic freedom (Ren and Li 2013; Tierney and Lanford 2014). Yet, while both academic freedom and university autonomy touch on the idea of liberty, they are markedly different. Academic freedom highlights freedom of thought and expression in teaching, research and student cultivation. It centres on freedom as a necessary condition for critical and reflective thinking, and inquiry, by faculty and students. In contrast, university autonomy concerns the operation of the university as an institution in a social context. If we understand university as a sphere, as noted, university autonomy is largely determined by the university's relationship with other spheres especially the spheres of state and society. This subsection primarily concentrates on the relationship between the university and the state.

The Anglo-American tradition sees the university as a distinctive type of public sphere independent of other spheres. Perhaps the Habermasian idea of the public sphere may imply that the university should be an independent sphere with the other spheres not imposing restraints. However, the idea of the public sphere as discussed is more focused on the academic freedom of the university and its capacity to critically reflect on social and political issues. This does not shed much light on university autonomy. An examination of university autonomy begins with an investigation of the scope of state and society, revealing the university–state and university–society relationships.

It is generally agreed that university autonomy is a precondition of effective university operation and should be guaranteed (Pan 2009: 9). Exactly what is meant by university autonomy is much more variable. University autonomy covers a range of aspects such as courses, research, public service and overall mission. As indicated in Chapter 3, the central concern of classical liberal thinkers is the scope of the state. Their intention is to protect individual liberty by limiting the power and functions of the state. Yet, classical liberal thinkers also make the state a watchdog whose main responsibility is to guarantee the functioning of other spheres. The first point suggests maximum university autonomy, the second point less so.

Ideally, classical liberal thinkers would favour absolute university autonomy, for at least three reasons. First, if university affairs are not solely determined by university faculty but are controlled by external entities, the university is no longer a self-governing community of scholars and there is no difference between a university and a bureaucracy (Pan 2009: 11). Second, under political and social pressure, universities can lose its academic freedom, the protection of which is essential to academic activities (Y. Cai 1986; Pan 2009: 11). Third, the university may lose the status of a public sphere if controlled by external social and political powers (Wolff 1992). However, the above reasons are focused primarily on academic freedom rather than university autonomy. As long as university autonomy sufficiently protects academic freedom, the above conditions can be realized.

In Anglo-American countries, there is no absolute university autonomy, though universities in both the United Kingdom and the United States have enjoyed a large measure of self-government (Pritchard 1998). On the one hand, there has been increasing intervention of university affairs from the business sector. For example, in American universities, the business community can make a difference through their members who have seats on universities' boards of trustees (Nelson 2010: 1–2). Commercial companies, such as pharmaceutical companies, might also intervene in research and circulation of research results in higher education. On the other hand, the UK and US governments also exercise control over universities in multiple ways, including exercising public accountability. It seems that certain external controls are acceptable providing they do not harm academic freedom. Yet, it is still unclear to what extent the university is free of external control.

Pan (2009) claims that absolute university autonomy hardly exists. States control universities in different ways and intervene in their affairs to varying degrees (Green and Hayward 1997; Pan 2009). But both the state–university relationship and judgements about it vary by country and culture. It is problematic to discuss university autonomy without paying attention to its context, as the case of China makes clear.

The modern university appeared in China in the late nineteenth century. Unlike the Imperial academies, where there was no tradition of autonomy, the universities founded between the late Qing Dynasty and 1949 followed international models, particularly the model of American universities with its tradition of university autonomy and academic freedom. However, those universities disappeared after 1949. Firm state oversight has been exercised since 1949, though the degree of autonomy has varied. Higher education has experienced decentralization and (re)centralization (H. Wu and Li 2021) with state control swinging back and forth (H. Wu and Li 2021; Zha and Hayhoe 2014).

Given the lack of a Chinese tradition in university autonomy, it is less surprising that researchers benchmark governance in Chinese universities' against their US and UK counterparts. This benchmarking is often associated with criticism.

Zha and Hayhoe (2014) argue that Chinese universities lack university autonomy and this hinders the evolution of Chinese higher education. They remark on Chinese universities' 'serving governmental agendas' and 'social embeddedness' (Zha and Hayhoe 2014: 42). As discussed earlier, the practical focus in knowledge does not necessarily restrict positive academic freedom. It may not be a problem of academic freedom nor university autonomy. However, Zha and Hayhoe (2014) do suggest that researchers rely too much on liberal templates. Altbach (2016) even argues that American governance is the only way to protect university autonomy, and the only way to make universities successful. However, benchmarking does not enhance mutual understanding and cooperation. It does not protect university autonomy in China. University autonomy cannot be discussed as abstract or normative. The discussion must be contextualized.

China is searching for a Chinese mode of university governance, with an aim of protecting Chinese universities' institutional autonomy within China's political system. For example, the unique dual-governance system in Chinese universities might be a positive way forward (S. Han and Xu 2019). In the Chinese language, *zizhu*, meaning self-mastery, is more often used to discuss university autonomy in China than self-governance (*zizhi*) (Hayhoe 2011: 17). While self-governance highlights legal independence from the state, self-mastery reflects the university's engagement with the state and the social responsibilities it bears, in addition to the university's autonomy over various matters including student recruitment, course design and research.

All the same, contemporary university autonomy is problematic. Among Chinese universities, some – often elite universities – enjoy greater autonomy whereas others are gripped by the state (see, e.g., Chapter 9 of Pan 2009; Ren and Li 2013; L. Wang 2010). Non-elite universities must strictly follow government regulation concerning the arrangement of courses and the design of curricula while elite universities have much more autonomy. Some elite universities independently decide on the opening of new courses and programmes. The urgent need is to develop a coherent and equitable governance system on Chinese soil under which university autonomy is well protected though not absolute.

As with academic freedom, university autonomy would benefit from enhanced mutual trust and reciprocity between university and state, and between university and society. The tension between university autonomy and the demands of public accountability can be addressed if there is mutual trust between the university and elsewhere in society. When universities are trusted and well supported, they will gain a higher level of institutional autonomy and better protect academic freedom.

8

The Resources and Outcomes of Higher Education

The *Gong*/Public and *Si*/Private

8.1 Introduction

This chapter explores the fourth theme in the context of higher education: *gong* and *si* in the Chinese tradition, and the public and private in the Anglo-American tradition. As this chapter will show, the distinction in English between 'public' and 'private' can refer to differing spheres of social action (e.g., state versus non-state, market versus non-market) or value creation (non-market government or philanthropic provision versus market-based value). As well as its use in a dualism of public and private, the term 'public' can refer to a universal and inclusive social space, as in 'public opinion' or 'public communication'.

In Chinese, *gong* has multiple meanings. It can refer to specific non-individual collective spheres such as the state or humanity as a whole. It also has normative meanings parallel to those of 'public', including common, universal, open and fair. Similarly, *si* may be understood as individual, personal and secret or normatively, as selfish. *Gong* and *si* are often used together to indicate the relative relationship between them. In Chinese society, there is a normative preference for *gong* over *si*. In this chapter, the relative relationship is illustrated by a pair of Chinese terms: *dawo* (the larger self) and *xiaowo* (the smaller self).

As Marginson and Yang (2021) argue, the English term of 'public' is not universal and has approximations rather than parallels in the Chinese language. Similarly, the Chinese concept of *gong* is non-universal, and there is no parallel in English. However, there are large overlaps between *gong* and public, and between *si* and private. *Gong* and *si* are often used as the Chinese translations of the English notions of public and private, and vice versa. Arguably, *gong* and *si* are the closest Chinese approximations to public and private; and conversely, public and private are the closest English approximations to *gong* and *si*. Hence, I use *gong* and *si* when discussing the Chinese tradition of the resources and outcomes of higher education.

The public – and specifically public good of higher education – lies at the heart of this book. Connotations of the public and private largely mould higher education systems (Nixon 2011). At the risk of over-simplification, the relationship and boundary between the public and private affects public policies, the status of the university and resources of the university from the state (Marginson 2007; Pusser 2006). At the individual level, people's interpretations of the public and private direct their attitudes towards the university and strategies of investing in higher education (Monks 2000). However, as was discussed in Chapter 1 in setting out the study, in different national-cultural contexts there are varying understandings of the public and private.

8.2 *Gong* and *Si* in the Chinese Tradition

8.2.1 *Gong/Si* and *Dawo/Xiaowo*

Before the spring and autumn period (770–476 BCE), *gong* and *si* were used to describe physical objects, like farming tools and clothing. Since then, the two terms started to contain abstract and metaphysical meanings (C. Huang 2005). Confucius (551–479 BCE) and Mencius (372–289 BCE) emphasize the differentiation between *gong* and *si*. At their time, *gong* was the larger concept which contained *si*, and ideally, there was no conflict between them (C. Huang 1991). In the Northern Song Dynasty (960–1127 CE), *gong* referred to righteousness, and *si* meant private goods and personal desire. Si Maguang (1019–086) claims that people ought to prioritize *gong* (C. Huang 2005). During the Southern Song Dynasty (1127–1297 CE), *gong* meant the heavenly principle and private represented people's will. Neo-Confucian master Zhu Xi (1130–1200) argues *gong* to be legal while *si* was illegal (Zhu and Lv [1175] 2001).

Xunzi (about 316–237 BCE) avers that public interests should take precedence over private interests, and people should use public norms to constrain private desire. Anyone who was able to contribute to the public good could become a decent gentleman (*daru*). While there was a tension between public and private interests in Imperial China, the ideal situation was to find a balance to satisfy both. However, if that was not possible, then the prevailing moral criterion favoured the public (see later).

Moral requirements of prioritizing the public over the private are justified by the relative relationship between *dawo* and *xiaowo*. 'Self' (*wo*) is a critical term in seeking to understand public-private relations in China. Chapter 2 discussed how the Chinese tradition views *xiaowo* and *dawo* pertain to different spheres of social action. In a pair of *dawo* and *xiaowo*, *xiaowo* is the private and *dawo* is the public. As *dawo* is larger than *xiaowo* and therefore more important, *xiaowo*, the private interests, is to be sacrificed for *dawo*, the public interests.

However, always nesting *xiaowo* in *dawo* deliberately overlooks potential tensions between them, which as noted are not well recognized or discussed in the Chinese tradition. C. Huang and Jiang (2005a) argue that a clear boundary between *dawo* and *xiaowo*, and therefore between the *gong* and *si*, is lacking and this exacerbates the tension. People can face dilemmas in choosing between personal will and moral obligations. For example, if someone's father committed a crime, it could be hard to decide whether to report the crime (a public responsibility) or hide the fact (one's private family interests) (Y. Han 2009). In Imperial China, people might rather commit suicide than violate moral principles or report their father (Huang 2005).

K. Cheng and Yang (2015: 127) remark that the Chinese structure of spheres of social action is hierarchical in nature and individuals are relative to the social fabric. The hierarchy may leave individuals and other *xiaowo*s susceptible to *dawo*s. The private is unprotected. It is essential to identify a clear boundary between public and private. Although laws and policies have been introduced in China to protect private property, the boundary is still ambiguous, and awareness of the importance of the private is still lacking.

8.2.2 The Communicative Public

Whereas the Anglo-American tradition has developed the idea of the communicative public, represented by Habermas's (1989) public sphere, there is no equivalent idea in the Chinese tradition. As will be discussed later, in conjunction with the centrality of liberty and democracy, the liberal version of the public communication is a relational space that is universally inclusive, open to all actors and is independent from interference from other spheres (Marginson and Yang 2021).

In contrast, the tradition of the comprehensive state in China makes it scarcely possible to develop a universal communicative public outside the state. Instead, there is a sphere of communication within the state sphere. The Chinese university remains inside the state's boundary and part of that sphere of communication. Such a sphere within the state's boundary underscores the constructive contribution of communication to the state and, under some circumstances, has been compatible with free speech. For example, the intellectually cosmopolitan Jixia Academy during the Warring States period, fully supported by the state and within the state sphere, had full freedom to provide fearless advice to the state on statecraft.

Largely because the communicative public lies within the boundary of the state, freedom of expression and discussion was and is in continuous flux. From time to time, in many Chinese dynasties, there was a group of officials named *jianguan* whose job was to make comments and criticisms (S. Cheng 2001).

8.2.3 The Collectivist Tradition in China

The collectivist priority of *gong* over *si* is a fundamental tenet of Chinese society. In contrast with liberal individualism, in the Chinese tradition Confucian individualism is not in conflict with collectivism but supports it (Bell 2017a; Rosemont Jr. 2015). However, as Chapter 2 explored, in the modern period, the connotations of collectivism have changed. Despite the influence of Western liberalism and individualism, the prioritizing of public interests is still central. However, interpretations of the collective spheres of social action, and the way individuals connect to them, have changed. This demonstrates the evolution of a Chinese social imaginary.

Collectivism and Confucian Individualism

Hofstede (1980) argues that individualism views individuals as separate entities, distinguishable from social milieus, while collectivism asserts that individuals are extensions of the social systems to which they belong, and there is only a blurred distinction between the individual and the group (Hofstede 1980). According to Earley and Gibson (1998: 265), the distinction between individualism and collectivism depends on the form of 'the social connectedness among individuals'. At the cultural level, there are guiding principles and normative patterns that prescribe behaviour. Individualism prioritizes individuals' interests. Collectivism argues that the group's interests and goals should be primary (Earley and Gibson 1998; Parsons and Shils 1951).

As demonstrated in Chapter 2, role-bearing Confucian individualism, which supports collectivism, is a foundation of the Confucian order. In this setting, individuals' interactions with the family and other social groups cultivate and sharpen their collective consciousness and self-sacrifice, through *xiushen*. Contemporary China adopts a similar strategy to strengthen individuals' collective consciousness and their responsibilities towards *dawo*. Higher education, especially its moral education (partly manifested in political education), plays an essential role in carrying out this strategy.

The Evolution of the Collective Spheres in China from Mid-Nineteenth Century Onwards

As discussed in Chapter 2, the Imperial Chinese state was a civilizational state rather than a nation-state. The state had limited influence on grassroots society, whereas semi-autonomous local units grounded partly in extended kinship undertook joint responsibility for social organization and control.

The establishment of the People's Republic of China in 1949 marked the decisive appearance of a modern nation-state in China. Amid its efforts to remake collectivism as socialist collectivism while reducing the influence of the family unit, the state became the most solid collective sphere. Collective interests still took priority but understanding of the collective spheres changed. In the new order, the interests of the state exceeded those of the family and *tianxia*. This led to criticisms of the Chinese Communist Party (CCP) for merely 'serving the interests of Chinese nationalism' regardless of interests of the world or other local associations (Schwartz 1965: 14).

In retrospect, the CCP's primary concentration on national development alone can be seen as a transitional strategy. Deng Xiaoping's idea of 'development is the absolute principle'[1] suggests that the long-standing idea of *tianxia*, universal harmony and peace grounded in respecting diversity, had lost influence. However, as Marginson and Yang (2020) note, China's Belt and Road Initiative launched in 2013 suggests a return of *tianxia* at the official level. China is now using the new term of 'a shared future for human beings (*renlei mingyun gongtongti*)' to re-engage *tianxia* in the global platforms. This is further discussed in Chapter 9.

The Chinese family experienced significant suppression through a series of socialist mobilizations in the Mao period. By the end of the Mao era, the Confucian spheres of social action had been replaced by smaller families, people's communes and the state. The individual as a sphere of social action still barely gained recognition at this stage (see more details about this in Chapter 2).

The important spheres of social action changed again after the policy of reform and opening up which began in 1978. The new capitalist influences on

---

[1] 发展才是硬道理。

Chinese society were unprecedented and weakened China's collectivist tradition. Rural areas saw the decollectivization of agriculture and the release of people from communes (Y.-m. Lin 2011). People gained the right of free migration. With growing opportunities for labour and business in the cities, large-scale rural-to-urban movement occurred. According to Muhlhahn (2019), China's 2010 census shows that more than 261 million Chinese citizens were living in places other than where they registered in the household system. In urban areas, the government implemented policies to establish markets and encourage competition (Zang 2011b). A large proportion of state-owned enterprises were privatized and many new 'people-managed' enterprises, big or small, emerged. A wide range of local units again became a vital sphere of social action. These local units were formed based on varying types of *guanxi* (social networks/relationships).

Although traditional moral bonds and people's loyalty to the family had weakened in the Mao era, many aspects of Chinese people's traditional life were maintained. Family loyalty and obligation survived in rural areas (Johnson et al. 1993). Along with an end to the suppression of the family, the post-Mao era saw the state's advocacy of traditional Chinese ideas including Confucian filial piety. There was a revived enthusiasm for lineage rituals and sentiments, renovating the ancestral house and recompiling genealogical records (C. Liu 2011; Huning Wang 1991). The family became a more important sphere again. However, average family size shrank because of frequent migration and the one-child policy implemented in the late 1970s (Zang 2011a).

In the absence of the large traditional family, the traditional role of the family system in monitoring members' values, daily lives, marriage and career was correspondingly weakened. However, close bonds among nuclear family members did not vanish. Perhaps relations between parents and children became closer because they were no longer mediated by the large kinship hierarchy. In China, parents' devotion to raising and cultivating their children, and children's support for their parents, has not changed. This is reflected in the family's investment in children's education, including shadow education, and the familial pension system (Chou 2010; Y.-J. Lee and Xiao 1998; Wei Zhang and Bray 2017). Arguably, since the Mao era, there has been a revitalization of the traditional idea of glorifying and illuminating the family.

As large kinship systems have shrunk in importance and people's communes have disappeared, spheres of social action based on *guanxi* have become more important. People who are more distant relatives, previously part of large family networks, often maintain a loosely connected but larger social nexus.

New forms of social nexuses have been created, forming a significant sphere of social action (Gold et al. 2002). In general, *guanxi* between members of smaller social nexuses are closer than relationships in larger nexuses. However, despite the resemblance between Confucian-nested circles and social nexuses based on *guanxi*, relationships between different social nexuses are more complicated than in classical Confucianism. It is not easy to identify smaller and corresponding larger entities because different associations can be independent and unrelated. For example, an individual can simultaneously belong to an association of fellow provincials and an association of schoolfellows. Further, while people's *guanxi* network expands and social nexuses diversify, most of these social nexuses are not as robust as the traditional family in their stability and the intensity of their influence on, and regulation of, members' mentalities and behaviours.

Grounded in differing degrees of loyalty and intimacy, social nexuses are imposing varying levels of influence on the individual. Often, members of new social nexuses are not bonded as closely as were traditional families. People tend to prioritize closer *guanxi* and the welfare of individuals and more closely connected social nexuses. At the same time, the autonomous individual has become more important than before.

The Rise of the Autonomous Individual in Contemporary China

The traditional role of the individual in social spheres brought with it ethical obligations and restraints. Yet, when not situated in relational social nestings, individuals were more or less free from those obligations. There existed 'a recognized phenomenon that Chinese individuals unabashedly show a kind of egocentric behaviour outside the family, particularly in a non-kin social context' (A. Y. King 2018: 53). Today, however, the individual in China is gaining a more autonomous status (Y. Yan 2003). Individuals are nested in multiple, but more loosely connected, social nexuses, some of which may extend abroad. There is a lack of comprehensive and decisive social nexuses, like the traditional family, below the level of the state. Moved by pragmatism and materialism, the individual's primary concerns focus on the economic potentials of national development and modernization. More and more people tend to embrace self-centred and profit-first ideas, even within family life (Y. Yan 2003: 6–7). Chinese people have become increasingly individualistic. Even though collectivism is officially endorsed by the government, the collectivist idea of prioritizing *gong* over *si* is under challenge today.

Nevertheless, the ideas of 'individual' and 'private' understood in China still differ from the capitalist notion of 'individual' and 'private'. Individual and private are still relative to the social fabric. While old social nestings gradually vanish and lose influence, new social nexuses appear and gain importance. For certain social nexuses such as the family and the state, the idea of *xiaowo* and *dawo* still make a difference in guiding individual behaviours.

8.2.4 Collectivism in Shaping Chinese Higher Education

Collectivism has played an essential role in shaping China's higher educational culture and modern higher education system. Three unique characteristics of the contemporary Chinese higher education system embody the evolving collectivist tradition.

The first characteristic is that the primary missions of higher education institutions are state-oriented, reflective of the state as a significant sphere of social action. This also dictates the importance of the state–university relationship. Traditionally, higher education was organized and supported by the state (Jie Xu 2000). The state decided higher education content, as it often used higher education as a tool of governance. Higher education, together with the civil service examination (*keju*), was the main channel for cultivating and recruiting officials. It also contributed to the creation and dissemination of state-approved moralities and values. Through higher education and *keju*, state-approved virtues and moralities were installed as the content of learning and tests, ensuring that those values would prevail.

Contemporary Chinese higher education draws on both the Chinese educational tradition and modern university organization. On the one hand, the traditionally close relationship between higher education and the state is maintained. Collins (2016) argues that Chinese higher education is structured as an extension of the state and has been deliberately designed and guided to support the state's pursuit of modernization. The state sees higher education and science as crucial to national development, and the 'strong nation-state shaping of structures, funding and priorities' is a distinctive element of Chinese higher education (Marginson 2011c: 587). Like many Western countries, China views higher education as a useful tool to enhance national competitive capacity. Many aspects of higher education, including programme provision, number of students, some curricula and the appointment of presidents, are state-supervised. Correspondingly, the state provides strong support for universities

– more than half of higher education's total financial income is from the state (China-MOE 2013). Notably, modern Western theories such as human capital theory and Samuelson's concept of public goods also provide rationales for the state investment in higher education (Marginson 2006).

The second characteristic is that there is a tight linkage between higher education and family. As noted, the family is an essential sphere in the Chinese tradition and is particularly important in higher education practice. The legacy of the linkage is still evident in China today, being partly embodied in parents' investment in their children's education and the idea that successful students bring glory to their families. Despite the growing importance of the individual as a sphere of social action, and the correspondingly decrease in the importance of family, Bodycott and Lai (2012) find that in higher education, the Chinese family rather than the individual student is still the critical locus of decision-making. They argue that the family's impact is evident not only in initial decision-making but in an individual student's social and academic well-being within and beyond higher education (Bodycott and Lai 2012). Western notions such as higher education as a positional good and as cultural capital for social reproduction have become integrated with traditional Confucian values concerning the public and private good of higher education (Bodycott and Lai 2012; Marginson 1997). This mix of values is arguably what the Chinese family now upholds concerning higher education.

The third characteristic is the clear preference for the practical use of knowledge over the pursuit of pure knowledge, similarly influenced by the collectivist tradition. Due to the state's reliance on higher education to cultivate and recruit officials, the practical use of knowledge, especially that which is useful for governance, has long been highly valued by the Chinese people. According to Needham (1969), China was superior to the West between the first century BCE and the fifteenth century CE in terms of technological advantage. He argues that 'the Chinese civilization was much more efficient than the occidental in applying natural human knowledge to practical human needs' (Needham 1969: 190). However, China did not make much progress in pure knowledge and theoretical understanding, as this was regarded as not valuable (Huff 2009: 241). Without the pursuit of pure knowledge, China gradually lost its technological advantage. However, since the late nineteenth century, modern higher education has been bonded to the project of national salvation, with the most valued knowledge produced and disseminated by higher education shifting from classical knowledge to modern scientific and technological knowledge serving modernization.

8.3 The Public and Private in the Anglo-American Tradition

The examination of the spheres of social action in this section focuses on outcomes of transactions in those spheres and implications for the public and private. I also explore two further spheres not discussed in Chapter 3 but essential when investigating the public and private in higher education: the spheres of the market and communication.

8.3.1 The Public and Private: Spheres of Social Action

Outcomes of Transactions and the Dualism of Public/Private

In *On Liberty*, Mill claims that every individual enjoys absolute liberty as long as no one else is involved or influenced without consent (see Chapter 3). The requirement that others should not be harmed or inconvenienced specifies the limit of the individual sphere. It is a private transaction if an activity does not involve or influence other agents. Public transactions, whose outcomes involve or influence others, are only legitimate when those that are involved/influenced give their consent or when they are necessary to prevent harm to people.

Dewey also interprets the public/private dualism in relation to the outcome of transactions. As discussed in Chapter 3, Dewey ([1927] 2016) argues that the only distinguishing factor of the public and private is the scope of the influence of consequences. On many occasions, the consequences of private acts contribute to the community's welfare, although no one else is directly involved or influenced. Similarly, one of the most-cited quotes of Adam Smith ([1827] 2000: 26–7) says, 'it is not from the benevolence of the butcher, the brewer, or the baker that we expect our dinner, but from their regard to their own interest.' It is human beings' pursuit of private interests that spontaneously serves the community. Some may also call this phenomenon the collective consumption of private goods (Spann 1974).

Dewey provides a helpful definition of the public. Arguably, there are two attributes of Dewey's public that deserve attention. First, the differentiation of the public and private does not rest on who participates in human activities but on immediate consequences of transactions for other human beings. Second, connotations of the public are not fixed. They are in constant change and relative to the private, which to a degree parallels with Confucian interpretations. In other words, the public is manifested on two scales: the private draws certain boundaries according to consequences of acts, and the boundary of the public is always more extensive than that of, and includes, the private. Though Dewey did not set up a limitation of how large the public is, he did identify a clear boundary between the public and private, rather than blurring the boundary as the Chinese tradition does.

The Public-as-State/Government and the Public/Private Dualism

As Chapter 3 explained, the state should take charge of, and regulate, possible public consequences upon others. Seemingly, the state identifies with the public for Dewey. For example, based on Dewey's theory, Marginson (2018h) states that the public can be understood as state ownership and/or control. Indeed, Dewey's depiction of public-as-state has become an influential strand of the public/private dualism in the Anglo-American tradition – so that the public simply means the state or government and the private means the non-state sector (especially the sphere of individual/family and the market sphere).

However, for Dewey, the public is not always equivalent to the state. It is also understood more broadly. In Dewey's notion of public, the public can be interpreted on multiple scales, including the global scale (see also Chapter 3). Equating Dewey's public with the state can unduly narrow the notion. Dewey sees matters as public because they have to be resolved by politics – that can refer to both the state and grassroots democracy. Here, he intersects with two foundational ideas in the Anglo-American tradition: the limited liberal state and the inclusive democratic space. I shall return to these two foundational ideas.

However, there are problems with focusing solely on the outcome of transaction to unpack the public/private dualism. First, the long debating topic – the relationship between public and private – is not touched on. The zero-sum assumption (Marginson 2018f) regarding public goods and private goods is not well-addressed or refuted, but left aside. Second, the notion of a public act is a plain description of a type of activity that has consequences for people besides those who are directly engaged. Drawing on this definition, the term 'public goods' refers to public consequences. It does not concern whether or not those 'goods' augment the common public welfare and people's lives.

The Sphere of the Market and the Public/Private Dualism

The market is an important private sector in the Anglo-American tradition. The economic perspective, represented by Samuelson's (1954) formula of public/private, provides another approach to depicting the public/private dualism.

The economic perspective views society as composed of two parts: the market sector where the exchange of goods follows the law of market and the non-market sector with governmental or philanthropic intervention. In the Anglo-American tradition, the core objective is to maximize the scope of the market sector, as directly pursued in strategies of laissez-faire (Viner 1960). However, like Adam Smith, liberal economists acknowledge that in several areas, governmental and philanthropic intervention and provision is needed (Cornes and Sandler 1996: 3). Some economic activities affect people not directly engaged, the outcomes of which are 'externalities' (Cornes and Sandler 1996; Dybvig and Spatt 1983). There are two kinds of externalities: positive and negative (Dybvig and Spatt 1983). Higher education and science are examples of positive externalities, whereas pollution generation is a negative externality. Paralleling Dewey's arguments, public actions are needed in relation to transactions that generate externalities, to maximize the positive externalities and minimize the negative externalities (Dybvig and Spatt 1983). Actions by non-government agents outside the market such as philanthropists are also valued as public in the economic sense.

There are also certain activities that can hardly be conducted within the sphere of the market, or that follow the law of the market. Neoclassical economic theory calls this situation market failure. The provision of collective goods is one area subject to market failure (Randall 1983). Therefore, when there is market failure, public actions by non-market agents, not following the law of the market, are needed.

Similarly, scholars/researchers point to the phenomenon of 'the tragedy of the commons', which needs to be addressed by collective actions (Ostrom 1990: 2). Olson (1965: 2) argues that 'unless the number of individuals is quite small, or unless there is coercion or some other special device to make individuals act in their common interest, rational, self-interested individuals will not act to achieve their common or group interests.' He notes that it is not the pure number of individuals but how noticeable each person's actions are that determines the effectiveness of collective action. The key here is the free-rider problem, which is also one primary reason for market failure. In many cases, 'coercion or some other special device' is necessary if individuals are to collectively deal with the tragedy of the commons. This provides a further rationale for public intervention or provision (Ophuls 1973), or privatization – 'end[ing] the common-property system by creating a system of private property rights' (R. J. Smith 1981: 467). Public intervention or provision justifies governmental, philanthropic and other collective actions in relation to common-pool goods; privatization aims to turn common-pool goods into pure private goods.

With this approach to the public/private dualism, economists examine the spectrum of goods between the two poles of pure public goods and pure private goods. 'Private goods could be parceled out among individuals and efficiently allocated by markets, whereas public goods could not be divided among individuals, owing to nonrivalry of benefits and nonexcludability problems' (Cornes and Sandler 1986: 4). This definition draws on the two criteria for identifying public goods, proposed by Samuelson (1954): non-excludability and non-rivalry. Collective provision is essential for non-private goods, which consists of pure public goods, and impure public goods, including club goods and common-pool goods (Cornes and Sandler 1996; Randall 1983). There is more on this in 8.4.

The Sphere of Communication and the Communicative Inclusive Public

The sphere of communication, a social space in which agents communicate and express, provides another insight into the notion of 'public'. This sphere points to a different social connotation of the public: the communicative inclusive public.

The communicative inclusive public imagines a shared inclusive space – the sphere of free communication – in which agents are related and communicate in the forms of expression, communication and electoral behaviours (Marginson and Yang 2020). It is relational and network-based, a shared space in the sense of a universal assembly, though methods of how this public is constructed can vary across contexts. In the French tradition, this relational inclusive public is state-constructed in many respects. In the United Kingdom and the United States, it is partly constructed by commercial agents represented by social media platforms. The sphere of communication differs from the individual and collective spheres illustrated in Figure 3.1, which are agent-based, although certain agents may wish to dominate the sphere of communication.

In the Anglo-American tradition, the communication sphere is informed by the emphasis on liberty, especially freedom of thought and expression, as well as the idea of inclusive and grassroots democracy. While the public/private dualism centres on distinguishing in zero-sum fashion between the scope of public and the scope of private, the communicative inclusive public universally embraces all agents, including all that are 'private'. There is no wholly independent 'private' when 'public' is interpreted as 'the communicative inclusive public', paralleling with the Chinese idea of *tianxia*.

Many scholars/researchers see the public sphere as an ideal type of communication sphere (Calhoun 1993; Castells 2008; Habermas 1989), which was explored in Chapter 7. Here I consider why and in what way the public sphere represents the universal communicative public. Although ideally the sphere of communication is universal, the scope for *free* and *bottom-up* communication in a common space can vary. This scope rests on society's normative values. For example, in Imperial China, there was no emphasis on the universal inclusive democratic space or liberty in the modern Anglo-American sense.

The public sphere described by Habermas (1989) is an early public sphere in the sense of the communicative universal public, though it was not wholly universal. His example is eighteenth-century London where people met, formed their opinions and communicated in places such as salons, coffee shops and broadsheets. This was a bottom-up process of networked communication open to the social elite and the literati. It provided critical reflexivity, rationalizing 'public authority under the institutionalised influence of informed discussion and reasoned agreement' (Habermas 1989: xii).

Enabling individuals to participate in the public sphere is another purpose for the public. Individuals are carriers of public opinion. Places for communication are not exclusive but available to all individuals. As Habermas (1989: 1) states, 'we call events and occasions "public" when they are open to all, in contrast to closed or exclusive affairs – as when we speak of public places or public houses'. 'Open to all' means that no one, regardless of social background or status, should be excluded from the public sphere. Sen (1999) further points out that 'open to all' not only requires an individual's negative freedom to participate but positive freedom to discuss and express.

8.3.2 The Public and Private: Value Creation

The previous subsection suggested two connotations of the 'public' – the public/private dualism and the communicative inclusive public. This subsection focuses on normative values in the Anglo-American tradition informed by the tradition of the limited liberal state and the civic republican tradition,[2] and examines how those values have coloured the two connotations of public.

Chapter 3 has demonstrated that an essential aim of the Anglo-American tradition is to protect individual liberty, from which develops liberal individualism.

---

[2] The civic republican tradition, also known as classical republicanism or civic humanism, 'can be traced back to ancient Greek and the work of Aristotle and to the writings of Cicero in ancient Rome, and that these ideas were then borrowed, critiqued, adapted and extended within the writings of Niccòlo Machiavelli, James Harrington, Jean-Jacques Rousseau and James Madison' (Peterson 2011: 8). While the civic republican tradition is important to the ideas of universal public and (the) common goods, a detailed exploration of this tradition is not attempted in this book.

Lukes (1973: 37) lists five associated normative values: 'equal individual rights, limited government, laissez-faire, natural justice and equal opportunity, and individual freedom, moral development and dignity'. Arguably, these are public-related normative values that the Anglo-American tradition has developed to discursively regulate the relationship between spheres of social action, and colour interpretations of the public/private dualism.

As discussed, in Anglo-American societies, there is a long-standing tension between individuals and human associations. Individualism addresses that tension. Lukes (1973) identifies four ideas basic to liberal individualism: the dignity of man, autonomy, privacy and self-development. These ideas are consistent with the limited liberal state, including the absence of state intervention, or minimum state intervention, in civil society, the market and the sphere of civil communication. The liberal tradition draws a clear boundary around the state and installs a normative preference for private over public. It also values free decision-making by the individual/family in the market.

Protecting the sphere of individual/family does not mean wholly isolating the individual from collective spheres. As Chapter 3 demonstrated, Dewey refutes the idea that individuals and communities are two divergent extremes. As he saw it, atomic individualism justifies the free self-interest of the socially advantaged and worsening social inequalities.

Methodological individualism is a branch of atomism. It is influential in Anglo-American public debates, including those concerning higher education (Lukes 1973). According to methodological individualism, the collective outcomes of higher education are simply the sum of individuals' private interests (Marginson 2011b). This leaves the collective contributions of higher education largely overlooked.

Methodological individualism is doubtful as a guiding principle in policy. Even some of its supporters argue that 'the merit of methodological individualism should be investigated in terms of methodological fruitfulness, not in terms of its political uses (or abuses)' (Schumpeter 1980: 1). Methodological individualism is an ideal case that privileges the individual sphere over the collective sphere. It is impossible to draw on 'what is in any conceivable sense an individualistic system of values' (Weber [1922] 1968: 18) as a mode of universal explanation. Nevertheless, the method and its solely individualistic system of values have been widely applied. One result has been to divert attention from a more constructive individualism, whose key, according to Dewey ([1916] 2011: 167), is to enable and support the individual's development of free agency. The pursuit of the limited state by itself cannot do this and tends to subtract from the resources needed.

8.4 Relevant Concepts of Collective Goods (Plural) based on the Connotations of the Public

This section examines different kinds of collective goods informed by the connotations of the public in the two traditions. These goods include public goods based on the public/private dualism and common goods drawing on the communicative inclusive public. Enlightened by the Chinese tradition, I also introduce the concept of normative collective goods, which can connect agents to the singular form of 'the collective good'.

Marginson (2011b) argues that public goods (plural) originates from economics and is often used for objective and empirical descriptions. Samuelson's economic definition now dominates the discursive usage of the term 'public goods'. In contrast, the singular form – the public good – is normative in nature and entangled with public-related values (Calhoun 1998; Mansbridge 1998; Marginson 2011b). It highlights the collective attribute of activities, interests and resources (Marginson 2011b).

The UNESCO-developed notion of '(the) common goods' intersects with the communicative inclusive public – though it is perhaps more local and less society-wide than the full sweep of communicative society – and calls for the bottom-up and collective production of collective goods. Compared to public goods, common goods as defined by UNESCO have a more normative orientation. Common goods stress solidarity and cooperation, and collective interests (Locatelli 2019). However, 'common goods' are still descriptive in nature. The normative term is the 'common good'. Here I refer to the singular 'public good' and 'common good' together as *the collective good*.

Connotations of the public good(s) and private good(s), in both Anglo-American and Chinese societies, are dominated by Anglo-American interpretations (Tian and Liu 2018). A comparison of the two traditions' ideas of collective goods, on a more normatively symmetrical basis, is developed in Chapter 10.

8.4.1 Economic/Governmental Public Goods: Collective Goods in the Sense of the Public/Private Dualism

Marginson (2018h) argues that the plural form of public good(s) can be depicted in two dimensions. The first dimension draws on economic theories of public goods, as in Samuelson (1954), as discussed earlier. Economic public goods are non-rivalrous and/or non-excludable. The economic public goods, though alien to the Chinese tradition before its introduction from the West, concept has gained prominence in the Chinese context. Tian and Liu (2018: 9) argue that 'Chinese scholars began to discuss public good(s) in 1990, from an economic point of view. In general, over the past 30 years, Chinese scholars' discussions about "public good(s)" have mainly focused on meanings, classifications and externalities.'

Defining public goods by non-rivalry and non-excludability has problems. First, it is problematic to apply this definition to non-capitalist societies, including a gift economy or an economy grounded in government-owned/administered property (Marginson 2018h; Ostrom 2010). Second, the definition is naturalistic, assigning the category 'public' according to what is seen as the intrinsic nature of the good, and cannot encompass the fact that the public/private nature of certain goods can change according to the social or political arrangements (Marginson 2018h). For example, whether higher education is non-rival and/or non-excludable, and the extent in each case, varies in different societies. With the growing private input in higher education, whether higher education is a public good and contributes to public goods or not becomes more debatable (Locatelli 2019). Third, the definition fails to embrace normative values, such as equality, that are intrinsically important to society. Fourth, it fails to identify many collective goods that cannot be individualized or given meaningful price values (Marginson 2018h).

The second dimension Marginson (2018h) employs is the state/non-state dimension, offering the example of Dewey's depiction of public/private. The concept of public goods in this dimension is that of governmental public goods. These are state-addressed/provided or state-owned goods, and non-market-produced. It seems that governmental public goods are often economic public goods. But economic public goods may also include non-state collective goods, including certain common goods.

The concept of governmental public goods is widely employed across the world. In the Anglo-American tradition, the concept provides a second definition of the necessary roles and functions of the state, alongside the limited liberal state (Locatelli 2019). In the limited liberal state, the state's essential responsibilities are largely informed by 'market failure'. This leads to a limited list of governmental public goods, but Anglo-American states can range wider than this, beyond the strict limit implied by liberal doctrine, for example, in equity policy in higher education.

Governmental public goods can be different across countries, depending on the prevailing political system. For example, with the traditions of the comprehensive state and collectivism in Chinese society, the state undertakes larger responsibilities, and more goods are state-owned or state-produced. Higher education is largely a governmental public good in China, as the bulk of financial source of higher education comes from the state, but less so in the United States, where even the so-called public universities do not primarily rely on government funding. However, in all countries, governmental public goods, like economic public goods, are not necessarily beneficial to all. In other words, solely working with the state/non-state dimension does not guarantee the essential character of the goods: how beneficial, how accessible, how broadly distributed.

8.4.2 Common Goods and Public Goods in a Traditional Chinese Sense: Collective Goods in the Sense of the (Communicative) Inclusive Public

There is also the notion of common goods. The common goods concept is closer to the communicative inclusive public than the public/private dualism and moves a step beyond communication to include collective action. Many scholars/researchers recognize the problems associated with the concepts of economic and governmental public goods, and suggest the use of 'common goods' rather than public goods to discuss higher education's collective contributions (see, e.g., Locatelli 2019; Tian and Liu 2018; UNESCO 2015). Here the notion of common goods suggests joint activity by a wide array of agents engaged in both defining and producing common goods, respects the potential for diverse interpretations in practice, based on differing cultural contexts, and has a normative orientation in favour of collective welfare.

Dupré (1994: 173) defines common goods as goods 'proper to, and attainable only by the community, yet individually shared by its members'. UNESCO (2015) asserts that the concept of common goods includes collective goods produced by multiple stakeholders, such as diverse organizations in civil society, arguing that this cannot be fully covered by the notion of public goods.

The common goods concept highlights two attributes: collectively produced/shared and collectively beneficial. To be collectively produced or shared does not require production or ownership by the state. Common goods can incorporate collective goods produced or owned by many entities. Meanwhile, the idea encourages and opens up space for inclusive and bottom-up participation (UNESCO 2015: 78), which is itself a common good contributing to democracy, consistent with the civic republican tradition, especially its local communal forms. The attribute of collective interests is at the base of the normative orientation of common goods. The term 'common goods' does not refer to outcomes of common action but only those consequences that are collectively beneficial. UNESCO (2015) states that common goods concern the good life of individuals and the goodness of life that is common to all persons. On the other hand, the goodness of life may be interpreted in varying ways across contexts. Nevertheless, all of this contrasts with 'public goods'. As was noted earlier, no presumption can be made about the collective interests of public goods, however they are defined. Another attraction of common goods for scholars/researchers is that the term falls outside the zero-sum public/private dichotomy (Szadkowski 2019; UNESCO 2015) and provides space for private/individual and common interests to advance together.

Although it does not share the civic republican tradition, the Chinese tradition nevertheless develops a concept of traditional Chinese public goods that seems to highly overlap with UNESCO's common goods. Arguably, although the concepts of economic public goods and governmental public goods are now highly visible in China, they are distinct from the concept of public goods in a traditional Chinese sense.

> In China, the meaning of 'public good' goes far beyond the idea of 'good' or 'wealth'. ... They are goods for public benefit, which are produced on the basis of public demands, relying on public power and through consensus and cooperation. ... In this sense, the meaning of public goods in China is more related to common goods, which are collective in nature, beneficial to all, and perhaps fostering social inclusion, integration, tolerance, equality, and human rights, with a distinct feature of intrinsic value and shared participation. (Tian and Liu 2018: 10)

As discussed in 8.2, there is no absolute private in the Chinese tradition. The public is relative to the private and at the utmost means *tianxia* (all under heaven). The public-as-*tianxia* to a large extent overlaps with the universally inclusive public in the Anglo-American tradition. In *tianxia*, all creatures belong to one community as a whole; *tianxia* is collectively shared by all. There is also the anthropocosmic worldview (see Chapter 2) – that people are expected to work collectively and in a harmonious way with other creatures and nature, for the collective good of all under heaven. This idea is embodied in the Chinese phrase of *tianxia weigong* (all under heaven belongs to all and is for all) (see Chapter 9). It can be argued that *tianxia weigong* parallels with the concept of global common goods. For global common goods, in line with the globally inclusive public, all agents in the world, including grassroots agents, collectively communicate and act for the universal interests. This is a wholly inclusive and bottom-up process, similar to the process of producing public goods in the traditional Chinese sense, at the village level. Though formal democracy was absent in the despotic Imperial state, the conjoint communicative experiences in Chinese local communities, where the Imperial state's power hardly reached, nurtured the democratic spirit of the Chinese people (J. C. Wang 2012: 105–6).

> Those [communities] which were important, which really counted in forming emotional and intellectual dispositions, were local and contiguous and consequently visible. . . . The state, even when it despotically interfered, was remote, an agency alien to daily life. Otherwise it entered men's lives through custom and common law. (Dewey [1927] 872016: 134)

Using the concept of (global) common goods does not mean the concepts of economic and governmental public goods have no purpose. The three concepts emerge from different connotations of the public – the market/non-market of the public/private dualism, the state/non-state of the public/private dualism or the (communicative) inclusive public. Together, they are able to address different kinds of collective goods. Because the three kinds of collective goods concern heterogeneous qualities, they are not directly complementary. Putting them together does not enable a satisfactory categorization of collective goods. This is attempted on a different basis in Chapter 10.

8.4.3 Normative Collective Goods: Connecting Agents with the Singular Form of the Collective Good

The Chinese tradition's particular emphasis on virtues and morals leads to another kind of collective goods, one that connects different agents within a social order. For Confucianism, the collective good (singular) with the highest status is the maintenance of harmony and order. *De* (德), meaning virtues or morals, is fundamental to achieving this aim. In the Chinese tradition, *de* centres on the individual's moral consciousness and the conduct of external behaviour in a moral and virtuous way. It is believed that good governance should be based on *de*, rather than coercive measures. When every individual acts in accordance with *de*, harmony and order is realized.

The term *gongde* combines the characters of *gong* (the public) and *de*. *Gongde* consists of numerous *de* that are related to collective life and need to be obeyed and practised by the universal public, that is, by every individual under heaven. In other words, *gongde* refers to the normative values that have a collective impact by shaping an individual's personality and guiding external behaviours. The typical values in the Chinese tradition include Confucian *wuchang* – *ren* (humanity and benevolence), *yi* (righteousness), *li* (propriety), *zhi* (wisdom) and *xin* (integrity).

The Chinese tradition's emphasis on *de* indicates the need to bridge the gap between agents and their external actions contributing to the collective good. People are not born with the *de* that would lead them to behave for the sake of the collective good. They have to learn how to behave. This idea has a parallel in the Anglo-American tradition. As discussed, Olson (1965: 2) notes that rational, self-interested individuals do not necessarily act for the collective good. Here the Anglo-American tradition resorts to external coercion, or privatization, to sustain the collective good. The Chinese tradition falls back on normative values.

In the Chinese tradition, individuals are expected to self-cultivate, especially through the process of moral perfectionism. They become morally virtuous and able to behave in a way that sustains the collective good, closing the gap between agents and the collective good. Here, values directly stipulate the scope of, and the relationship between, the Chinese spheres of social action. These values are also collective goods, in the sense that they *are jointly produced and/or accepted by the collective, permeate through different spheres of action to shape an agent's behaviour and the relationship between the spheres (and thus influence the public/private dualism), uphold the scope of the (communicative) inclusive public and colour the interpretations of what is commonly beneficial.* These values are not captured by the three kinds of collective goods previously discussed – economic public goods, governmental public goods and common goods. Instead, they belong to another specific kind of collective goods – normative collective goods. Arguably, these normative collective goods are key to agents' joint production of the collective good, including common welfare. Normative collective goods are not only important in the Chinese tradition, they also play a significant role in the Anglo-American tradition. The production of collective goods requires individual agents to behave in certain ways that are steeped in values. This is manifested in moral and citizenship education programmes.

8.5 Higher Education and the Gong/Public and Si/Private

Connotations of the *gong*/public and the *si*/private are essential to higher education. However, there is still a lack of clarity about what the *gong*/public and *si*/private and the collective good(s) mean in higher education (Naidoo 2004; G. Williams 2016).

Marginson (2018h) points out four reasons why there is a lack of clarity. First, with respect to public/private dualism, higher education differs in various aspects including 'location of activity (state sector versus outside), the source of funding (government versus household or private organization) and the nature of the activity' (Marginson 2018h: 323). Some scholars/researchers such as Hazelkorn and Gibson (2018) investigate the location of higher education activity by looking at the 'publicness' of higher education – whether higher education sits inside or outside the state sector. Some focus on financial sources of higher education (see, e.g., Carnoy et al. 2014). Growing competition for funds, corporatization and the expanding role of student tuition fees reflect the changing pattern of higher education finance (Marginson 2013b). Likewise, studies on the nature of the activity look at higher education activities and their consequences. Research on the collective good contribution of higher education belongs to this group (e.g., Calhoun 2006). The second reason is the diversity of political and educational traditions across the world. The third reason is the different approaches taken across the social sciences. The fourth reason is a 'sustained and influential assault on notions of the public good or public interests, which has partly obscured the public dimension in higher education and other sectors' (Marginson 2018h: 323). In addition to scholarly work such as the writings of Hayek and Friedman, the marketization of higher education and the emergent of for-profit higher education embody an aspect of this assault (Locatelli 2019). Despite these obstacles of understanding, elaboration and clarification of public and private in higher education are urgently needed in order to better understand and develop higher education, and in order to better understand the similarities and differences between societies.

8.5.1 To What Extent Does Higher Education Produce Collective Goods?

It is widely agreed that higher education produces collective goods (Filippakou and Williams 2015; Pusser 2006), though there are many different takes on which collective goods higher education brings forth.

Externalities as Public Goods in Economic Sense

The term 'externalities' of higher education, as public goods in an economic sense, is one of the dominant approaches to capture higher education's collective goods.

Some economists define the benefits from higher education that are received by individuals simply as private goods (see, e.g., Blundell et al. 1999; Monks 2000). These private goods include higher economic returns, better employability, augmented social status and reputation, better life quality, better health outcomes and the growth of individual capability (Kelly et al. 2010; Marginson 2016b; J. Williams 2016). Meanwhile, economists are also aware of collective interests following from the production of these individual private goods (Spann 1974), in the form of externalities. For example, accompanying the growth of individual capability is the greater productivity of the labour force, as economic externalities (Glewwe et al. 2014; Marginson 2019); and the instilling of common core virtues into social members, possibilities for social mobility and an improvement in shared social literacy, as social externalities (Tilak 2008: 455). However, economics lacks rigorous methods for calculating the exact amount of economic externalities generated in higher education and tend to overlook social externalities produced by higher education (see later) (Chapman and Lounkaew 2015; Marginson 2013a).

The production of knowledge, as an important collective good, is a core activity of higher education (Calhoun 2006). Research in higher education advances scientific and technological knowledge, which is essential in the development of national economic and political capacity and, more importantly, the development of humanity (McMahon 2009). For example, policy consultancy, innovation spill-overs, more advanced medical treatment for better health and strategies to tackle global climate change all rely on research to create knowledge. Meanwhile, there is also knowledge in humanities and social sciences created by higher education. Besides their contributions to addressing social problems, such knowledge is often closely related to normative collective goods. For example, curricular design in moral and citizenship education plays a crucial role in instilling common values into young members of society.

Nevertheless, 'higher education is under some pressure to focus primarily or exclusively on individualistic economic benefits' (Marginson 2014c: 52). The knowledge-related aspect of higher education, especially in relation to humanities and social sciences knowledge, is less recognized in policy discourses and this can lead to neglect also within internal university priorities (Marginson 2014c; J. Williams 2014).

Normative Collective Goods

Higher education's contribution through the formation and distribution of normative collective goods is often neglected. Normative collective goods, outcomes grounded in the goals and values of society, are intangible and hard to measure, although it is possible to identify normalizing practices that implement values: for example, neoliberal governance that structures higher education so as to be closely aligned with the market economy.

Arguably, a central purpose of higher education is to 'foster a vibrant public good, which includes increased democratic participation, equality before the law, [and] positive social transformation' (Letizia 2015: 1). In contemporary contexts, higher education is engaged with the promotion of social justice (Pusser 2006; J. Williams 2016). Meanwhile, in the Chinese tradition, there is arguably an emphasis on higher education to propose, update and disseminate values. All of these aspects demonstrate higher education's function in creating normative collective goods. Values, including liberty, solidarity, inclusion, tolerance and equity, are essential in upholding a harmonious collective sphere of social action (Marginson 2018b; McMahon 2009).

Values become public values only when they are accepted and practised by members of societies (Jørgensen and Bozeman 2007), which also rests on education including higher education through educating individuals. As Nixon (2011: 32) states, 'higher education is centrally concerned with how people develop their life projects, negotiate their life choices, and configure their life purposes. It is, first and last, concerned with human flourishing.' The formation of these values requires knowledge creation in higher education. Many of the influential and widely accepted values in societies are proposed by thinkers who have connections with higher education, in addition to those values coming from government, media and think tanks. Compared to the situation in Anglo-American societies, thinkers connected with higher education are arguably more influential in the Chinese society. These thinkers either engage in higher education activities or work in higher education (see also Chapter 7).

The contents of values are debatable in society and vary in different societies. Corruption of values may also happen (Marginson 2016a). The growth of a virulent blood-and-soil form of nationalism in the twenty-first century is regarded by many scholars/researchers as a sign of the corruption of values (see, e.g., Brubaker 2017). Higher education as a public sphere is expected to provide a free space for critical reflection on public issues, including values. Ideally, as discussed, higher education-fostered and incubated reflexivity is an important reference point for decision-making by states and social and economic leaders (Pusser 2006). However, the marketization and privatization of higher education have resulted in the evacuation of values inside and outside higher education (Marginson 2006).

In sum, higher education produces collective goods. The externalities concept is an Anglo-American way of opening up the terrain of collective goods, but it still underplays them – as it sees them as secondary to market transactions – and it altogether misses the dimension of normative collective goods. Anglo-American economics institutionalizes values indirectly, through the method of methodological individualism and the limited state and zero-sum approach to the public and private. But this is a clumsy way of creating and normalizing values, and as has been shown, problematic. The extreme individualist economic values are not broadly supported in higher education, as they exclude much of what it does. Thus, it is necessary to re-emphasize the normative collective goods that higher education produces.

8.5.2 Is Higher Education Organized So as to Produce Such Collective Goods?

Subsection 8.5.1 has discussed the collective goods produced by higher education. However, it is not clear whether the organization of higher education is conducive to producing such collective goods. The organization of higher education includes financing and accessibility.

In relation to financial sources, one way to support higher education's production of collective goods is to sustain it with the public purse. Public financial support can be applied to research, students, infrastructure, as well as teaching and learning activities. However, higher education's collective goods are not only generated for the state sphere. Other social spheres also benefit. In turn, these spheres may also need to support higher education financially. This resonates with UNESCO's argument of viewing higher education as a common good, being supported collectively by various state and non-state actors in society (Szadkowski 2019; UNESCO 2015).

Some scholars/researchers are concerned that an increase in public funding can be associated with reduced institutional autonomy (J. Williams 2016). In addition to the dangers associated with state involvement, funding from other spheres such as the market sphere and the social sphere may also result in reduced autonomy for higher education and pose a threat to academic freedom. This problem suggests that it is important to explore possible ways of balancing the autonomy of higher education with the external influences flowing from funding support. As discussed in Chapter 7, the idea of mutual trust may be helpful.

The financing and regulation of higher education partly determine whether or not it is located in the public sector. While higher education is responsible for responding to public demands (e.g., by producing collective goods), the Anglo-American tradition would argue that the independent status of higher education should be maintained. Higher education itself should determine, after critical reflection, whether and how to respond. This is different in the Chinese tradition where the comprehensive state applies.

The availability of student places and social access has long been a debatable topic in higher education. Scholars/researchers have pointed out the resulting problems of defining a public good based on non-rivalry and non-excludability. Goldin (1977: 53) asserts that this definition creates an unavoidable choice: 'shall every one have equal access to that service (in which case the service will be similar to a public good) or shall the service be available selectively: to some, but not to others?' This raises an important question about higher education – accessibility or excellence? (Collins 2016; Marginson 2013a, 2016a). According to Calhoun (2006), social accessibility of higher education is a virtue, one more important than other virtues. But this does not mean that accessibility always trumps quality or excellence. Balance is desirable. Societies employ various strategies to reach that balance (I shall come back to this point in the next subsection).

How Collective Goods Are Understood

The provision of collective goods in practice is affected by the scholarly and policy-related discussion about those collective goods, including the lack of clarity in that discussion and the partial neglect of the collective dimension, especially the neglect of higher education's role in producing normative (values-oriented) collective goods.

In attempting to determine whether activity in higher education is public or private, scholars often focus on locality, financial sources and accessibility. The state/non-state notion of the public determines whether higher education is a governmental public good in terms of locality (Labaree 1997; Marginson 2018h). In relation to financial sources, higher education is seen as a governmental public good if the bulk of higher education's financial income is from the public purse (Calhoun 2006; Labaree 2016). The concept of economic public goods is used to explore whether higher education is a public good in relation to accessibility (Goldin 1977; Hazelkorn and Gibson 2018). However, arguments made at a descriptive level vary in different societies and different periods (Marginson 2018h). Countries have varying attitudes towards how higher education should be organized to produce collective goods.

Marginson (2006) argues that in Anglo-American countries, the decrease of state financing to higher education has been associated with a shift to the view of higher education as mainly a producer of private goods. In the United States, where the public purse is not the main financial source for higher education, the sector is understood more as a private good rather than a public good (Labaree 2016), and is read in terms of a meritocratic and competitive ideology and regarded as a commodity. The 'student as consumer' discourse has gained prominence in the United States since the 1970s when a rise in tuition fees occurred (Slaughter and Leslie 1997). Clark (1986) regards the attributes of US higher education as limited state authority, academic oligarchy and high market-orientation. Higher education in the United States is seen as an independent domain that enjoys high-level autonomy. In this framework, the federal government has limited regulatory authority and operates from a distance. Knowledge is seen as contributing to public goods and thus research funding, to a certain extent, comes from the federal government's support.

In the 1960s in the UK, the state sought to equalize the participation of all citizens through public funding, although higher education still catered mostly for elites at that time (Fisher 2006; Tilak 2008). In 1963, the state issued the *Robbins Report* in which higher education was seen as a public good, and contributing to the public good, and one that should receive financial support from the public (Committee on Higher Education 1963). In exchange, higher education was expected to expand massively to meet growing social demand. At that time, the state was widely perceived by the public as a 'benevolent dictator' because of its responsibility to safeguard all citizens' economic and social well-being (Desai 2003). However, in the past three decades, heavily influenced by the restructuring of the welfare state in the 1980s, the UK higher education system has been increasingly associated with political and economic ideologies related to neoliberalism (Robertson 2010). The marketization of higher education and the rise of the practices of the student consumer have been joined with successive governments' attempts to shift the funding of higher education away from the state and on to students as customer beneficiaries (Naidoo and Williams 2015). Governments have created the conditions for a quasi-market, while at the same time market mechanisms are deployed to achieve governmental goals (Naidoo and Williams 2015).

In contrast, China's higher education continues to be organized in a way that enables the production of collective goods, notwithstanding the diverse financial sources (Tian and Liu 2018). As discussed in Chapter 2, modern universities emerged in China in the late Qing Dynasty. Prior to the massification of higher education in the late twentieth century, the state regarded higher education as an indispensable part of the state system and gave it full support. The market played no role. The mission of higher education was to support the state and produce collective goods. In the last two decades of the twentieth century, there was rapid massification, privatization and governmental deregulation in Chinese higher education. With the rise of private actors in China's higher education system, the distinction between the public and private became more blurred, and higher education's public role came under debate.

While the worldwide trend to privatization and marketization makes higher education less like a public good, massification has made higher education more available to the public. In terms of accessibility, higher education is becoming more like a public good. Now, all three countries under discussion in this book – China, the United States and the United Kingdom – have entered Trow's stage of universal higher education (Trow [1973] 2010; UNESCO 2018), though in different ways. The California Master Plan is a representative strategy of massification, the central idea of which is pursuing 'equality with excellence' (Kerr 2011). In the three decades of its golden age of higher education, California made higher education available to most of its residents while maintaining the high quality of the University of California campuses at the top of the institutional hierarchy. The quality of the University of California was sustained by generous financial support from the state government (Kerr 2011). However, this pattern is being challenged, largely because of the decrease of public financial support, reflecting changing attitudes towards higher education's contributions to collective goods.

9

Global Outcomes of Higher Education

Global Public/Common Goods and *Tianxia Weigong* (All under Heaven Belongs to/is for All)

9.1 Introduction

This chapter focuses on the fifth and final key theme: global public/common goods, or global collective goods, in the Anglo-American tradition and *tianxia weigong* (all under heaven belongs to/is for all) in the Chinese tradition.

Higher education contributes to a wide range of public and/or common goods, many of which are located within national borders: for example, higher education's contribution to a country's 'human power', social cohesion and economic competitiveness (Hüfner 2003; Nyborg 2003; Tilak 2008). Indeed, the mainstream narrative about higher education's collective outcomes focuses on national public/common goods. While some aspects that transcend the national border are sporadically discussed, such as knowledge advancement and the international mobility of talent, higher education's outcomes in the global sphere remain under-researched. However, in the contemporary context, such an examination is urgently needed.

There are at least two reasons to investigate collective goods in the global sphere. The first is the existence of worldwide common problems. In a certain respect, states across the world face similar problems due to ever-increasing globalization. These include the threat of international terrorism, financial instability, climate change and epidemics. These problems challenge the sustainable development not only of any single country but of humanity as a whole. There is an urgent need for countries to establish common solutions for these common problems (Kaul et al. 1999b; I. Taylor 2014). Addressing common problems requires joint efforts. For example, the mitigation of global climate change can be scarcely realized by a single country. Second, as pointed out by Amartya Sen (2006: 129–30) (see also

Chapter 3), a country's, and even an individual's, behaviour can have effects that flow across national borders. The cost and benefits of individual, institutional or national conduct in one country can be carried by people in other countries (Kaul et al. 1999b; Rao et al. 1999; Sen 1999). This calls for discussion of global collective goods. Here methodological nationalism creates constraints that must be overcome. I shall come back to this later.

Further, higher education in particular works with collective goods in the global sphere. Higher education systems are routinely connected across borders (Marginson 2018b, g). In a global common space, the outcomes of higher education often reach beyond national borders. For example, knowledge as a major theme of higher education is intrinsically a collective good shared by the whole of humanity (see more on this in 9.2), notwithstanding the language hierarchies and unequal power between research systems. However, national and local governments are the main supporters of higher education in most countries. The legitimacy of public finance for higher education rests largely on its production of national and local collective goods. In contrast, the production of global collective goods is not always understood, is often short of support and is sometimes restricted by governments (e.g., countries' immigration regulations may limit the flow and mobility of academics and students).

Against this backdrop, the chapter focuses on the ideas of collective goods in the global sphere in relation to higher education. In this process, cross-border activities in higher education are discussed. Compared to the other four key themes, more abundantly investigated in academia, global public goods only started to attract attention in the late twentieth century (Kaul et al. 1999b). It was not until the twenty-first century that scholars/researchers started to examine global common goods (Anand et al. 2007; UNESCO 2015). There is not much scholarship to draw on. This chapter is both a reflection on the existing discussion and an explorative search for new insights by introducing the Chinese idea of *tianxia* and *tianxia weigong* into the discussion.

9.2 Global Public/Common Goods in the Anglo-American Tradition

9.2.1 The Dualistic Worldview and Methodological Nationalism

As presented in Chapters 5 and 8, the dualistic worldview of I and non-I is fundamental to the Anglo-American interpretation of 'the public'. This worldview also shapes the interpretation of 'the world'. The assumption of continuous conflict between I and non-I is a foundational pillar of the current world order, in which the world as a whole is subsumed under self-interested nation-states (Chernilo 2011; B. Wang 2017: 7). As the state's legitimacy derives from within the boundary of the nation-state rather than beyond it, states that understand the world in the terms of I and not-I are routinely self-interested and responsive only to domestic needs (T. Zhao 2011: 2, 3, 16). This bordered outlook has been described as 'methodological nationalism':

> Methodological nationalism takes the following ideal premises for granted: it equates society with nation-state societies, and sees states and their governments as the cornerstones of a social sciences analysis. It assumes that humanity is naturally divided into a limited number of nations, which on the inside, organize themselves as nation-states, and on the outside, set boundaries to distinguish themselves from other nation-states. It goes even further: this outer delimitation, as well as the competition between nation-states, presents the most fundamental category of political organization. Indeed, the social science stance is rooted in the concept of the nation-state. It is a nation-state outlook on society and politics, law, justice and history, that governs the sociological imagination. (Beck 2007: 287)

Though the limitations of methodological nationalism have been repeatedly addressed by social scientists (see, e.g., Beck 2007; Chernilo 2011; Shahjahan and Kezar 2013), it still largely shapes discussion of global public/common goods.

How then do nations cooperate and on what basis? In a methodologically nationalist world, the device for cooperation is multilateralism. In the ideal multilateral world order, nation-states relate as equals (Bell 2017b; Callahan and Barabantseva 2011). Each state has equal international status and equally participates in the international decision-making process. It is expected that states will work together and make international agreements so as to maintain a peaceful international environment, and produce the agreed global public goods (Kaul et al. 2003, 1999b; I. Taylor 2014). In the multilateral order, in addition to governmental cooperation, social forces including non-governmental organizations are also encouraged to work jointly to produce global common goods.

This idea is not always achieved. In reality, smaller states are not always the equals of larger states in international affairs (B. Wang 2017: 1–2). International agreements are not always effective in regulating every state's behaviours, as was shown in the US-Iraq war. In the multilateral order, the collective welfare of the globe is often subordinate to the interests of individual nations.

The nation-state framework may work well with national issues but causes problems at a global level. Scholars/researchers search for ways through these problems. A common strategy in the Anglo-American tradition is to both work with the interstate global system and encourage non-governmental organizations' participation (Kaul et al. 2003). This strategy is acknowledged in UNESCO's development of the idea of global common goods (Anand et al. 2007; UNESCO 2015). Alternatively, some scholars/researchers familiar with the Chinese tradition argue that the nation-state framework is itself a decisive problem and must be addressed in order to move forward (B. Wang 2017: 7–8; T. Zhao 2011: 15–6, 32). The idea of *tianxia* has been suggested as an alternative perspective in understanding and intervening in the world (see, e.g., Bell 2017b; Duara 2017; H. Lee 2017; Z. Xu 2018; T. Zhao 2011, 2019). I consider this pathway in 9.3.

9.2.2 Global Common Challenges and Global Public/Common Goods

Global Public Goods

Global public goods refer to those public goods that extend beyond national borders and are shared by people from different countries. For example, I. Taylor (2014: 13) argues that global public goods are goods whose 'benefits are sufficiently widely dispersed across the globe'. In Taylor's definition, benefiting every country across the world is not a necessary requirement of global public goods. As long as a public good is shared by more than one country, it is a global public good (I. Taylor 2014). Kaul and colleagues (1999a: xxi) add intergenerational aspects and recognition of social groups. Global public goods are public goods 'whose benefits reach across borders, generations and population groups'. The mitigation of climate change is a global public good not only because it benefits people across the world but also because it benefits future generations. In addition, Kaul et al. (1999a: 3–4) argue that certain goods transcend national borders but benefit certain groups in countries, often advantaged populations. If we are to view the internet as a global public good, its benefits should be accessible to all groups, particularly those with low income and living in remote areas.

Given these provisos and caveats, the extant interpretations of global public goods largely rest on the connotation of public goods themselves – the key issue is what is included in that category. Nevertheless, when exploring global public goods, scholars/researchers tend to only consider the economic definition of public goods (see, e.g., Kaul et al. 1999a; I. Taylor 2014). Here global public goods are defined as goods that are non-rivalrous and non-excludable, as well as beneficial across countries, generations and groups (Kaul et al. 1999a). Given that solely relying on the economic interpretation of public goods is problematic at the national level, it is also problematic at the global level and in additional ways. Locatelli (2019: 157) makes the point that policies following the economic interpretation of global public goods may 'potentially perpetuate the harmful facets of economic globalization via the spread of capitalism'.

Nevertheless, the economic exposition does identify one important attribute of global public goods, which is related to market failure. According to Samuelson (1954), as the market is unable to produce public goods, it is the government's responsibility to provide them. This indicates that the provision of global public goods is in need of a global government. In reality, a 'global government' does not exist. Arguably, today's turmoil, as illustrated by the failure of international coordination in relation to climate change and the Covid-19 pandemic, shows that global public goods are seriously underprovided, and there is a great need for international organizations with authority, if not some kind of global government (Deneulin and Townsend 2007; Kaul et al. 1999b).

There are constant international efforts to cope with cross-border conflicts and to produce global public goods of peace, sustainability and security (Kaul et al. 2003). Some methods derive from the idea of global governance (Dingwerth and Pattberg 2006; Held and Maffettone 2016). There are numerous multilateral organizations, such as the United Nations and the World Health Organization. These organizations reflect the hopes of Dewey and others that international cooperation and multilateral organizations would be sufficient to sustain global public goods (Dewey [1921] 1976: 218–19; Kaul et al. 2003; I. Taylor 2014). Nevertheless, exacerbating international conflicts, long-standing inequality gaps and persisting under-provision of many global public goods show that new approaches may be needed. With the role and nature of nation-states unchanged within present interstate relationships, it seems difficult if not impossible to develop a mechanism for countries to sustain a high level of cooperation, share the cost of global public goods and distribute global public goods effectively. In a methodologically nationalist world, simply unpacking global public goods as public goods at a global level is very unlikely to deliver the necessary results.

Global Common Goods

Some scholars/researchers have suggested a framework other than 'global public goods' to mitigate conflicts between countries, narrow inequality within or between countries and secure the provision of jointly valued outcomes. UNESCO (2015) suggests the concept of global common goods as a constructive alternative. This no longer centres on the public/private dualism, and it places more emphasis on agency and delivery than does the concept of global public goods.

The idea of global common goods suggests a universal common sphere, devoted to collective welfare and comprised of diverse agencies. As discussed in Chapter 8, the problems of the economic definition of global public goods are largely due to the narrow notion of 'goods'. We need to understand 'goods' as those conducive to human well-being and the good life rather than merely goods in the transactional economic sense (Deneulin and Townsend 2007); and we need a concept that addresses the good life of humanity as a whole as well as that of individual human beings. Here, global common goods resonates with a cosmopolitanism that views all human beings belonging to a single relational community with shared moralities (Kleingeld and Brown 2019). This humanistic approach embraces a wider range of goods than does economic global public goods (Locatelli 2019; UNESCO 2015), from a peaceful environment to the progress of arts. Meanwhile, as Deneulin and Townsend (2007) argue, enabling every individual to live a good life is an important global common good, which reprises Amartya Sen's (1999) argument in *Development as Freedom*.

As the humanistic approach shows, in contrast with global public goods, global common goods makes normative values explicit. UNESCO (2015) lists several values as global common goods: cultural and social diversity, social harmony, respect for life and human dignity, equal rights and justice, and a sense of human solidarity and shared responsibility for our common future. This universalist vision is carried through in the notions of agency and delivery associated with the common goods concept. In addition, a plurality of contributions from the whole of humanity is called for. As E. Zhang (2010) sees, the term 'public' in global public goods may suggest that global public goods are provided only by the public in the sense of government. The concept of global common goods overcomes this limitation, as common goods have been defined 'as those goods that, irrespective of any public or private origin, are characterized by a binding destination and necessary for the realization of the fundamental rights of all people' (UNESCO 2015: 77).

The inclusion of diverse communities in producing global common goods is a new approach to world governance, one that no longer relies entirely on nation-states and makes effective use of the extensive and often intensive cross-border activity of non-state actors in a globalizing world. The engagement of plural actors also opens the possibility of more effectively addressing cultural and regional diversity (UNESCO 2015: 78).

Nevertheless, as it has been used so far, the concept of global common goods has not broken entirely with the methodological nationalist standpoint. The intrinsic problems of 'global public goods' that arise from the assumption of zero-sum relations between nation-states, and nation-state's being primarily responsive to national interests, persist with 'global common goods'. Further, non-state social forces lack potency in tackling global conflicts – non-governmental agencies are vulnerable to interventions with governments that have a monopoly of force. The idea of global common goods does not go far enough conceptually to solving the under-provision of global public/common goods. Thus, I now turn to the Chinese *tianxia weigong* as a means of rethinking the idea of global public/common goods in the Anglo-American tradition.

9.3 Rethinking Global Public/Common Goods through *Tianxia Weigong*

This section introduces the idea of *tianxia* and *tianxia weigong* as a potential alternative perspective to the Anglo-American discussion of global collective goods. From here on, the term 'global collective goods' is used to refer to both global public goods and global common goods taken together. While the global public goods concept is useful as it points to the market failure and financing problem, as well as distributional issues including justice, it is limited by the fact that it understands goods in only economic terms. The global common goods concept adds in agency and diversity and normative collectivity and non-state actors, which is also helpful. Both contribute to understanding global collective goods, though they share the common limitation of a nation-state world.

There are primarily two approaches to the interpretation of *tianxia* in academia – the normative approach and the realpolitik approach (B. Wang 2017: 5, 12). As discussed throughout this book, the *tianxia* idea is rooted in the Confucian anthropocosmic worldview. *Tianxia*, as the entity that is the largest in scope in the Confucian social imaginary, represents the idea of the entire world of shared values and cultures, including nature as well as humanity. This worldview stands in dramatic contrast with the world of methodological nationalism and the mindset of Hobbesian zero-sum competition, deeply embedded in Anglo-American societies.

9.3.1 *Tianxia* as a Normative Appeal

Tianxia implies transcendence of the nation-state perspective. It normatively constructs a universal order of *tianxia* unbounded by ethnicity or geography.

Tianxia literally means 'all under heaven'. In the Chinese tradition, it is a symbolic ideal reflecting a universal civilizational order and the pursuit of the ideal kingly way (Jilin Xu 2017; Z. Xu 2018). For Confucianism, the ultimate aim is to bring harmony and peace to all under heaven. There is no boundary to the civilizational order or the reach of *tianxia*. *Tianxia weigong* (all under heaven belongs to/is for all) demonstrates an idea of 'no other' in all under heaven. All is under heaven and, all under heaven belongs to all and should serve the good of all (B. Wang 2017; T. Zhao 2011). This is very different to the dualistic worldview of I and non-I/other. In the framework of *tianxia* and *tianxia weigong*, due to there being no 'other', the relationship between different entities, including either individualistic or collective entities, is not zero-sum but potentially reciprocal and harmonious (T. Zhao, 2011: 9, 33–6). The foundation of *tianxia* is the Confucian reciprocal relationship, which is supported by Confucian moral and ethical doctrine (see also Chapters 5 and 7) (Duara 2017: 71).

According to B. Wang (2017: 1), '*tianxia* refers to a system of governance held together by a regime of culture and value that transcends racial and geographical boundaries'. The emphasis on culture, value, and mutual acceptance and recognition, rather than racial and geographical boundaries, is consistent with the civilizational state (see more in Chapter 2). In other words, a *tianxia* system is not an '*inter*-national' system, consisting of independent nation-states. Instead, it appeals for transcendence of the 'inter-national' world so as to understand the world as a world per se.

According to Zhao Tingyang, whose work is largely responsible for the revival of the *tianxia* idea in the twenty-first century (Duara 2017: 70), the *tianxia* idea requires us to think *through* the world, not to think *of* the world (T. Zhao 2011: 3). Thinking *through* the world highlights at least three aspects. First, thinking through the world understands the world as a collective agent shared by human beings as well as all other creatures on earth. The world, in this case, is not an aggregation of independent nation-states. It is a single entity with sub-collective agents such as states. Second, the priority for the different levels of entities, or spheres, is the good of *tianxia* rather than parochial interests. For example, at the individual level, every human being becomes responsible to serving the good of *tianxia*. This is consistent with the Chinese collectivist tradition that prioritizes the collective good over the individualistic good. In discussing the terms of *dawo* and *xiaowo*, *tianxia* refers to the *dawo* that transcends all other existing entities which are *xiaowos*. Third, to think through the world paves the way for discussing global/world citizenship. In the perspective of *tianxia*, the national identity of the individual is secondary to being a member of *tianxia*. This reverses the dictum of the former British prime minister Theresa May, who said: 'If you believe you're a citizen of the world, you're a citizen of nowhere.' The *tianxia* viewpoint is not a mere abstraction. It may not exist for Theresa May, but it already exists in China.

Thinking through the world consolidates human beings' responsibility to serve the world and to focus only on the good of the world and not state interests or other parochial interests. It is in this sense that the Chinese approximation of the Anglo-American global collective (public/common) goods is the *collective goods of tianxia*, rather than *collective goods that transcend national borders*. Collective goods of *tianxia* are goods that benefit and belong to all under heaven. The starting point is *tianxia*, not the nation-state. National goods becomes private in relation to collective goods of *tianxia*: the state is *xiaowo*, *tianxia* is *dawo*. Correspondingly, global collective goods, or more precisely, collective goods of *tianxia*, take precedence over parochial goods in the behaviours of country, organization and agent.

I move now to the normative core of *tianxia*: values. Values of *tianxia* that are particularly emphasized include the pursuit of order and harmony, and embracing diversity, as aspects of a harmonious and peaceful *tianxia*. The central concern of Confucianism is order and harmony, as repeatedly discussed in previous chapters. Harmony without conformity (*heer butong*) reflects the Confucian pursuit of order as well as its openness to, and respect for, diversity. This requires flexibility, mutual understanding, respect and dialogue (Fang 2003). Mere tolerance as in the Anglo-American tradition is not enough. Parallel to Smith's natural sympathy and Kant's sympathy in humanity, the Confucian movement from *qin qin* (affection for one's kin) to *fan ai zhong* (affection for all humanity) is a journey to the realization of harmony without assimilation. Confucianism endorses a series of moral values, represented by the Five Constant Virtues (see Chapter 5), as a foundational pillar to uphold the social order. The pillar of virtue, to a large extent, constituted formal/legal regulations in guiding people's daily life in Imperial China. The notion of *tianxia* takes Five Constant Virtues to the level of the world as a whole.

9.3.2 *Tianxia* in Realpolitik

T. Zhao (2011, 2018, 2019) imagines how the idea of *tianxia* may be implemented in realpolitik. He argues for a political entity/sovereignty at the *tianxia* level. In Zhao's imagination, the world is an organic whole, and there are lower-level entities below *tianxia*/the world, but these are not nation-states (Callahan 2004; Hui 2017; T. Zhao 2003, 2011). An example of *tianxia* system in history is the Zhou Dynasty (1046–256 BCE) in China.

> In Zhao's view, the contemporary extension of the *tianxia* model would involve a world government controlling a larger territory and military force than that controlled by the autonomous substates. These substates would be independent in most respects, except in their legitimacy and obligations, for which they would depend on the recognition of world government. Rather than being based on force and self-interest, the cultural empire would use ritual as a means to limit the self and its interests. *Tianxia* is a hierarchical worldview that prioritizes order over freedom, elite governance over democracy and the superior political institution over the lower level. (Duara 2017: 70)

Duara (2017) interprets a *tianxia* system in association with cosmopolitanism. He points out that the *tianxia* idea reflects the cosmopolitan thought of all humanity belonging nonexclusively to a single community (Duara 2017: 67). While existing nation-states centre on humans' belongingness in terms of locality, race and religion, *tianxia* is based on the belongingness to humanity and the world. Correspondingly, institutions or representatives of the *tianxia* community need to 'make sovereign decisions in some (mutually agreed upon) areas of political society' (Duara 2017: 67). Existing international organizations like the United Nations are not the kind of institutional representatives in *tianxia*. Perhaps the closest existing institution is the European Union, although it is operating at a regional, not global, level. In the *tianxia* framework, institutions at the global level produce collective goods of *tianxia* for all humanity.

In Zhao's imagination, meritocracy, not democracy, is used for selecting political leaders for global institutions (T. Zhao 2011: 19–20). *Tianxia* incorporates the people's will (*min xin*) (T. Zhao 2011: 19). Democracy is only one technical method for revealing the will of people. Democracy is not an end in itself, the end is the people's will. In Zhao's opinion, the best way to capture the will of the people is meritocracy. Elites lead in *tianxia*.

However, such realpolitik discussion of *tianxia* has been challenged and criticized, primarily concerning interstate relations. A central concern is equality between states, a foundational pillar of the existing interstate relationship, albeit not always well implemented. In the *tianxia* system, at least in scholarly discussion, it is acceptable to have hierarchy between states (X. Yan 2011: 97, 104). Some critiques argue that in Imperial times, such as under the Zhou Dynasty and the Han Dynasty, *tianxia* was structured with China as the 'inner' part and neighbouring countries as the 'outer' part, as manifested in the Chinese-centric tributary system. This 'inner' and 'outer' relationship is a structural parallel of centre–periphery relations today (Callahan 2008; T. Liang 2018). Some *tianxia* scholars/researchers justify such a hierarchy by attaching to it a graded system of responsibilities. Countries with higher positions take larger responsibilities for maintaining the order of *tianxia*, including help for those in need. Hence the government of Imperial China provided protection for recognized tributary countries. In the contemporary context, X. Yan (2011) offers the example of China's relations with the Association of Southeast Asian Nations (ASEAN). Yan argues that bigger countries should take greater responsibilities in cooperation and in the production of global collective goods – although this does not strictly follow the equality principle, nevertheless, it arguably benefits both smaller countries and the world (X. Yan 2011: 105). Yan's argument is consistent with Zhao's 'thinking through the world', which prioritizes the good of *dawo* over *xiaowo*. But liberty and equality are less emphasized.

Critics of the *tianxia* system point to the potential for major countries to influence or dominate weaker ones. Callahan (2008) questions China's use of *tianxia*. He sees *tianxia* not as a regime of culture and authority but the projection of a global hegemon (Callahan 2008; Callahan and Barabantseva 2011). Many Chinese scholars/researchers state that with the rise of its economic power, China needs to expand its soft power and that one way of facilitating this is through reimagining the world order. *Tianxia* is one way that China can establish its own discourses (W. Ding 2018), for example, around the Belt and Road Initiative. These interpretations are not inconsistent with Callahan's critique. However, there have long been critics inside and outside China of the embedding of a centre–periphery construct in *tianxia*, thereby repeating the Imperial tribute system (e.g., Imperial China as the centre while countries who paid tribute to Imperial China as periphery) (Callahan and Barabantseva 2011; Chirot and Hall 1982; Fairbank 1968; Hui 2003). Xiaotong Fei (2015), a Chinese sociologist who works with the structure of social relations as nested circles, makes the point that the individual's affection becomes thinner when the circle expands. The same might apply to the affection of the hegemonic centre in a centre–periphery world order. However, B. Wang (2017: 17) states that while a *tianxia* system might be hierarchical, there would not be coercion by the country with greatest power. They point out that in Chinese history the Imperial state seldom interfered with or invaded tributary countries.

Mutual trust is a core requisite if the *tianxia* idea is to be taken forward. However, mutual trust between agents/institutions/countries with diverse races, cultures, values and languages is not easy to achieve. Fei (2015: 50) emphasizes self-cultural awareness, summarized as 'an appreciation of one's own culture, an understanding and appreciation of other cultures, and mutual respect, would result in people's living together harmoniously, which then leads to the status of unity in diversity.' Although scholars/researchers may argue a *tianxia* system would work on the basis of voluntary participation rather than coercion, as discussed, however, the *tianxia* idea may be vulnerable to coercive mechanisms of domination. Perceptions of this danger may prevent it from being employed in the contemporary world. Ge (2017:11) argues that '*tianxia* is either a utopian imagining or an "invented tradition." In history, we have a hard time finding a monarchy that possessed this tripartite legitimacy.'

Another obstacle facing the *tianxia* idea is that the emphases on harmony over diversity, stability over liberty and meritocracy over democracy are major divergences from the Anglo-American worldview (B. Wang 2017: 13). The Confucian notion of solving practical problems of statecraft through norms, values, behaviours and accepted rituals rather than law, contract and the final backing of state coercion also diverges from the Anglo-American worldview.

Nevertheless, despite the difficulty in employing the *tianxia* idea in realpolitik, the problems of the current world order, including unresolvable power struggles and the under-provision of global collective goods, point to the value of considering the idea of *tianxia*. Given the urgency of the problem of global collective goods, the late Ulrich Beck and scholars/researchers from East Asia have worked on ways to integrate cosmopolitan visions and the *tianxia* worldview. Beck (2016: 257) proposes a cosmopolitan sociology that addresses the 'fundamental fragility and mutability of societal dynamics shaped by the globalization of capital and risks today'. According to Beck (2016) and S.-J. Han, Shim and Park (2016), cosmopolitanism can be consolidated and rendered more effective when the normative layer of the *tianxia* worldview is added.

9.3.3 *Tianxia Weigong* and Collective Goods of *Tianxia*

UNESCO (2015) argues that global common goods enables a more humanistic consideration in comparison to global public goods. However, a humanistic perspective still rooted in the dualistic I/not-I worldview and an 'inter-national' global setting is not enough to challenge methodological nationalism or develop social and political machinery sufficient to address the existing global problems. The *tianxia* worldview can add more to the mix.

While the implications of the *tianxia* idea for realpolitik are unclear, the idea sheds new light on global collective goods. *Tianxia weigong* understands the world as an organic collective whole. In line with the Chinese collectivist tradition, there exists no 'private' in all under heaven. All under heaven belongs to all and is for all. Belonging to all reflects the fact that the world is collectively shared not only by human beings but by all creatures on earth, while being for all highlights the absolute priority of collective goods over individualistic/private goods.

Tianxia weigong moves decisively beyond methodological nationalism. The world is a public realm and all humans are responsible to contribute to the good of the world. Here 'global collective goods' become understood not as 'public/common goods', but more in the sense of the collective goods of *tianxia*. Global collective goods are goods that benefit all under heaven and require human beings' concerted contribution. Not just the public authority but many agents and agencies carry joint responsibility to produce such collectively shared goods. These global collective goods are not marginal to national goods: the importance of global collective goods is not lower than that of parochial goods.

In the long term only a world government, responsive to the world while effectively engaging the many agents, institutions, localities and scales within it, can fully sustain the production of global collective goods. Further, even though such a world government could hardly be established in the current world order, the normative idea of *tianxia* of thinking *through* the world – of prioritizing global collective goods and consolidating all agents' and agencies' responsibilities to produce global collective goods – is still worthy of consideration. This approach can be considerably advanced in higher education now. In fact, organizations such as research intensive universities, collaborating on a large scale, can produce very significant global collective goods.

9.4 Global Collective Goods, Collective Goods of *Tianxia* and Higher Education

9.4.1 The Student

Through the acquisition of skills and knowledge, graduates contribute to a country's combined human power. They also promote world economic prosperity; each country's economy is an integral part of the global economic system (Griffiths and Arnove 2015). Meanwhile, studies show that higher education graduates are more likely to be internationally mobile (Marginson 2018d). International mobility on the one hand is a global collective good, contributing to the enhancement of both combined and individual capabilities and combined freedoms (Tran 2016). On the other hand, it leads to other global collective goods, such as interaction among people from different countries and communities. Such interaction contributes to the mutual understanding between, and the respect for, each other, which are fundamental to the maintenance of a peaceful and harmonious world environment (Fang 2003; Fei 2015).

The enhancement of individual capability is a crucial global collective good as it plays an essential role in promoting both the individual's well-being and humanity's well-being (Boni and Walker 2013; Sen 1999). To take one example, receiving higher education can improve students' own and their families' health conditions (see, e.g., Hartog and Oosterbeek 1998). Furthermore, the Covid-19 pandemic has shown that the health of one person can have global effects.

In addition, global normative collective goods can centre on values essential to the well-being and flourishing of all. For example, diversity is an essential global common good, as emphasized by UNESCO (2015). As noted, diverse development and interpretation is itself an important global collective good. Likewise, higher education's daily operation also calls for diversity. As Chapter 5 shows, the manifoldness of the environment is essential to individual development. Likewise, values of tolerance, equality and mutual respect are shared by the whole of humanity; and many of these values, as normative collective goods, are also crucial to the functioning and evolution of higher education, for example academic freedom and the diversity of persons, methods and ideas (Altbach 2001; Bodycott and Lai 2012).

Students' identification with, and internalization of, values involves moral and citizenship education, including education for global citizenship (Jarvis 2002; Ramirez and Cha 1990). Most national governments have policies on preparing students to become desirable national citizens (Kennedy et al. 2014). There are less programmes inside universities centring on world and global citizenship education (Moon and Koo 2011). Through educating individual students, higher education could play a vital role in attaining and maintaining a harmonious, peaceful and desirable world. Indeed, research shows that higher education influences attitudes and perceptions. Marginson (2018g) points to the clear divide between higher education graduates and others in the Brexit vote and Donald Trump's election in 2016. University-educated individuals are less likely to reject science and experts, for example, in relation to global climate change, and are less readily mobilized as an unreflective source of populist power (Marginson 2018g; Swales 2016).

9.4.2 Knowledge

Higher education contributes to global collective goods/collective goods of *tianxia* through the production of knowledge. UNESCO (2015: 79) understands knowledge as 'encompassing information, understanding, skills, values and attitudes'. Knowledge is a common heritage which belongs to and is contributed by the whole of humanity (Stiglitz 1999; UNESCO 2015). Normally, knowledge produced in higher education should be available to all human beings.

In this regard, higher education does not always live up to the expectation. There is a world trend towards the privatization of knowledge, including knowledge production, dissemination and reproduction (Cozzi and Galli 2011; Maskus and Reichman 2004; Stiglitz 1999). This is evident in higher education, resulting in concerns and suspicions about whether higher education contributes to global collective goods in the knowledge domain (Szadkowski 2019). For example, medicinal knowledge produced by higher education is not always accessible to every individual across the world. This suggests that higher education needs to pay special attention in order to make knowledge accessible. The open-access mode of publication is one solution (Molloy 2011). Making knowledge more accessible involves educating the public, including fashioning the communication of knowledge to render it comprehensible and improve its reception.

Knowledge is also an intermediate global collective goods that is vital to the production of many other global collective goods. Scholars' philosophical discussions about justice, liberty and equity feed into the attainment and maintenance of a fairer and more peaceful world (Rao et al. 1999; I. Taylor 2014). Studies in science and social science often target global problems and attempt to propose solutions. A strong example is research on climate change, which involves many thousands of people in almost every country, visible to each other, and collaborating extensively, largely from the bottom up. This kind of knowledge has the potential to influence global policies. When this book was being written, the world was facing the global epidemic challenge of the novel coronavirus Covid-19. International collaboration in research, open-access publishing of the results of research, and providing the worldwide public with relevant knowledge and information, is of paramount importance in the common fight against this global challenge (X. Xu 2020). Further, scientific knowledge produced by universities is also transferred to technological applications that benefit people and social groups across the world, including future generations (Hou 2011).

9.4.3 Global Equity

Many higher education institutions and agents assist the development of emerging countries (Novelli 2013). One mechanism is the recruitment of international students, especially specific targeting of international students from certain countries (Mazzarol and Soutar 2002). Numerous universities have established scholarship programmes for international students from low-income countries, often based on the World Bank category. It is hoped that well-educated international students will contribute significantly to their home countries, though in reality, these countries often face the problem of brain drain (Beine et al. 2008).

Higher education's commitment to global equity is also embodied in international research collaboration. Some international collaborative research projects focus on emerging country problems: for example, social science research's focus on local responses to the global financial crisis; medical research focusing on epidemic diseases such as dengue fever and malaria; and projects designed to assist with food security or urban water supply. Aid-based assistance extends also to professional development. Universities in wealthy countries may organize training programmes for teachers and other professionals from emerging countries.

9.4.4 National and Global Perspectives

Despite higher education's commitment to global collective goods, in most countries the primary concerns are still fixed within the national border. For example, compared to global equity, universities and academics focus mostly on equity in national terms (Bowen et al. 2005; Clancy and Goastellec 2007; Q. Jia and Ericson 2017).

Higher education across the world is primarily funded by national, provincial and sometimes local government. Institutions and their agents are primarily responsive to the needs of nations and proximate communities. The operation of higher education institutions must abide by national regulations. National governments mostly prioritize their own interests when making decisions. While many countries have commitment to global collective goods, such as promoting international mobility, and international research cooperation, national goods generally have primacy. In higher education, the prioritization of national goods is apparent in at least four ways.

First, there is often (though not always) an emphasis on addressing national issues when providing *research funding* for higher education. Sometimes funding provided by governments is targeted to specific research topics or more generally designated areas of national priority. When governments invest in topics that are mostly relevant to domestic issues, research for producing global collective goods can be under-supported (Bayer and Urpelainen 2013).

Second, the aforementioned *privatization of knowledge*, which to a certain extent is reinforced by the Intellectual Property Rights regime (Cozzi and Galli 2011; UNESCO 2015: 80), arguably hampers the global dissemination and reproduction of knowledge produced by higher education. We need a better balance between making knowledge available for humanity and protecting intellectual property rights.

Third, national governments may focus strongly on higher education's role in preparing *students as national citizens* (Calhoun 2006; Jiao Li 2006; H. Qi and Shen 2015). Moral and citizenship education often contains a nationalist strand with global elements less visible (Jarvis 2002). The nationalist element, such as certain ideas of patriotism, does not always contribute to the cultivation of global citizens.

Fourth, as previously discussed, *international mobility* is a global collective good, but countries' immigration and visa regulations often contain barriers restricting mobility (Neumayer 2006). Mostly, the more influential is the nationalist strand in politics, the stricter will be the visa regulations. Arguably, the limitation posed on students and academics by such regulations impedes higher education's production of global collective goods. For example, at the time when this book was written, the US government was making efforts to impose limits on Chinese international students. In May 2020, the US government was under criticism from American universities because it planned to cancel the visas of Chinese graduate students and researchers in the United States, who had ties to certain universities which were believed by the government to be affiliated with the People's Liberation Army.[1] This policy threatened to affect thousands of Chinese graduate students and researchers who played important roles in the production of knowledge in the US higher education (Gaule and Piacentini 2013).

Higher education is intrinsically globally connected. Single countries operating alone are no longer able to deal with many higher education issues, such as mobility and international research collaboration. Methodological nationalism retards attention to such issues while blocking from view the existence of the cross-border dimension, the need to be more globally effective and the potential means of doing so. Informed by the *tianxia weigong* idea, I argue that the organization of higher education can be adjusted as follows, in response to the five aspects listed earlier:

(i) *Research:* to better respond to global challenges and issues, it is essential to provide national government and non-government financial support for research on global topics. The anthropocosmic worldview of the Chinese tradition, which stresses the harmonious balance between humanity and nature, provides a framework for global ecological research grounded in *tianxia*.

(ii) *Privatization of knowledge:* knowledge is a global collective good belonging to all under heaven. There is a need to better balance the relationship between knowledge available for humanity and protecting intellectual property rights.

(iii) *Students as citizens:* while higher education is often effective in preparing national citizens, states need to further emphasize the importance of preparing global citizens.

International mobility: In *tianxia*, there is no 'other' and belongingness is not based on locality, race and culture. Regulations limiting international mobility of academics and students, and international research collaboration, rarely have an intrinsic justification and need to be reconsidered.

---

[1] See, for example, https://www.nytimes.com/2020/05/28/us/politics/china-hong-kong-trump-student-visas.html (accessed on 30 August 2020).

Part III

Trans-Positional Approaches to the Public (Good) in Higher Education

10

Comparison and Combination
Complementarities, Hybridizations and Synergies

10.1 Introduction

Building on Chapters 5–9, this chapter conducts Trans-positional assessment II. It compares the two traditions and searches for complementarities, hybridizations and synergies between them. The comparison and combination are done one pair at a time (note that the fourth pair, *gong* and public, and the fifth pair – *tianxia weigong* and global public/common goods – are discussed together. See 10.5). For each pair, I start with a systematic comparison and outline the findings using figures. Similarities and differences between the notions in each pair are identified. Some similarities/differences between the two traditions are reflected in the comparison of more than one theme (e.g., the differing worldviews). Based on the similarities and differences, I then attempt to search for the potential for combination. Combination can be in three forms: complementarities, hybridizations and synergies (see Chapter 1).

To reiterate, I do not attempt to comprehensively combine the two traditions in relation to the five themes. In addition, as will be discussed, both the potential for combination and the absence of combination are both seen as possible.

10.2 The First Pair: *Xiushen* and *Bildung*

10.2.1 Comparison between *Xiushen* and *Bildung*

As Figure 10.1 shows, *xiushen* and *Bildung* differ regarding the view of the world, the assumption of the individual's natural personality and capacity, the process of individual development including the interplay between individual and the

194 Higher Education, State and Society

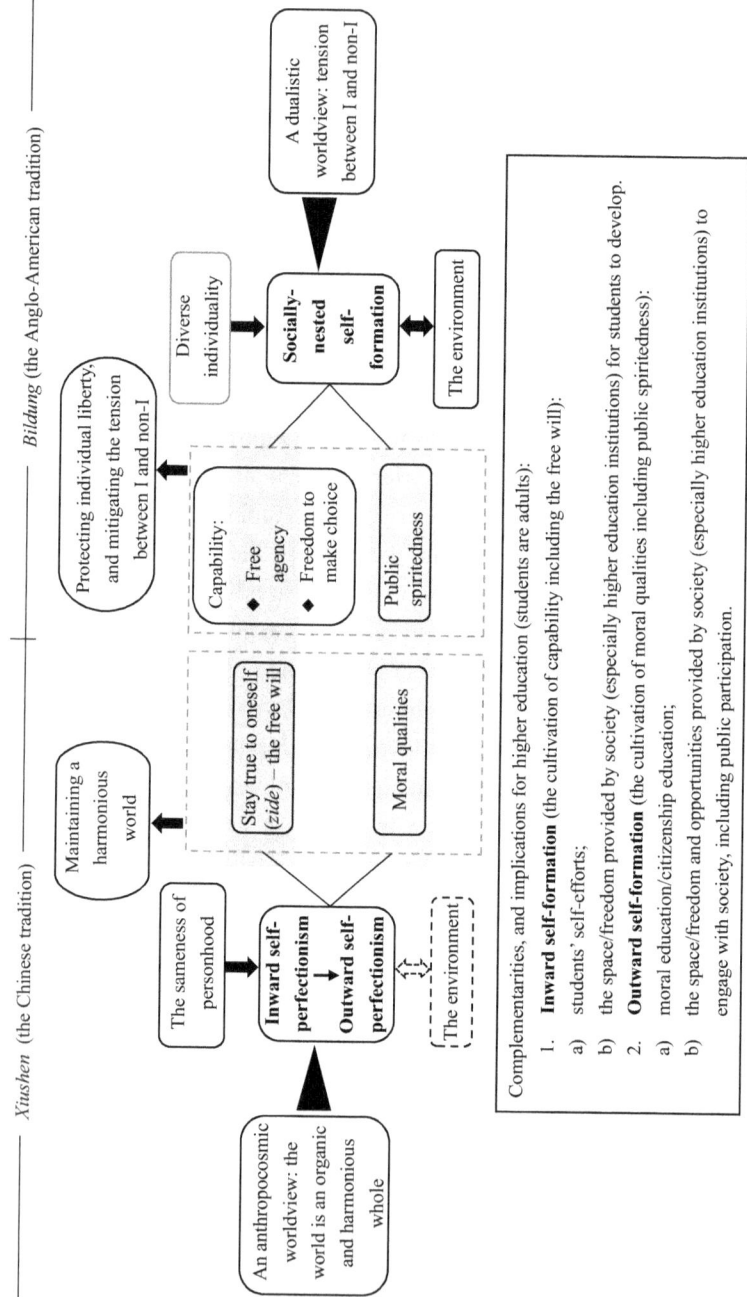

Figure 10.1 An outline of the comparison and complementarity between *xiushen* and *Bildung*.

environment, and the primary aim of individual development. Nevertheless, their views overlap on two specific aspects of the individual's development: the cultivation of an individual's free will/agency and the cultivation of moral qualities/public spiritedness. The grey area shows how the two traditions overlap (this applies to other figures in this chapter too).

Differences between Xiushen and Bildung

The anthropocosmic worldview vis-à-vis the dualistic worldview and the aim to maintain a harmonious world vis-à-vis the aim to protect individual liberty while mitigating the tension between I and non-I. The difference between the worldviews of the Chinese and Anglo-American traditions is fundamental to the comparison of *xiushen* and *Bildung* (and the other pairs too, see later). As demonstrated in previous chapters, Confucianism views the world as an organic and harmonious whole, consisting of the expanding entities (from the self to *tianxia*). *Xiushen*, as a process of individual self-perfectionism, aims to ensure that individuals genuinely work for the maintenance of the harmonious world.

In contrast, the Anglo-American tradition follows the dualistic worldview that views the world as composed of I and non-I/the other. There is constant tension between I and the other. While *Bildung* attempts to mitigate the tension between I and non-I, its priority is to protect and enhance individual liberty. Here individual liberty embraces both negative freedom that protects individuals from external intrusion and the cultivation of an individual's free agency as positive freedom.

The sameness of personhood vis-à-vis diverse individuality. The two traditions disagree on the natural personality and capacity of human beings. While Confucianism asserts that human beings are born with the same personhood, the Anglo-American tradition believes in the diversity of essential individual attributes. With this difference, *xiushen* and *Bildung* have developed varying approaches to individual development, especially concerning the role of environmental support (see later).

Inward and outward self-perfectionism *vis-à-vis* socially nested self-formation. Drawing on the varying worldviews and assumptions of human beings' natural capacity and potential, the two traditions further diverge in terms of the process of individual development.

Confucianism views *xiushen* as an individualistic process, not relying on the external environment. Also, as all individuals share the same natural capacity and potential, it is believed that the success of the individualistic process of *xiushen* is mainly determined by the individual's own efforts. There are two broad stages of *xiushen*: inward and outward self-perfectionism. It was expected that, through higher learning, individuals gradually developed and exercised their capacity for critical reflection and thinking and moral qualities.

The impact from the environment is deliberately overlooked, in relation to both the inward and outward self-perfectionism of *xiushen*. Despite the claim of *xiushen* being a highly individualistic process, individuals de facto self-cultivate with external support and through the interplay with the other. For example, the teacher's guidance plays an important role in higher learning (and thus inward self-cultivation), and outward self-perfectionism is realized through an individual's interaction with collective spheres.

In contrast, *Bildung* is understood as a process of socially nested self-formation, although liberalism to a large extent follows an individualistic tradition. The environment is pivotal to *Bildung*. It is agreed by both the German tradition and liberalism that there are at least two environmental prerequisites for *Bildung*: freedom of development and the manifoldness of situation. The two prerequisites are associated with the assumption of the diversity of natural individuality. As human beings are born with diverse natural individuality, *Bildung* should not follow a certain template but be rendered consistent with the individual's individuality.

Nevertheless, while liberalism draws attention to the environment, it focuses less than might be expected on the agency of the individual in the process of development, including determination, self-effort and resilience. Both of the presence of the importance of the environment and the absence of the individual agency in *Bildung* are complementary to Confucian *xiushen*. *Xiushen* centres on the individual's agency, such as self-efforts and determination, while overlooking the effects of the environment. This complementarity is enlightening to the discussion of student development, equity and liberty in higher education (see later).

Similarities: The Free Will/Agency and Moral Qualities/Public Spiritedness

Xiushen and *Bildung* start with different worldviews and assumptions about natural individuality, and disagree on the process of individual development. However, they have reached a consensus on two aims of individual development.

The first is the development of the free will in Confucianism and free agency in liberalism. As discussed, *xiushen* aims to enable the individual's development of the free will through inward self-perfectionism. The keystone of this development is to ensure individuals are attuned to the way through constant repossession of the way. Similarly, Sen's concept of capability consists of two components: free agency and freedom to make choice. For *Bildung*, the development of free agency centres on the training of the ability to reason. Freedom to make choice builds on an individual's free agency, manifested in the ability to truly understand the available options, and further requires negative freedom within which to make choices. Although freedom to make choices is not embraced by Confucianism, the liberal emphasis on the development of free agency substantively overlaps with the Confucian emphasis on the development of free will.

Xiushen and *Bildung* also agree on the 'public' aspect of individual development: the cultivation of moral qualities in *xiushen* and the cultivation of public spiritedness in *Bildung*. The moral qualities particularly stressed by *xiushen* include the individual's responsibility to contribute to the good of the collective spheres and to maintain a harmonious world. The public spiritedness in liberalism is key to the mitigation of the tension between individual and community. Arguably, despite varying attitudes towards individual liberty, both of the Chinese moral quality and Anglo-American public spiritedness emphasize the individual's engagement with community and aim to make individual development conducive to community-building. Both expect to achieve a harmonious and well-ordered society consisting of members with these desirable qualities. See Figure 10.1 for an illustration of the above comparison (note that Figure 10.1 also shows the complementarity between *xiushen* and *Bildung* that will be discussed in the next subsection).

10.2.2 Searching for Complementarity and Implications for Student Development in Higher Education

It is evident that both *xiushen* and *Bildung* have strengths and weaknesses. On the one hand, *xiushen* affirms every individual's equal potential and natural capacity, and foregrounds an individual's agency (here agency primarily refers to qualities including diligence and determination). But it fails to encourage diverse pathways of individual development or to consider the influence of the environment on individual development. On the other hand, *Bildung*'s stipulation of the environment is more successful in enabling diverse development of individuals in accordance with their manifold individualities. Nevertheless, in scholars' discussions of *Bildung*, the importance of individual agency (especially diligence and determination) in individual development is seldom recognized. The assertion of the diversity of individuality, arguably, reflects the Anglo-American tradition's attitudes towards inequality of individual capacity and talent (see also 10.3). Together with the idea of equality of opportunity, it seems that individuals with 'lower' talent or capacity may be provided with fewer opportunities, which can stand in contradiction with the idea of social equity.

I propose a complementarity of *xiushen* and *Bildung* that takes into account both *agency* and *environment* in individual development, and recognizes human beings' *equal potential, and diverse individuality, to be developed*. This combination suggests that **theoretically the optimum situation for individual development arises when individual agency is harmonized with the external environment**. This situation is also ideal for social equity, as I shall attempt to argue in 10.3.

Specifically in the context of higher education, the complementarity points to two aspects: student's agency and the necessary support from the environment (including from higher education institutions, as well as society). As discussed, there are two similarities between *xiushen* and *Bildung*: the shared emphasis on the development of the free will or free agency and the cultivation of moral qualities or public spiritedness. Here the book understands free will and free agency as equivalent in the sense that both of them centre on the individual's capacity for critical thinking, reflection and reasoning. I shall expand on the complementarity with respect to the two similarities.

Individuals' capacity for critical thinking, reflection and reasoning is expected to be an important aspect of student development in higher education. If both individual agency and environment are considered here, then while society, especially higher education institutions, need to provide the space for students to develop, it is also necessary to emphasize student agency and the student's own efforts, devotion and determination. The emphasis on students' agency not only points to the need for the individual's own efforts and determination but implies the need to support and enable *every* individual student to develop. In other words, although individuality is diverse, informed by the idea of *xiushen*, every student is educable and with equal potential. It is possible for any student to achieve their goals as long as she/he is minded to develop, provided she/he has the necessary external support.

In addition, in relation to the question of free space for development, one distinctive aspect is the freedom of discussion including public discussion. According to liberalism, public discussion is essential to the development of free agency. As most students are adults when they commence higher education, they already possess the basic capacity for reason and critical thinking, which enables them to participate in public discussion, in which such capacity is further developed. This freedom of discussion is also enlightening for academic freedom in higher education, though academic freedom depends on whether and how higher education is located in the broader public setting, and is not the same in each culture (see also 10.4).

One of the primary aims of the cultivation of moral qualities/public spiritedness in higher education is to make higher education graduates desirable members of society. On top of graduates' ability to reason and think critically, their sense of responsibility to society is crucial. The desired moral qualities include the individual's commitment to actively serving the collective good and maintaining a harmonious world in the Chinese tradition. Such moral qualities are cultivated not only through inward self-perfectionism but also through external moral education. In the Anglo-American tradition, individuals who are publicly spirited actively participate in public affairs and work on mitigating the tension between I and non-I. According to liberal thinkers, public spiritedness can be cultivated through public participation. Therefore, to support students' cultivation of moral qualities including public spiritedness, higher education can be helpful in at least two ways: providing moral education or citizenship education, and encouraging and providing opportunities for students to engage with society. In addition, moral education and citizenship education should be organized in a way that is compatible with students' development of free will and free agency.

10.3 The Second Pair: *Gongping*/Equity

10.3.1 Comparison between *Gongping* and Equity

The two traditions on social equity are different but overlap. The Anglo-American tradition's social equity is mainly originated in the Enlightenment, whereas the Chinese *gongping* has been shaped by both Chinese philosophical schools of thought represented by Confucianism and the modern Western ideas of social equity. Much of the overlap is a result of Western influence on the Chinese tradition.

A summary comparison is illustrated in Figure 10.2. This presents the philosophical rationales for, and constitutes of, social equity in each tradition. The two dotted boxes for the Chinese tradition, in addition to the one primary philosophical rationale (social order including social justice), reflects the

200 Higher Education, State and Society

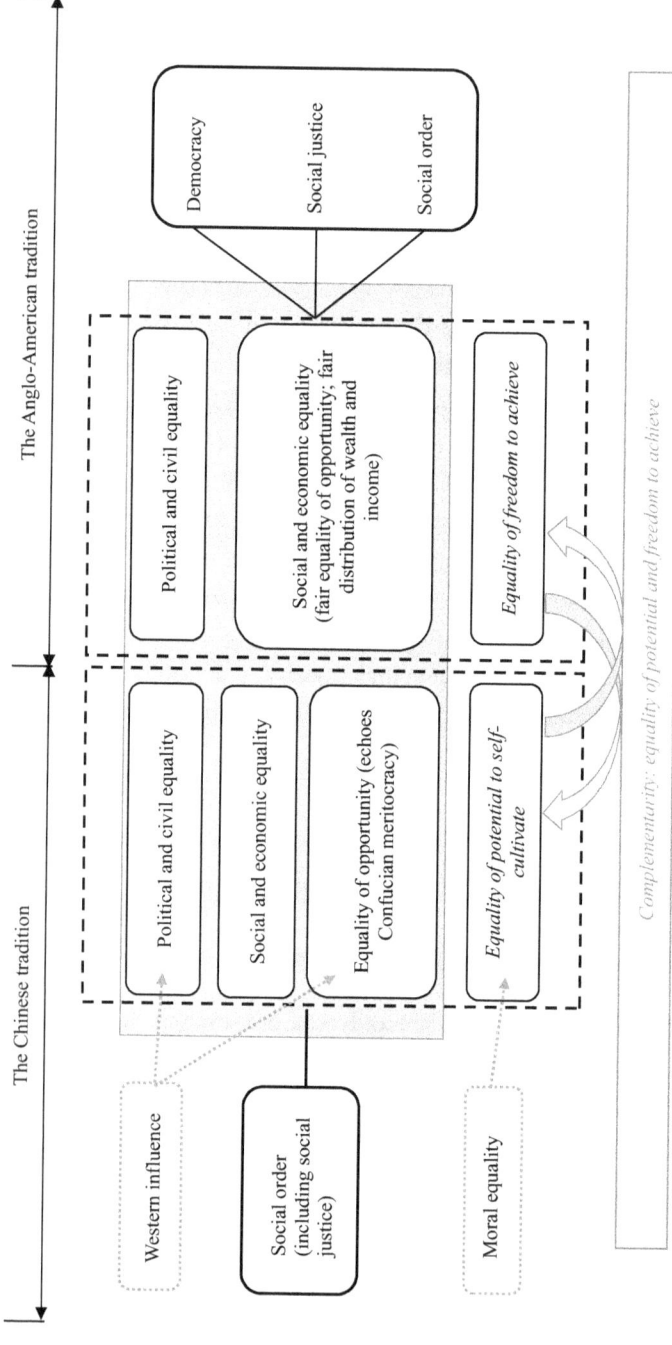

Figure 10.2 An outline of the comparison of (social) *gongping*/equity between the Chinese and Anglo-American traditions.

influence from the West on the ideas of social equity and the importance of Confucian moral equality, respectively. The dotted lines connecting the dotted boxes and the specific constitutes of Chinese social equity show how the ideas in the two boxes have impacted social equity in China.

The two traditions diverge concerning the philosophical rationales for social equity. For the Anglo-American tradition, the primary rationales are democracy, social justice and social order. Among the three, social equity is a necessity for the first two rationales but merely a good in relation to the third. In the Chinese tradition, there is one primary rationale for social equity – social order, in which social justice is also included. For the Chinese tradition, social equity is regarded as beneficial for the maintenance of social order and therefore a necessity. It is also beneficial to social justice, which further contributes to social order.

As discussed in Chapter 6, with three philosophical rationales, there are three primary constitutes in the Anglo-American tradition: political and civil equality, social and economic equality (requiring fair equality of opportunity and fair distribution of wealth and income), and equality of freedom to achieve. In the Chinese tradition, there are four constitutes – political and civil equality, social and political equality, equality of opportunity and equality of potential to self-cultivate. Three of these have one common rationale in the Chinese tradition. In addition, two other factors have impacted the four constitutes. One is the Western influence, associated with political and civil equality, and equality of opportunity. The other is the idea of Confucian moral equality, which leads to equality of potential to self-cultivate.

Despite varying rationales, the two traditions overlap substantially regarding the components of social equity. Except for equality of freedom to achieve in the Anglo-American and equality of potential to self-cultivate in the Chinese tradition, all constitutes in either tradition have resonance in the other, as indicated by the grey area in Figure 10.2.

One of the main differences in relation to the components of social equity lies in Anglo-American equality of freedom to achieve versus the Chinese equality of potential to self-cultivate. As noted, the difference is derived from a contrasting assumption on human beings' talent and capacity. In the Anglo-American tradition, Rawls's idea of fair equality of opportunity maintains that individuals with similar talent and aspiration should have equal opportunity. Though Sen moves forward from this to propose equality of freedom to achieve, his focus is still on the provision of external opportunities, means and resources for individuals to achieve. The domain of the individuals' personal character, their internal formation and support for this process, is arguably under-recognized. Both equality of freedom to achieve and equality of potential to self-cultivate centre on individual development. However, Sen's capability concerns the expansion of substantial freedom, especially human agency, and there is no specific destination of this process. Whereas, in the Chinese tradition, Confucian *xiushen* aims at achieving the status of internal sagehood and external kinglihood.

The two equalities – equality of freedom to achieve and equality of potential to self-cultivate – are contrasting, in that they understand natural capacity and talent differently. Meanwhile, they centre on different aspects of individual development, that is, the external and internal factors, and, in that respect, they can be reconciled using complementarity, as will now be discussed.

10.3.2 Searching for Complementarity and Implications for Equity in Higher Education

The overlapping constitutes of social equity – political and civil equality, social and economic equality and equality of opportunity – can act as a common bridge across the two traditions in discussing social equity. However, it is also necessary to note that their philosophical foundations vary, and correspondingly they are nuanced by contexts.

Political and civil equality. Political and civil equality is a fundamental constitute of social equity in both traditions. The manifestations of this equality may involve equal political rights (such as rights of voting and running for public offices) or equal status. However, the precise manifestations, and the means of protecting this equality, may vary across contexts.

Social and economic equality. The two traditions agree on the value of enhancing social and economic equality while acknowledging the formidability of eliminating inequality. They also agree on making meritocracy a primary means of addressing inequalities. However, they diverge from each other on the extent to which, and means whereby, the state may intervene to achieve such equality. The divergence is particularly associated with the attitudes towards the relationship between equality and liberty in the two traditions (this is not attempted here, but see more in Chapter 3 and, for example, Narveson 1984).

Equality of opportunity. Equality of opportunity is crucial to the enhancement of social and economic equality in the Anglo-American tradition. Influenced by the West, this form of equality has become an important aspect of social justice and the maintenance of social order in Chinese society.

Without trying to homogenize the social imaginaries and political systems, it is still possible to reinterpret and complement the partly contrasting concepts of 'equality of freedom to achieve' and 'equality of potential to self-cultivate'. Further, there appears to be a growing convergence at the level of fundamental assumptions. In the Anglo-American tradition, there is an increasing tendency to regard all human beings as educable.

To extend further the discussion in 10.2, these two ideas of equality also focus on two complementary aspects of individual development: externally, the individual's opportunities, resources and means; and internally, the individual's inner formation and personal character. The Anglo-American tradition only considers external supports, despite the fact that the main focus of equality of freedom to achieve is the development of agency. Further, external supports tend to favour individuals who are 'more talented' following the assumption of inequality of human talent and capacity. In many social fields, including higher education, in which there is a pronounced meritocratic tendency, prior achievements are often taken into account while the individual's potential is partly overlooked. Arguably, the Chinese tradition can fill this gap, thereby *complementing* the Anglo-American tradition in this respect.

In contrast, the Chinese idea of equal potential to self-cultivate assumes that every human has an equal possibility of becoming a sage through self-perfectionism, which is largely a personal journey in which success depends on personal efforts. As external supports are overlooked, socially disadvantaged individuals are left without the necessary opportunities and resources, reinforcing inequality. With its focus on external factors, the Anglo-American tradition can *complement* the Chinese tradition.

The personal journey of Confucian self-cultivation has changed in contemporary contexts. Becoming a sage is not the only aim of individual self-cultivation. Yet still, the idea of equality of potential to self-cultivate persists – any individual can pursue their understandings of what it means to be a good person. This parallels with Sen's equality of freedom to achieve, which entails having capacity to make and carry out decisions.

Taken together, the Anglo-American equality of freedom to achieve and Chinese equality of potential to self-cultivate are partly complementary – they are contrasting while paradoxically completing each other as the principle of complementarity suggests. The fact that each of them only considers part of individual development makes their complementarity meaningful. I propose the idea of *equality of potential and freedom to achieve* as a complementarity.

Equality of potential and freedom to achieve. Humans are equally educable and, in that respect, have equal potential to achieve. The pathway to achievement is not prescribed, but relies on personal choices and decisions.

The ability to make and implement decisions requires the development of individual agency. While the development of agency involves individual self-formation and requires personal characteristics such as diligence, resilience and perseverance, it also needs external supports including opportunities, resources and means. **Social equity can be maximized when external conditions are harmonized with individual effort – when social structure and agency are combined, collective conditions and the individual are combined, and the outer and inner self are combined.** Following this pathway, it is possible to achieve maximum personal empowerment of the maximum number of people. This is what constitutes equality of opportunity in the larger sense.

As mentioned in Chapter 6, Sen's idea of equality of freedom to achieve is *not* the dominant or mainstream liberal view. Arguably, Sen's capability approach is a social democratic version of liberalism and while it has a significant role in Anglo-American thought, it is not nearly as central as Confucian self-cultivation in China. The complementary I have achieved here is between Confucian thought and one strand of liberal thought.

10.4 The Third Pair: *Zhi* (the Free Will) and Liberty

In contrast with the attempt to search for combination for the other themes, this section shows that there is an absence of complementarity, hybridization or synergy for *zhi* and liberty.

10.4.1 Comparison between *Zhi* and Liberty

Zhi's emphasis on the development of individual's capacity for critical thinking and reflection arguably overlaps with the Anglo-American emphasis on individual agency (see Figure 10.3). Arguably, this overlap is the only similarity between the two traditions regarding this theme. The two traditions' ideas on liberty have originated in diverging foundations and followed different development pathways.

The sameness of personhood vis-à-vis diverse individuality. A fundamental difference between *zhi* and liberty lies in the assumptions of human beings' natural individuality, a difference running through all of the themes. I shall not repeat here.

Comparison and Combination 205

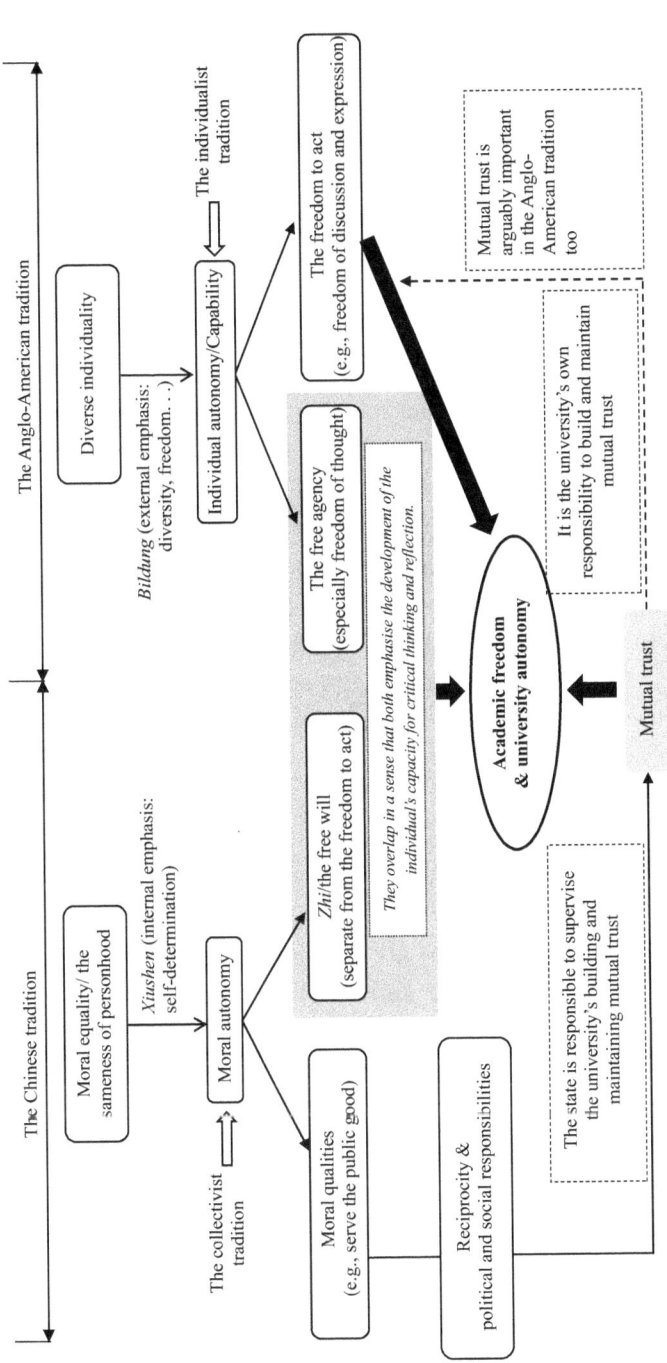

Figure 10.3 An outline of the comparison between *zhi* (the free will) and liberty.

***Xiushen*'s internal emphasis vis-à-vis *Bildung*'s external emphasis**. As has been demonstrated earlier, the two traditions hold varying views on the development of personhood/individuality.

Moral autonomy vis-à-vis individual autonomy. With varied approaches to individual development on top of distinct assumptions of natural individuality, the two traditions further disagree on two kinds of autonomy – moral autonomy vis-à-vis individual autonomy. Individual autonomy includes both the free will and freedom to act outwardly. Moral autonomy is limited to inward moral cultivation and perfectionism.

The emphasis of moral autonomy is on the cultivation of *zhi*/the free will. There is a separation of the free will and freedom to act. While an individual's free will, especially critical reflection and reinterpretation, is encouraged, the outward expression of free will is restrained. One important restraint comes from moral qualities, upheld by different sorts of collective spheres such as the state, society and family (partly manifested in collective-determination). Underlying these moral qualities are ideas of reciprocity and social and political responsibility to serve the collective good. Free discussion and expression are meant to be constructive and grounded in good will. In this framework, there is a need for mutual trust, whereby the authority believes in the good will of the people, and conversely, the people have confidence in the authority to protect their freedom.

In contrast, individual autonomy in the Anglo-American tradition incorporates both the free will and freedom to express that free will. The cultivation of the free will (inward consciousness) requires a free and diverse environment, and the freedom to express free will requires freedoms such as the freedom of participation, discussion and expression. In the Anglo-American tradition, it is argued that inward consciousness is a product of the interaction between human beings and the external environment. In this framework, inward cultivation and moral autonomy form a basis for outward freedom of action. In Sen's (1999) eyes, the individual's free agency, as positive freedom, is an essential condition for the exercise of negative freedoms.

Arguably, the shared emphasis on the development of the individual's capacity for critical thinking and reflection, by the free will and the free agency, is the only commonality between the two traditions regarding the ideas of liberty in general. However, as will be explained in the next subsection, specifically concerning liberty in higher education, the two traditions also overlap with each other on the importance of mutual trust between higher education and society, and between higher education and the state. This emphasis centres on the development of individuals. Higher education, tasks of which include student development, is informed by such an emphasis.

10.4.2 The Absence of Combination, Implications for Academic Freedom and University Autonomy in Higher Education

I argue that it is formidable to complement, hybridize or synergize the two traditions regarding the ideas of liberty, given the fundamental contradictions between them, represented by the different statuses ascribed to the individual's freedom to act. Though the two traditions agree on the importance of the development of the individual's capacity for critical thinking and reflection, embodied in the ideas of the free agency and free will, the difference on the question of whether to protect the freedom to express the free will, as a right, can hardly be reconciled. This difference is associated with the varying statuses attached to *gong*/public and *si*/private.

The Chinese tradition is collectivist and prioritizes *gong* over *si*. Individual behaviours are expected to be consistent with moral qualities and expectations concerning the collective good. In contrast, individual autonomy, comprising free agency and the freedom to act, is essential and cannot be compromised in the Anglo-American tradition. Any attempt to combine the two traditions will undermine the foundational views of each tradition. The Chinese tradition's primacy of the public and limitation of individual behaviour for the sake of the harmony and order compromises the Anglo-American tradition's central claim of protecting individual autonomy. To follow the Anglo-American tradition and make individual autonomy, the priority is to compromise the Chinese tradition's perpetual pursuit of harmony and order.

Nevertheless, both the differences and the only commonality are relevant to the discussion of academic freedom and university autonomy in higher education. As Figure 10.3 illustrates, each of moral autonomy and individual autonomy has two components – moral autonomy includes both the free will and moral qualities, and individual autonomy includes both free agency and the freedom to act. The overlap is between the free will and free agency, with regard to their shared emphasis on the individual's capacity for critical thinking and reflection. Four different components can be derived here: the free will, the free agency, moral qualities and freedom to act. As discussed, though these four components can hardly be hybridized into one set because of the contrasting underpinning views, as discussed, each of them sheds light on academic freedom and university autonomy.

The free will and the free agency. The free will and the free agency are important to academic freedom in higher education. As Chapter 7 shows, it remains unclear how to define the scope of academic freedom in higher education. One crux lies in the freedom of discussions on social and political issues. Some scholars/researchers may argue that faculty and the student's broad engagement in discussing social and political issues should not be protected by academic freedom because that engagement is not an indispensable component of either teaching or research. In other words, in the absence of the general freedom to discuss social and political issues, teaching and research activities may not be greatly affected.

Nevertheless, as discussed, such freedom is essential to the provision of a desirable environment for *Bildung* and the development of free will. In both traditions, the capacity for, and voluntary regulation of, critical reflection are key elements of free will and free agency. Hence the student's freedom of broad engagement in social and political discussions in the classroom becomes an important condition.

Moreover, a main role for higher education is to cultivate good citizens for society. A good citizen is expected to have the capacity and the public spiritedness to engage in public issues. Both Kant (1996) and von Humboldt (2000) highlight the importance of the development of reasoning in making students good citizens, which requires the freedom to discuss political and social issues, and calls for the student's active engagement in such discussions.

Arguably, the freedom required for the development of the student's free will and free agency and public spiritedness is compatible with both traditions, and therefore it can and needs to be included in academic freedom in higher education in both contexts. In the Chinese tradition, this freedom is only protected in conditions in which discussions are constructive, take place on the basis of good will and follow the principle of reciprocity. There is a need for mutual trust, which is discussed further.

The freedom to act. The idea of the freedom to act is closely associated with views on academic freedom and university autonomy in Anglo-American societies. Freedom of discussion and expression, which involve action, is a rationale for academic freedom. Meanwhile, the freedom to act, as a negative freedom, is a rationale for university autonomy. According to Berdahl et al. (1971: 8), the university has the freedom to control its own activities. Following Mill's idea of self-protection, as long as the action does not influence others, the freedom to act ought to be protected. In Anglo-American higher education systems, in ideal circumstances, this kind of university autonomy is formally protected.

Nevertheless, in many cases, university activities have direct or indirect impacts on society or the state, breaking Mill's principle of self-protection. Further, modern universities are often financially supported by the public. This suggests a need for public supervision of university activities and performance. Indeed, in the United Kingdom and the United States, the government exercises control over universities in different ways. There is also a lack of mutual trust between, on one hand, the university and, on the other hand, the state and society. Even in Anglo-American contexts, where freedom to act is normal, although not always equitably distributed, mutual trust plays a crucial role in higher education. The need for mutual trust is another overlap between the two traditions with regard to *zhi* and liberty in higher education.

Moral qualities. In the Chinese tradition, the idea of moral autonomy does not require the freedom to act. But there are certain moral qualities inherent in an individual's expression of the free will, including reciprocity and serving the public goods. In higher education, it is expected that university activities constructively contribute to the collective good. This makes mutual trust essential to academic freedom and university autonomy in higher education.

As noted, mutual trust is a common point between the two traditions, a key to maintaining academic freedom and university autonomy in both contexts. It is more fundamental in the Chinese tradition. In China, mutual trust is a precondition of academic freedom and university autonomy, theoretically and practically. In the Anglo-American contexts, where academic freedom and university are theoretically protected, mutual trust has become *de facto* important in protecting them in practice.

However, there is a difference between the two traditions – in the Anglo-American tradition, it is the university's own responsibility to build and maintain mutual trust; whereas in China, the state is responsible for supervising the university's role in building and maintaining mutual trust. Ideally, in the Anglo-American tradition, the university is an independent sphere, freed from external control, though this is often not the case in reality. In the Chinese context, the university is an integral part of the state system. In the Anglo-American tradition, academia is an autonomous community, fully responsible for sustaining public trust. In China, it is the comprehensive state's responsibility to regulate academia and make it trustworthy.

10.5 The Fourth Pair: *Gong*/Public and the Fifth Pair: *Tianxia Weigong* and Global Public/Common Goods

This section considers two key themes that are intrinsically interrelated: the fourth theme of *gong*/public and the fifth theme of *tianxia weigong* and global public/common goods. The two themes are examined together because they focus on the same aspect of higher education – the public and private modalities of higher education – although the fifth pair particularly focuses on this aspect at the global level.

10.5.1 Comparison between *Gong* and Public, and *Tianxia Weigong* and Global/Common Public Goods

Figure 10.4 outlines the findings of the comparison. For both traditions, the terms *gong*/public contain multiple meanings.

As discussed in Chapter 8, the two traditions interpret the *gong*/public based on distinct political ideas. The Chinese *gong* to a large extent draws on the pre-Qin (221–207 BCE) ideas represented by classical Confucian teachings. *Gong* takes precedence over *si*, accompanied by a tradition of the comprehensive state that has no limits. In contrast, the Anglo-American tradition's 'public' has been largely shaped by two post-Reformation ideas – those of the limited liberal state, and the civic republican tradition that envisions a bottom-up democratic space. The primacy of the individual/private sphere, especially of the protection of individual rights and the division of power, is key. These ideas are embodied in the forms of the modern nation-state in Anglo-American societies.

In the Chinese tradition, there exists no absolute *si* or private. *Si* is nested within *gong*, and thus the public is always relative to the private. As illustrated by the escalating nested circles in Confucianism (from the self to *tianxia*), *gong* to the utmost means *tianxia*, all under heaven. Chapter 9 explains the twofold meaning of *tianxia*. On the one hand, *tianxia* reflects a normative appeal of 'no other' in all under heaven. *Gong*, to the utmost, identifies with this normative *tianxia*, echoing the universal public in the Anglo-American tradition. Manifested in the idea of **gong-as-tianxia** or **tianxia weigong**, all under heaven belongs to all and is for all. With a civilizational state that had limited influence on grassroots society in Imperial China, individual members of society were expected to contribute to collective goods in a concerted way, mainly through local collectives such as the clan and local community. In this sense, the traditional Chinese notion of 'public

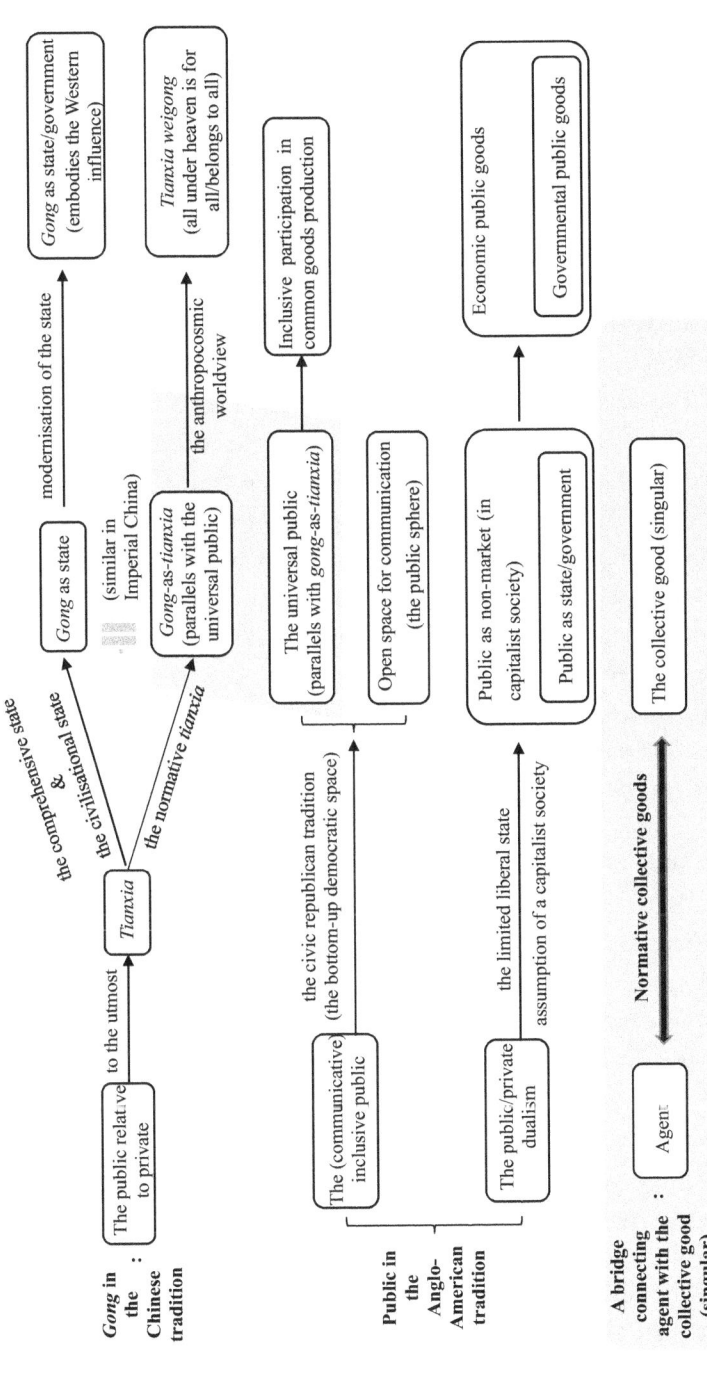

Figure 10.4 An outline of the comparison between the Chinese *gong* and the Anglo-American public.

goods' parallels with the notion of 'common goods' in the Anglo-American tradition (see later).

On the other hand, *tianxia* has a realpolitik meaning – that of the Chinese civilizational state as the legitimate representative of *tianxia*. There emerged the idea of ***gong*-as-state**. Arguably, in Imperial times, the normative claim of *gong*-as-state was equated with *gong*-as-*tianxia*. Nevertheless, the modernization of the Chinese state in the twentieth century and after has shifted the meaning of *gong*-as-state towards the Anglo-American public-as-state. The modern Chinese state is no longer a pure civilizational state that resembles the state as the legitimate representative of *tianxia* in Imperial China, but to a large extent can be understood as modern nation-state (although one that retains elements of the civilizational state, as discussed in Chapters 2 and 8). I argue that today the *tianxia* idea is largely normative. Nevertheless, the tradition of the comprehensive state has been retained, so that higher education sits within the state. Higher education is regarded as an integral part of the public, in that respect. Sitting within the state has significant implications for Chinese higher education including the relationship between the government and universities, higher education finance, access to higher education and other areas. These matters were examined in Chapter 8.

The Anglo-American tradition interprets the public in two ways: **the (communicative) inclusive public** based on the civic republican tradition and **the public/private dualism** on the basis of the tradition of the limited liberal state.

The Anglo-American tradition imagines an open space for communication that allows and encourages free, inclusive and bottom-up discussion. A typical example is Habermas's public sphere. Ideally, the university is a public sphere, being an open space for discussion and protected by the ideas of institutional autonomy and academic freedom. This *communicative* inclusive public marks a distinctive difference between the two traditions.

To move forward, in a democratic Anglo-American society, arguably not only communication but concerted grassroots participation in collective affairs may be incorporated in the openly inclusive space. In other words, *the inclusive public* can go beyond *the communicative inclusive public* and involve an open space for action. In this sense, there is **the universal public**, which partly parallels the Chinese idea of *gong*-as-*tianxia*. This open space for action does not mean there is no limitation on action, but it does entail the inclusive and bottom-up participation of social members in collective affairs, without them being directly surveilled or regulated by the state. This is in line with the

UNESCO (2015) interpretation of (global) common goods. Common goods require joint participation by a wide range of agents. It is notable that UNESCO (2015) views education, including higher education, as a (global) common good, in the double sense that education is both a participatory sphere in its own right and one of the means of developing and distributing the capabilities of common and effective participation by all agents. This argument is also made by Amartya Sen (1999: 42) in *Development as Freedom*.

The public/private dualism centres on the scope of, and the relationship between, the spheres of social action. Generally, Anglo-American societies view the world as composed of four spheres: the sphere of the state, the sphere of the market, the sphere of civil society and the sphere of the individual/family. The sphere of the individual/family, which is private, has normative primacy. The private takes precedence over the public, which is in contrast with the Chinese tradition. The sphere of the individual/family is seen as independent and autonomous, though it also overlaps with the other three spheres that are collective. Higher education should sit somewhere between the state, the market and civil society.

There are two primary approaches to the concept of public in the framework of the public/private dualism. The first is the economic approach, claiming **public-as-non-market**. Here we find the assumption of a capitalist society – society consists of two parts (i.e. market and non-market). However, not every society is a capitalist society, or a capitalist society in this way, and thus public-as-non-market does not work well everywhere. The second approach is the political approach that draws on the idea of **public-as-state/government**. Here, the state/government is public whereas non-state/government (market, civil society, individual/family) is private. It is evident that, in capitalist societies, public-as-state/government is combined with public-as-non-market. However, compared to the economic approach that only suits a specific kind of society, public-as-state/government may work across a larger set of contexts, as long as government is responsive to the needs of the populace (Dewey [1927] 2016: 130).

Nevertheless, despite the prerequisite assumption of a capitalist society, the economic public has become one of the dominant discourses of 'the public' worldwide, including in contemporary Chinese higher education discourse. For example, the idea associated with economic public goods, translated as *gonggong wupin* or *gonggong chanpin* in Chinese, provides a rationale for the state's financial investment in higher education, while also playing an important role in reforms that establish a cost-sharing mechanism in Chinese higher education finance.

The notion of public goods in a traditional Chinese sense, which is similar to the concept of common goods, is distinct from that of economic public goods.

There is another similarity between the two traditions that is suggested by the Chinese tradition's particular focus on the moral perfection of individuals. The similarity lies in the two traditions' shared need of *a bridge* to connect the individual agent with his/her active contribution to the collective good in the singular form. Here the collective good involves normative judgements about what is desirable for the augmentation of the collective welfare. This similarity draws on the agreement by both traditions that individuals are *not* naturally concerned with the collective good. Their genuine and active willingness to contribute to the collective depends on their acceptance or acquisition of certain collectively oriented values – **normative collective goods**. The two traditions' emphasis on cultivating the individual's willingness in this regard is embodied in widely implemented programmes of moral education or citizenship education in both Chinese and Anglo-American societies. In this respect, higher education is among the main producers of normative collective goods in society.

In sum, there are numerous differences between the two traditions, while the only overlaps/similarities are between the ideas of *gong*-as-*tianxia* and the universal public, between the concept of common goods and the traditional Chinese sense of public goods, and between the shared emphasis on normative collective goods as the bridge to connect agent and the collective good. Notably, despite the overlap between *gong*-as-*tianxia* and the universal public, the two traditions diverge concerning their further developments of *tianxia weigong* and inclusive participation in public/common goods production. While *tianxia weigong* highlights thinking *through* the world and imagines the world as an organic whole, the idea of global public/common goods builds on the methodological nationalism that subsumes the world under nation-states.

> Arguably, however, the differences between the two traditions have been mitigated to a certain degree. This is partly due to the openness and heterogeneity of the Chinese tradition. Since the late nineteenth century, the Chinese tradition has continuously absorbed elements from the West including the Anglo-American tradition, and Marxism and Leninism. For example, the modernization of the state has led to a partial convergence between *gong*-as-state (in a traditional Chinese sense) and public-as-state/government (in the Anglo-American tradition); and the capitalization of the Chinese economy and the introduction of liberal individualism have expanded the autonomy of the individual. It seems that Chinese society is attempting to reach a new balanced combination of the individual and collective, and a new balance between individualistic goods and

collective goods. The outcome of these tendencies remains to be seen. In higher education, both higher education's production of pecuniary private/collective goods and non-pecuniary collective goods are well recognized and considered in China, indicating the mixed influence of traditional Chinese ideas and the Western ideologies. (Hongcai Wang 2014)

10.5.2 Searching for Hybridization and Synergy, and Implications for Higher Education's Collective Outcomes

The two traditions have fundamental differences concerning the ideas of *gong* and public. For example, they differ on the views of the composition of society and the world. Further, liberal individualism and Chinese collectivism, and the primacy of *gong* in the Chinese tradition and the primacy of the private in the Anglo-American tradition, also seem to be contradictory. The differences and contradictions indicate the difficulties in complementing *gong* and public, and in searching for a common conceptual framework for discussing the outcomes of higher education.

On the one hand, to base the common conceptual framework on the Chinese *gong* and *si* would violate the independent status of the individual and private in the Anglo-American tradition. On the other hand, to establish the framework centring on the Anglo-American public and private would assume a limited liberal state, Western-style capitalist society and the division of power, which are all to a certain extent alien to the Chinese tradition. Seemingly, the contradictions mainly come from the differing political and cultural ideas and assumptions underlying the concepts of *gong*, public, *si* and private. Therefore, efforts to establish a common conceptual framework for discussing the outcomes of higher education may need to avoid those concepts which have normative underpinnings, while working with those that are more descriptive and neutral with regard to political ideologies. Here I attempt to do so through hybridizations and synergies, using the terms of 'collective' and 'individualized' (in a normatively neutral way here) instead of *gong*/public or *si*/private.

***The collective good*, and the universal public and public-as-*tianxia*.** As discussed, one of the similarities between the two traditions is the universal public in the Anglo-American tradition, and public-as-*tianxia* in the Chinese tradition. The two ideas share the similar emphasis on the universal reach of collective outcomes. In both cases, these outcomes involve normative judgements, as they need to be understood as augmenting the collective welfare. Outcomes of higher education in relation to this similarity are captured by the concept of *the collective* *good* in the singular form. Kinds and levels of space may be added before 'the collective good' to refer to the particular outcomes associated with various kinds/levels of collectivity; for example, the global collective good (drawing on the collective good of *tianxia*), the national collective good, the local collective good or the non-pecuniary collective good.

***Collective goods*, common goods and the traditional Chinese sense of public goods**. Drawing on the bottom-up democratic space in the Anglo-American tradition, the concept of common goods calls for inclusive, open and bottom-up participation of agents in producing common goods. This idea has resonance in the concept of public goods in a traditional Chinese sense. As Tian and Liu (2018) claim, perhaps the closest approximation of the traditional Chinese sense of public goods in the Anglo-American tradition is the UNESCO notion of common goods. As I see it, both common goods and public goods in the traditional Chinese sense can be regarded as collective goods. This concept of collective goods inherits the idea of bottom-up and collective participation. Here, higher education is a kind of collective good itself, calling for participation and contribution from a wide range of agents. It also contributes to collective goods.

***Collective goods* and *gong*/public-as-state/government**. As noted, modernization has turned the Chinese state to a large extent into a modern nation-state; and accompanied by the influence of Western ideologies, the idea of public-as-state/government in China overlaps with the Anglo-American tradition, even though the boundary of the state differs in each case. In this sense, outcomes of higher education that have relevance in the state/government may be called (governmental) public goods, which is also a form of collective goods.

To use the notion of collective goods rather than public goods has its advantage. In addition to the meaning of state-owned/produced goods, the term 'public goods' can also be interpreted from an economic perspective, but as pointed out, public-as-non-market assumes a capitalist society and a limited liberal state, and does not work well in the Chinese context. However, the visibility of the idea of public goods (in economic sense) in Chinese discourse on higher education reflects the fact that non-market collective goods not only exist in China but are important in the Chinese context. On one hand, to simply stop using the term 'public goods' may not work practically. On the other hand, the problems arising from applying the term of 'public goods' across contexts, which has haunted ideological assumptions, need to be addressed. I suggest using collective goods to capture various kinds of 'public goods' while avoiding unnecessary ideological assumptions/underpinnings associated with the latter term.

Therefore, the notion of collective goods, embracing a range of publicly related goods such as public goods (including governmental and economic public goods, and public goods in the traditional Chinese sense) and common goods, may be an alternative term to capture the collective outcomes of higher education across contexts. Again, various terms can be added before the term of 'collective goods' to reflect the different kinds of collective goods – for example, pecuniary collective goods, normative collective goods and legal collective goods. As will be discussed later, collective goods also include the repercussions of certain individualized goods.

Collective goods and normative collective goods. Normative collective goods, as a bridge connecting individual agent with the collective good in the singular form, specifically contribute to the cultivation and enhancement of the agent's genuine and active willingness to contribute to the collective good.

***Individualized goods* and non-absolute *si* vis-à-vis the absolute private.** One of the fundamental differences between the two traditions lies in the status of the *si* and private. There is no absolute private in the Chinese tradition, and the pursuit of *si*/private reflects moral degeneration in the normative sense. Expressions such as *yiji zhisi*, meaning to one's individualized and selfish ends, embody the inferior status of *si*. This Chinese understanding is in contradiction to the central status of the private and individual in the Anglo-American tradition. Despite the contradiction in terms of the normative position, both individualized private goods in the Anglo-American tradition and the idea of individualized and selfish ends in the Chinese tradition point to a kind of non-collective goods – individualized goods.

The *direct* influence of individualized goods is limited to the individual person. However, individualized goods may have repercussions for collective entities. For example, higher education's augmentation of graduates' salary may generate an increase in governmental income (e.g., tax income) and the growth of the national economy; higher education graduates' improved agency and health awareness may further contribute to the improvement of the health conditions of the family and society. The repercussions of individualized goods may be captured by collective goods. But individualized goods per se are not collective.

Individualized goods are well acknowledged in the Anglo-American tradition, but are downplayed and discouraged in the Chinese tradition (including both indigenous Confucian ideas and the contemporary Chinese ideas that are largely shaped by Marxism) to a certain extent. The handling of individualized goods in China may change, partly because of the growth of individual autonomy. Meanwhile, the pecuniary returns of higher education for individual students and graduates are gaining importance in the Chinese context.

11

Conclusion

As noted at the outset of this book, higher education produces collective goods and does so in all societies. However, societies vary in the incidence of such goods and also in how they are understood. There is considerable variation across the world in the connotations of collective goods, in understandings of what collective goods higher education can produce, in society's expectations about higher education's collective goods and in the policies designed to support the production of collective goods by higher education. This variation, to a large extent, is a result of varying philosophical and cultural ideas underlying the conceptions of the public (good) across contexts. Drawing on different social imaginaries, associated with connotations of the primary spheres of social action, including the spheres of the individual, society, state and world, and different interpretations of the relationship between these spheres, the two traditions studied in this book demonstrate distinctive approaches to the state, society, higher education and the public (good) of higher education.

The book suggests that the Anglo-American higher education tradition is characterized by a strong focus on individualized interests, a central concern of the development of individual agency, belief in the value and legitimacy of atomized competition, preference for a limited liberal state in interaction with higher education and (in some but not in all quarters) an advocacy for higher education as a public sphere. It is also suggested that the Chinese higher education tradition is characterized by a strong focus on serving collective goods, higher education that is largely supported by a comprehensive state and higher education that is incorporated within the sphere of the state.

These characteristics of higher education, which arguably further shape higher education practices, have partly emerged from how each tradition frames the interaction between higher education and the primary spheres of social action. For example, as Chapter 8 noted, the individual, as the smallest entity in the Chinese tradition, may compromise her/his interests for the sake of collective interests; whereas in the Anglo-American tradition, the individual's interests take priority, at least nominally, although the individual is also subordinate to market forces. This divergence accounts for a difference between higher education in the two traditions: the strong focus on collective goods in the Chinese higher education tradition versus the strong focus on individualized goods in the Anglo-American higher education tradition.

Chapter 8 also demonstrated that the Chinese tradition envisions the state as having a comprehensive role in human affairs and higher education as part of the state. Higher education serves the interests of the state and receives support from the state. The support of the state includes financial investment, institutional support and the state's efforts in building and maintaining mutual trust between higher education and society. In contrast, the tradition of the limited liberal state in the Anglo-American tradition imagines higher education as at least partly outside the state, with scope for critically evaluating and commenting on the state's behaviours (though Anglo-American states are not always comfortable with this practice). In the Anglo-American setting, higher education is solely accountable for winning the trust from society and the state. While the state is expected to financially support higher education as it is the state's responsibility to sustain the supply of public goods, the strong focus on individualized outcomes of higher education provides the state with an ongoing rationale to decrease its financial investment in higher education.

As argued in Chapter 5, the Chinese tradition assumes that all human beings are born with equal virtues and potentials. It is equally possible for all to realize what they wish if they dedicate efforts and perseverance to self-cultivation. Personal effort, rather than factors in the external environment, is seen as the key to the success of self-cultivation. According to Chapter 6, in the Chinese higher education tradition, with personal efforts so strongly emphasized, there is a comparatively weaker emphasis on how social inequities may influence the results of individual self-cultivation. In addition, as Chapter 7 suggested, Chinese self-cultivation concerns the development of the individual's free will, especially the capacity for critical thinking and reflection, in the context of the development and practice of certain moral qualities. Due to continuous concerns about moral qualities, a distinctive characteristic of Chinese higher education is the focus on *lide shuren* (fostering moralities and virtues through education).

In contrast, Chapter 5 argued that the Anglo-American tradition understands human beings as born with different and diverse talents and potentials. One of the dominant narratives, as noted in Chapter 6, is that due to the existence of social inequities, it is essential for society to provide equal opportunities for individuals who have similar talents and aspirations. According to Chapter 7, in addition to opportunities and necessary resources, the environment also needs to provide individuals with free space and diverse options for their development. Through higher education, individual students can develop their capability, including their capacity to make choices and to carry out such choices. There is less emphasis on moral and ethical qualities than in the Chinese tradition. Many in the Anglo-American world would argue that questions which particularly concern social philosophy are not for educators to prescribe but are matters of individual choice. The Anglo-American stress on the capacity to implement choice, on the basis of the freedom to act, without regard for the effects on others within the boundaries of legal conduct, distinguishes itself from the Chinese tradition, in which the social meaning of individual acts is primary. Arguably, it is this difference that makes it scarcely possible to combine the Chinese ideas of *zhi* and the Anglo-American liberty, and to develop universal ideas of academic freedom and institutional autonomy in higher education.

There are also tendencies to convergence between the two traditions, partly embodied in commonalities of higher education practices between the two contexts. In part, this convergence demonstrates a strong Anglo-American influence in the Chinese context. For example, in some respects, the Anglo-American approach to higher education's collective goods has become influential in China. As Chapter 8 demonstrated, the economic interpretation of public goods, based on a capitalist society, has become a strong narrative in capturing higher education's outcomes in China, although using this interpretation in the Chinese context can be problematic. In addition, as argued in Chapter 9, methodological nationalism has become a dominant narrative in unpacking the world order, with shaping effects in cross-border higher education activities, and China has also been touched by the dominant narrative of methodological nationalism. The traditional civilizational Chinese state has become largely a modern nation-state, embracing the current world order. Yet not completely so, as there are also attempts to rethink that world order in a Chinese way. The traditional Chinese idea *tianxia* provides an alternative view of the world, though its influence is limited even in China.

It should be noted that the commonalities of higher education practice are sometimes embodied in 'superficial' manifestations of the varying cultural and philosophical ideas. For example, both traditions emphasize the need to build and maintain mutual trust between higher education and the state, and between higher education and society. However, as suggested by Chapter 7, the two traditions diverge concerning how to build and maintain such trust – whether it is partly the state's responsibility, or the university's sole responsibility – due to their distinctive understandings of the state. At the same time, diverging cultural and philosophical ideas may gradually develop into more similar ideas in the contemporary context, indicating a converging tendency. For example, despite the varying assumptions about the natural talents and potentials of human beings in the two traditions, there is a converging tendency in higher education. Since the 1960s, there has been a growing trend in the Anglo-American context to see all individuals as educable, which parallels the long-standing Chinese assumption of the equal potentials of all human beings, with its origins in Confucian moral equality.

Building on the two traditions' approaches to the public (good) of higher education, the book proposes the following five trans-positional viewpoints, as first discussed in Chapter 10. First, drawing on the Chinese focus on individual efforts and perseverance in self-cultivation, and the Anglo-American focus on the support from the external environment in capability development, the book argues that theoretically the optimum situation for individual student development arises when individual agency is harmonized with the external environment. Second, following the first argument, social equity may be maximized when external conditions are harmonized with individual efforts – when social structure and agency are combined, collective conditions and the individual are combined, and the outer and inner self are combined. Third, on the basis of the two traditions' distinctive attitudes towards the freedom to act, this book suggests that although there is no universal idea of academic freedom and university autonomy, the two traditions agree that protecting these qualities in higher education (with various connotations embedded in the specific contexts) requires efforts to build mutual trust between higher education and society, and between higher education and the state. Fourth, partly due to the enduring global challenges and the under-provision of global collective goods, the comparative analysis suggests the need to be cautious about nationalist ideas underlying the concepts of global public/common goods. Cross-border higher education activities may benefit from thinking through a perspective of *tianxia weigong*. Fifth, taking into account the concepts of the public/common good(s) and the philosophical and cultural ideas underlying these concepts in the two traditions, the book claims that higher education's outcomes may be better captured by carefully distinguishing among a trans-positional set of terms, including the collective good, collective goods as common goods, collective goods as governmental-produced/owned public goods, collective goods as normative collective goods and individualized goods.

11.1 Contributions of the Book

Scholars/researchers have worked extensively on comparisons between the Chinese and Western traditions, in general and in higher education, and their work has informed this book. Many focus on introducing under-known Chinese thoughts to global audiences, for example, Tu Wei-Ming and William Theodore de Bary. The works of Tu and de Bary on Confucian thoughts, especially concerning individual self-cultivation and Confucian moral autonomy, have greatly influenced the argument of the book. Scholars/researchers also work on comparisons between the Chinese and Western traditions of social and political philosophical thoughts. Among them, works from Joseph Chan, Daniel A. Bell and Ambrose Y. C. King have been drawn on repeatedly in the book.

In relation to (higher) education, some scholars/researchers attempt to unpack Chinese educational thoughts for global audiences, suggesting how Chinese ideas can contribute to the development of (higher) education worldwide. Others attempt to draw on both Chinese and Western thoughts in looking for ways to develop China's higher education system. The works of the latter group have also heavily influenced this book. These scholars/researchers include Ruth Hayhoe, Rui Yang, Qiang Zha, Thomas H. C. Lee and Jun Li. However, arguably, their work still primarily leans towards Chinese educational thoughts and (higher) education practice in China, rather than attempting symmetrical or integrative comparisons between Chinese and Western educational thought.

For example, the books written or edited by Ruth Hayhoe, including *China's Universities, 1895-1995: A Century of Cultural Conflict* (1996) and *Portraits of 21st Century Chinese Universities: In the Move to Mass Higher Education* (2012), are primarily about higher education practice and educational thoughts in China, though through the lens of comparative education. The early works of Rui Yang primarily concern comparative education and the internationalization of higher education, with a particular focus on Chinese higher education; see articles such as 'Tensions between the Global and the Local: A Comparative Illustration of the Reorganisation of China's Higher Education in the 1950s and 1990s' (2000). However, Yang's recent works focus more on Chinese cultural and educational thoughts, higher education practice in China and possible ways to integrate Chinese and Western educational thoughts. See, for example, *Emulating or Integrating? Modern Transformations of Chinese Higher Education* (2018), *The Concept of Tianxia and Its Impact on Chinese Discourses on the West* (2015) and a commentary article written in Chinese, 'Integrating Chinese and Western Bodies of Knowledge Is an Important Pursuit of Chinese Higher Education' (2020).

Their works have greatly facilitated Chinese-Western mutual dialogue and enhanced mutual understanding, and have been invaluable sources of scholarship for this book. Nevertheless, while their works cover a range of topics of higher education, including the evolution of the university in China, world-class university building, academic freedom and university autonomy, and higher education internationalization, the public (good) of higher education has not attracted great attention from them. There have been very few works on the public (good) of higher education, though there is one significant book chapter, written by Kai-ming Cheng and Rui Yang (2015).

The book's conceptual comparison of ideas in relation to the public (good) of higher education between the Chinese and Anglo-American traditions, and the search for their combination, is among the first explorations in a largely uncharted territory – the cultural and philosophical underpinnings of the public (good) of higher education, considered on a trans-positional basis. Exploration of this territory could be foundational to the evolution of international cooperation in higher education, as well as being of value to academic scholarship.

China's modern higher education history had been a process of constant learning from the West and sometimes from Japan. The divergence and even conflicts between China's own historical pathway of higher learning and political and educational culture, and Western ideas of modern universities, have generated difficulties for China's higher education. Questions are repeatedly asked by researchers and scholars, for example, about what China can draw from the Western systems and experience, and whether and in what ways China's higher education ought to draw on China's own tradition and history. The key is to bring together the two distinctive traditions in shaping China's higher education in a conscious way. How to do this definitely has yet to emerge, but this book has aimed to contribute to this constructive project.

Despite the efforts of the scholars/researchers discussed earlier, in the Chinese as well as the international English literature, the knowledge and information flow have been largely unilateral – primarily from the West to China, not vice versa. In other words, while China is learning from the West, the West has yet to learn effectively from China.

However, a more balanced flow from China to the world can be important too. The richness of scholarship in the Chinese tradition and the achievement of China's higher education since the late twentieth century both indicate what the world may gain from this direction of flow. The bilateral and even multilateral flow of information and knowledge has become essential to higher education. In the era of globalization and internationalization, higher education exchange and cooperation are necessarily based on mutual respect and understanding. Real mutual respect and understanding depend on deep-rooted conceptual understanding on the basis of cultures and ideas, as well as empirical recognition of the existing manifestations of those ideas.

This book has attempted such a comparison and has sought to bring together key concepts in the Chinese tradition and the Anglo-American tradition, in relation to the public (good) of higher education. Five main aspects of higher education have been considered in the book, including student development, higher education equity, liberty in higher education and higher education's outcomes including those at the world level. Underlying the five aspects are fundamental political and educational cultural ideas in each of the two traditions: the social imaginary in each case; the boundary and responsibility of the state (including the relationship between the state and the university); the constitution of society, including practices of collectivism and individualism; the process of individual development and learning; and connotations of the 'good'. Arguably, taking the public (good) of higher education as the central theme of the comparison and combination has enabled me to carry out a comprehensive study covering different aspects of the intersection between higher education and the individual, state, society and the world.

Moreover, it is expected that the conceptual findings of this book can lead to mutual understanding, and contribute to mutual cooperation between the different contexts of higher education practice, in the Anglo-American countries and China. This book uncovers some of the reasons for long-standing differences between the higher education systems of China, the United States and the United Kingdom, differences that have affected higher education cooperation. For example, the different approaches to academic freedom and university autonomy are hindering cooperation, partly because they are not well understood. The findings of Chapter 7, especially regarding the Chinese separation of the free will and freedom to act and the Anglo-American insistence on both free agency and freedom to act, explain much of the long-standing conceptual differences. With greater mutual understanding, cooperation faces less hinderances.

11.2 Methodological Reflections

The trans-positional approach employed in the book points to a possible way to conduct cross-cultural comparison in scholarship. It is necessary here to reflect on methodological issues that emerged during this study. When I started this research, one of the primary tasks was to find a way to engage in this exploration and comparison of scholarship. There was not much methodological material to draw on. While working through Amartya Sen's works, I realized that his idea of trans-positional analysis could provide a methodological foundation for this research. However, he only proposes a broad philosophical approach. This approach has not been employed by him or others as a detailed and concrete methodological guideline for research. I endeavoured to find a way to operationalize it at a practical level. Yet, problems emerged in this process.

The first problem was that it was challenging to treat the two traditions equally when the starting point of this study was embedded in one tradition, not the other. If I went directly with the starting point of the public (good) of higher education (a Western construct), there would be a high risk that the comparison would become 'asymmetrical'. To deal with this problem, I decided to engage with a two-step trans-positional analysis, with the aim of the first step being to find a new starting point to explore the public (good) of higher education in the two traditions, one that did not lean towards either tradition. The second problem emerged in the process of searching for the new starting point, when I realized that the two traditions could hardly be treated as 'equal' if the book was to be written in English. In part, the English translations of certain Chinese terms were not able to capture all of the nuances of the Chinese terms.

Thus, I developed the lexical basis to address this problem. The lexical basis has worked well in forming the foundation for the comparison in this study. Arguably, establishing a lexical basis can be an effective tool to conduct cross-cultural comparison when the cultures are in different languages and especially when the respective sets of terms do not have identical meanings. The development of a lexical basis that incorporates terms from different languages and covers different topics of higher education can become a useful tool for higher education researchers and practitioners when doing other cross-contextual comparison and cooperation.

The third problem concerned my positionality throughout this study. To a large extent, the outcomes of this research rely on my interpretation and selection of materials. As a Chinese researcher who was raised and educated in mainland China for more than twenty years, my understanding of, and identification with, the Chinese tradition is strong. But this is partly mitigated by my studying and living in an Anglo-American country in the last four years. On the one hand, my previous weaker grasp of the Anglo-American tradition has been strengthened by a large-scale programme of reading the Anglo-American works. On the other hand, my understanding of the Chinese tradition provided me with access to resources for a detailed analysis of this tradition, which is still understudied in the field of higher education. Further, acknowledging that there is more than one well-developed tradition helped me to gain critical distance from each of them.

Another methodological limitation concerns the scope of this research. Although I have emphasized repeatedly that this research does not aim to give a comprehensive account of each tradition, I am aware that my selection of research materials is open to debate, even in relation to the specifically higher education-related materials. Arguably, any and every change of the research scope could potentially alter the research outcomes. Further, scholars in different theoretical disciplines and with different backgrounds, for example, scholars of postcolonialism, would perhaps have strong opinions regarding the limitations of solely using the perspectives of the dominant or mainstream scholars in each tradition. I made the selections for many reasons, but primarily in relation to the research questions, which highlight the public (good) in higher education, in the context of the length of a doctoral study. The appropriateness of materials was explained earlier in this chapter. Due to time and capacity limitations, I have focused mainly on a selection of key scholarly works. I hope that by conceptually exploring them, at least certain aspects of the two traditions in relation to the public (good) in higher education have been unpacked.

The topic of this book can involve lifelong thinking and exploration. In the end of this book, I would like to invite more scholars and researchers into this rich and intriguing research area. The more scholars and researchers there are, the more likely mutual respect and understanding may be realized.

References

Allison, R.E. (1998), 'Complementarity as a model for east-west integrative philosophy', *Journal of Chinese Philosophy*, 25 (4): 505–17.
Altbach, P.G. (2001), 'Academic freedom: International realities and challenges', *Higher Education*, 41 (1–2): 205–19.
Altbach, P.G. (2016), 'Chinese higher education: "Glass ceiling" and "feet of clay"', *International Higher Education*, 86: 11–13.
Altbach, P.G. and J. Balán (2007), *World Class Worldwide: Transforming Research Universities in Asia and Latin America*, Baltimore: JHU Press.
Anand, P., D. Gasper, S. Deneulin, and N. Townsend (2007), 'Public goods, global public goods and the common good', *International Journal of Social Economics*, 34 (1/2): 19–36.
Anderson, C.W. (1990), *Pragmatic Liberalism*, Chicago and London: The University of Chicago Press.
Arrow, K.J. (1974), 'General economic equilibrium: Purpose, analytic techniques, collective choice', *The American Economic Review*, 64 (3): 253–72.
Ash, M.G. (2006), 'The Humboldt illusion', *The Wilson Quarterly*, 20 (4): 45–8.
Ball, S.J. (2003), *Class Strategies and the Education Market: The Middle Classes and Social Advantage*, Abington: Routledge.
Bayer, P. and J. Urpelainen (2013), 'Funding global public goods: The dark side of multilateralism', *Review of Policy Research*, 30 (2): 160–89.
Beck, U. (2007), 'The cosmopolitan condition: Why methodological nationalism fails', *Theory, Culture & Society*, 24 (7–8): 286–90.
Beck, U. (2016), 'Varieties of second modernity and the cosmopolitan vision', *Theory, Culture & Society*, 33 (7–8): 257–70.
Becker, G. (1993), *Human Capital: A Theoretical and Empirical Analysis, with Special Reference to Education*, Chicago: University of Chicago Press.
Beine, M., F. Docquier, and H. Rapoport (2008), 'Brain drain and human capital formation in developing countries: Winners and losers', *The Economic Journal*, 118 (528): 631–52.
Bell, D.A. (2010), *China's New Confucianism: Politics and Everyday Life in a Changing Society*, Princeton: Princeton University Press.
Bell, D.A. (2017a), 'Against individualism: A Confucian rethinking of the foundations of morality, politics, family, and religion by Henry Rosemont Jr. (review)', *Philosophy East and West*, 67 (2): 565–8.
Bell, D.A. (2017b), 'Realizing tianxia: Traditional values and China's foreign policy', in B. Wang (ed.), *Chinese Visions of World Order: Tianxia, Culture, and World Politics*, 129–47, Durham and London: Duke University Press.

Bellah, R. (1976), *Beyond Belief: Essays on Religion in a Post-Traditional World*, New York: Harper & Row.

Berdahl, R.O., J. Graham, and D.R. Piper (1971), *Statewide Coordination of Higher Education*, Washington: American Council on Education.

Berlin, I. (1969), *Four Essays on Liberty*, Oxford: Oxford University Press.

Biesta, G. (2002), 'Bildung and modernity: The future of bildung in a world of difference', *Studies in Philosophy and Education*, 21 (4–5): 343–51.

Biesta, G. (2009), 'Good education in an age of measurement: On the need to reconnect with the question of purpose in education', *Educational Assessment, Evaluation and Accountability*, 21: 33–46.

Blanden, J. and S. Machin (2004), 'Educational inequality and the expansion of UK higher education', *Scottish Journal of Political Economy*, 51 (2): 230–49.

Blundell, R., L. Dearden, C. Meghir, and B. Sianesi (1999), 'Human capital investment: The returns from education and training to the individual, and the firm and the economy', *Fiscal Studies*, 20 (1): 1–23.

Bodde, D. (1957), *China's Cultural Tradition, What and Wither?* New York: Holt, Rinehart and Winston.

Bodycott, P. and A. Lai (2012), 'The influence and implications of Chinese culture in the decision to undertake cross-border higher education', *Journal of Studies in International Education*, 16 (3): 252–70.

Bol, P.K. (2008), *Neo-Confucianism in History*, Cambridge, MA: Harvard University Press.

Boni, A. and M. Walker (2013), *Human Development and Capabilities: Re-imagining the University of the Twenty-First Century*, Abingdon: Routledge.

Boudon, R. (1974), *Education, Opportunity, and Social Inequality: Changing Prospects in Western Society*, New York: Wiley-Interscience.

Bowen, W.G., M.A. Kurzweil, E.M. Tobin, and S.C. Pichler (2005), *Equity and Excellence in American Higher Education*, Charlottesville and London: University of Virginia Press.

Boyd, R. (2013), 'Adam Smith on civility and civil society', in C.J. Berry, M.P. Paganelli, and C. Smith (eds.), *The Oxford Handbook of Adam Smith*, 442–63, Oxford: Oxford University Press.

Bray, T. (1999), *The Shadow Education System: Private Tutoring and Its Implications for Planners*, Paris: UNESCO International Institute for Educational Planning.

Brubaker, R. (2017), 'Between nationalism and civilizationism: The European populist moment in comparative perspective', *Ethnic and Racial Studies*, 40 (8): 1191–226.

Burrage, M. (2010), 'Introduction', in M. Burrage (ed.), *Martin Trow: Twentieth-Century Higher Education: Elite to Mass to Universal*, 1–51, Baltimore: Johns Hopkins University Press.

Cai, Y. (1986), *Collections of Cai Yuanpei's Works (Cai Yuanpei Quanji)*, Beijing: Zhonghua Publisher (Zhonghua Chubanshe).

Calhoun, C. (1993), 'Civil society and the public sphere', *Public Culture*, 5 (2): 267–80.

Calhoun, C. (1998), 'The public good as a social and cultural project', in W.W. Powell and E.S. Clemens (eds.), *Private Action and the Public Good*, 20–35, New Haven: Yale University Press.

Calhoun, C. (2006), 'The university and the public good', *Thesis Eleven*, 84 (1): 7–43.

Callahan, W.A. (2004), 'Remembering the future: Utopia, empire and harmony in 21 century international theory', *European Journal of International Relations*, 10 (4): 569–601.

Callahan, W.A. (2008), 'Chinese visions of world order: Post-hegemonic or a new hegemony?' *International Studies Review*, 10 (4): 749–61.

Callahan, W.A. and E. Barabantseva (2011), *China Orders the World: Normative Soft Power and Foreign Policy*, Washington: Woodrow Wilson Center Press.

Cantwell, B. and S. Marginson (2018), 'Vertical stratification', in B. Cantwell, S. Marginson, and A. Smolentseva (eds.), *High Participation Systems of Higher Education*, 125–50, Oxford: Oxford University Press.

Cantwell, B., S. Marginson, and A. Smolentseva, eds (2018), *High Participation Systems of Higher Education*, Oxford: Oxford University Press.

Cantwell, B., R. Pinheiro, and M. Kwiek (2018), 'Governance', in B. Cantwell, S. Marginson, and A. Smolentseva (eds.), *High Participation Systems of Higher Education*, 68–93, Oxford: Oxford University Press.

Carnoy, M., I. Froumin, P.K. Loyalka, J.B. Tilak (2014), 'The concept of public goods, the state, and higher education finance: A view from the BRICs', *Higher Education*, 68 (3): 359–78.

Castells, M. (2008), 'The new public sphere: Global civil society, communication networks, and global governance', *The ANNALS of the American Academy of Political and Social Science*, 616 (1): 78–93.

Chan, J. (2002), 'Moral autonomy, civil liberties, and Confucianism', *Philosophy East and West*, 52 (3): 281–310.

Chan, J. (2013), *Confucian Perfectionism: A Political Philosophy for Modern Times*, Princeton: Princeton University Press.

Chang, H. (1997), 'Language and words: Communication and the Analects of Confucius', *Journal of Language and Social Psychology*, 16: 107–31.

Chang, W. and L. Kalmanson (2010), *Confucianism in Context: Classic Philosophy and Contemporary Issues, East Asia and Beyond*, Albany: State University of New York Press.

Chapman, B. and K. Lounkaew (2015), 'Measuring the value of externalities from higher education', *Higher education*, 70 (5): 767–85.

Chen, B. and Y. Feng (2000), 'Determinants of economic growth in China: Private enterprise, education, and openness', *China Economic Review*, 11 (1): 1–15.

Chen, D. (1919), 'The second query for the Eastern Magazine's journalist (Zai zhiwen Dongfang Zazhi jizhe)', *New Youths (Xin Qingnian)*, 2 (6): 86–99.

Chen, H. and C. Xiong (2011), 'Social equality: A re-examination of the concept (Shehui gongping: gainian zai bianxi)', *Exploration (Tansuo)*, 4: 160–5.

Chen, J. and Y. Zhong (2000), 'Valuation of individual liberty vs. social order among democratic supporters: A cross-validation', *Political Research Quarterly*, 53 (2): 427–39.

Chen, J.S. (2004), *The Rise and Fall of Fu Ren University, Beijing: Catholic Higher Education in China*, New York: Routledge.

Chen, Q. (2001), 'The study of ancient Chinese culture and system of remonstrating with the emperor (Zhongguo Gudai Yanjian Wenhua yu Zhidu Yanjiu)', Ph.D. diss, China University of Political Science and Law (Zhongguo Zhengfa Daxue), Beijing.

Cheng, C. (2004), 'A theory of Confucian selfhood: Self-cultivation and free will in Confucian philosophy', in K. Shun and D.B. Wong (eds.), *Confucian Ethics: A Comparative Study of Self, Autonomy, and Community*, 124–42, Cambridge: Cambridge University Press.

Cheng, K. and R. Yang (2015), 'A cultural value in crisis: Education as public good in China', in O. Filippakou and G.L. Williams (eds.), *Higher Education as A Public Good: Critical Perspectives on Theory, Policy and Practice*, 127–39, New York: Peter Lang.

Cheng, S. (2001), 'The recruiting system of Jianguan in the Tang Dynasty (Tangdai jianguan de xuanren zhidu)', *Social Science Front (Shehui kexue zhanxian)*, 3: 129–34.

Cheng, Y. and Q. Wang (2012), 'Building world-class universities in Mainland China', *Journal of International Higher Education*, 5 (2): 67–9.

Chernilo, D. (2011), 'The critique of methodological nationalism: Theory and history', *Thesis Eleven*, 106 (1): 98–117.

China-MOE. (2013), *Annual Report of China's Higher Education*. Available online: http://data.uis.unesco.org/ (accessed 25 February 2021).

Chirot, D. and T.D. Hall (1982), 'World-system theory', *Annual Review of Sociology*, 8 (1): 81–106.

Chou, R.J.-A. (2010), 'Filial piety by contract? The emergence, implementation, and implications of the "family support agreement" in China', *The Gerontologist*, 51 (1): 3–16.

Chu, Y. and A. So (2010), 'State neoliberalism: The Chinese road to capitalism', in Y. Chu (ed), *Chinese Capitalisms*, 46–72, London: Palgrave Macmillan.

Chu, Y.K. (1933), *Some Problems of A National System of Education in China*, Shanghai: The Commercial Press (Shangwu Yinshuguan).

Clancy, P. and G. Goastellec (2007), 'Exploring access and equity in higher education: Policy and performance in a comparative perspective', *Higher Education Quarterly*, 61 (2): 136–54.

Clark, B.R. (1986), *The Higher Education System: Academic Organization in Cross-national Perspective*, Berkeley: University of California Press.

Collins, C.S. (2016), 'Public good in Asian higher education', in C. Collins, M.N.N. Lee, J.N. Hawkins, and D.E. Neubauer (eds), *The Palgrave Handbook of Asia Pacific Higher Education*, 89–99, New York: Palgrave Macmillan.

Committee on Higher Education (1963), *Higher Education: Report of the Committee Appointed by the Prime Minister, under the Chairmanship of Lord Robbins, 1961-63*.

Available online: http://www.educationengland.org.uk/documents/robbins/robbins1963.html (accessed 25 February 2021).

Cornes, R. and T. Sandler (1996), *The Theory of Externalities, Public Goods and Club Goods* (2nd edn.), Cambridge: Cambridge University Press.

Cozzi, G. and S. Galli (2011), 'Privatization of knowledge: Did the US get it right?' Available online: https://mpra.ub.uni-muenchen.de/id/eprint/29710 (accessed 25 February 2021).

Craig, E., ed (1998), *Routledge Encyclopedia of Philosophy: Questions to Sociobiology* (Vol. 8), London and New York: Routledge.

de Bary, W.T. (1983), *The Liberal Tradition in China*, Hong Kong: The Chinese University Press.

de Bary, W.T. (1984), 'Neo-Confucian education and post-Confucian East Asia', *Bulletin of the American Academy of Arts and Sciences*, 37 (5): 7–17.

de Bary, W.T. and R. Lufrano (2001), *Sources of Chinese Tradition: From 1600 through the Twentieth Century*, New York: Columbia University Press.

de Ridder-Symoens, H. and W. Rüegg (2003), *A History of the University in Europe: Universities in the Middle Ages* (Vol. I), Cambridge: Cambridge University Press.

Deci, E.L. and R.M. Ryan (2004), *Handbook of Self-determination Research*, Rochester: University of Rochester Press.

Dee, J. (2006), 'Institutional autonomy and state-level accountability: Loosely coupled governance and the public good', in *Governance and the Public Good*, 133–55, Albany: State University of New York Press.

Deneulin, S. and N. Townsend (2007), 'Public goods, global public goods and the common good', *International Journal of Social Economics*, 34 (1–2): 19–36.

Desai, M. (2003), 'Public goods: A historical perspective', in I. Kaul, P. Conceicao, K.L. Goulven, and R.U. Mendoza (eds), *Providing Global Public Goods: Managing Globalization*, 63–77, New York and Oxford: Oxford University Press.

Deutsch, M. (1975), 'Equity, equality, and need: What determines which value will be used as the basis of distributive justice?' *Journal of Social Issues*, 31 (3): 137–49.

Dewey, J. ([1916] 2011), *Democracy and Education*, Essex: Simon & Brown.

Dewey, J. ([1921] 1976), 'As the Chinese think', in J.A. Boydston (ed.), *The Middle Works of John Dewey, 1899–1924* (Vol. 13), 217–27, Carbondale and Edwardsville: Southern Illinois University Press.

Dewey, J. ([1927] 2016), *The Public and Its Problems: An Essay in Political Inquiry*, ed. and introduction by M.L. Rogers, Athens: Ohio University Press.

Dewey, J. ([1935] 1987), 'Authority and social change', in J.A. Boydston (ed.), *The Later Works of John Dewey, 1925–1953* (Vol. 11), 130–45, Carbondale and Edwardsville: Southern Illinois University Press.

Ding, W. (2018), 'Bringing China's traditional culture into play in the Belt and Road Initiative (Fahui zhongguo youxiu chuantong wenhua zai "yidai yilu" jianshe zhong de jijizuoyong ji qi nuli fangxiang yu jianyi)', *Probe (Tansuo)*, 6: 185–92.

Ding, X. (2006), *The Decline of Communism in China: Legitimacy Crisis, 1977–1989*, Cambridge: Cambridge University Press.

Ding, X. (2007), 'Expansion and equality of access to higher education in China', *Frontiers of Education in China*, 2 (2): 151–62.

Dingwerth, K. and P. Pattberg (2006), 'Global governance as a perspective on world politics', *Global Governance*, 12: 185–203.

Donner, W. (1998), 'Perfect equality: John Stuart Mill on well-constituted communities. By Maria H. Morales. Lanham, Md.: Rowman and Littlefield, 1996. Pp. xiv, 219', *The Philosophical Review*, 107 (2): 337–40.

Duara, P. (2017), 'The Chinese world order and planetary sustainability', in B. Wang (ed.), *Chinese Visions of World Order: Tianxia, Culture, and World Politics*, 65–85, Durham and London: Duke University Press.

Dupré, L. (1994), 'The common good and the open society', in R.B. Douglas and D. Hollenbach (eds.), *Catholicism and Liberalism*, 172–95, Cambridge: Cambridge University Press.

Dybvig, P.H. and C.S. Spatt (1983), 'Adoption externalities as public goods', *Journal of Public Economics*, 20 (2): 231–47.

Earley, P.C. and C.B. Gibson (1998), 'Taking stock in our progress on individualism-collectivism: 100 years of solidarity and community', *Journal of Management*, 24 (3): 265–304.

Elman, B.A. (1991), 'Political, social, and cultural reproduction via civil service examinations in late imperial China', *The Journal of Asian Studies*, 50 (1): 7–28.

Elman, B.A. (2000), *A Cultural History of Civil Examinations in Late Imperial China*, Berkeley: University of California Press.

Espinoza, O. (2007), 'Solving the equity–equality conceptual dilemma: A new model for analysis of the educational process', *Educational Research*, 49 (4): 343–63.

Fairbank, J.K. (1968), *The Chinese World Order: Traditional China's Foreign Relations*, Cambridge, MA: Harvard University Press.

Fan, R. (1997), 'Self-determination vs. family-determination: Two incommensurable principles of autonomy', *Bioethics*, 11 (3&4): 309–22.

Fan, Z. (2004), 'Taixue in Han Dynasties', MA diss., Huazhong Normal University, Wuhan.

Fang, K. (2003), 'Harmony and diversity ("Heer butong: zuowei yizhong wenhuaguan de yiyi he jiazhi)', *Journal of Graduate School of Chinese Academy of Social Sciences (Zhongguo shehui kexueyuan yanjiushengyuan xuebao)*, 1: 26–33.

Fei, X. (2015), *Globalization and Self-cultural Awareness*, Heidelberg: Spinger.

Feng, G. ([1897] 2015), *Jiaobinlu's Protest (Jiaobinlu kangyi)*, Shanghai: Shanghai Shehui Kexueyuan Chubanshe.

Fewsmith, J. (1999), 'Elite politics', in M. Goldman and R. MacFarquhar (eds.), *The Paradox of China's Post-Mao Reforms*, 47–75, Cambridge: Harvard University Press.

Fichte, J.G. (1966), 'Grundlage der gesammten Wissenschaftslehre als Handschrift für seine yuhörer', in R. Lauth and H. Jacob (eds.), *J. G. Fichte-Gesamtausgabe der Bazrischen Akademie der Wissenschaften I*, 173–451, Stuttgart-Bad Cannstatt: Friedrich Fromman Verlag.

Filippakou, O. and G.L. Williams (2015), *Higher Education as A Public Good: Critical Perspectives on Theory, Policy and Practice*, New York: Peter Lang.

Fisher, S. (2006), 'Does the "Celtic Tiger" society need to debate the role of higher education and the public good?' *International Journal of Lifelong Education*, 2: 157–72.

Fleischacker, S. (2013), 'Adam Smith on equality', in C.J. Berry, M.P. Paganelli, and C. Smith (eds.), *The Oxford Handbook of Adam Smith*, 485–500, Oxford: Oxford University Press.

Forke, A. (1925), *The World-Conception of The Chinese: Their Astronomical, Cosmological and Physico-Philosophical Speculations*, London: Late Probsthain & Co.

Fu, C.W.-h. (1974), 'Confucianism, Marxism-Leninism and Mao: A critical stud', *Journal of Chinese Philosophy*, 1 (3–4): 339–71.

Fukuyama, F. (2011), *The Origins of Political Order: From Prehuman Times to the French Revolution*, New York: Farrar, Straus and Giroux.

Gaule, P. and M. Piacentini (2013), 'Chinese graduate students and US scientific productivity', *Review of Economics and Statistics*, 95 (2): 698–701.

Ge, Z. (2017), 'Imagining "all under heaven": The political, intellectual and academic background of a new utopia (Yixiangtiankai: Jinnianlai dalu xinruxue de zhengzhi suqiu)', *Thought (Sixiang)*, 33: 241–85.

Geng, Y. (1994), 'The origin of the new culture of China and its trend (Zhongguo xinwenhua de yuanliu jiqi quxiang)', *Historical Research (Lishi yanjiu)*, 2: 127–32.

Glewwe, P., E. Maïga, and H. Zheng (2014), 'The contribution of education to economic growth: A review of the evidence, with special attention and an application to Sub-Saharan Africa', *World Development*, 59: 379–93.

Goastellec, G. and J. Välimaa (2019), 'Access to higher education: An instrument for fair societies', *Social Inclusion*, 7 (1): 1–6.

Gold, T., D. Guthrie, and D. Wank (2002), 'An introduction to the study of guanxi', in T. Gold, D. Guthrie, and D. Wank (eds.), *Social Connections in China*, 3–20, Cambridge: Cambridge University Press.

Goldin, K.D. (1977), 'Equal access vs. selective access: A critique of public goods theory', *Public Choice*, 29 (1): 53–71.

Grant, M.J. and A. Booth (2009), 'A typology of reviews: An analysis of 14 review types and associated methodologies', *Health Information & Libraries Journal*, 26 (2): 91–108.

Green, M.F., and F.M. Hayward (1997), 'Force for change', in M.F. Green (ed.), *Transforming Higher Education: Views from Leaders around the World*, 3–26, Pheonix: ORYX Press.

Griffiths, T.G. and R.F. Arnove (2015), 'World culture in the capitalist world-system in transition', *Globalisation, Societies and Education*, 13 (1): 88–108.

Guo, B. (2003), 'Political legitimacy and China's transition', *Journal of Chinese Political Science*, 8 (1–2): 1–25.

Guo, S. and Y. Guo (2016), *Spotlight on China: Changes in Education under China's Market Economy*, Calgary: Sense Publishers.

Guo, X. (2012), *State and Society in China's Democratic Transition: Confucianism, Leninism, and Economic Development*, New York: Routledge.

Habermas, J. (1989), *The Structural Transformation of the Public Sphere: An Inquiry into A Category of Bourgeois Society*, trans. T. Burger, Cambridge, MA: The MIT Press.

Hahm, C. (2006), 'Confucianism and the concept of liberty', *Asia Europe Journal*, 4 (4): 477–89.

Han, S. and X. Xu (2019), 'How far has the state "stepped back": An exploratory study of the changing governance of higher education in China (1978–2018)', *Higher Education*, 78: 931–46.

Han, S.-J., Y.-H. Shim, and Y.-D. Park (2016), 'Cosmopolitan sociology and Confucian worldview: Beck's theory in East Asia', *Theory, Culture & Society*, 33 (7–8): 281–90.

Han, Y. (2009), *Collected Commentaries on Hanshi Waizhuan (Hanshi Waizhuan jishi)*, Beijing: Zhonghua Book Company (Zhonghua Shuju).

Hartnett, R.A. (2011), *The Jixia Academy and the Birth of Higher Learning in China: A Comparison of Fourth-Century BC Chinese Education with Ancient Greece*, Lweiston: Edwin Mellen Press.

Hartog, J. and H. Oosterbeek (1998), 'Health, wealth and happiness: Why pursue a higher education?' *Economics of Education Review*, 17 (3): 245–56.

Harvey, D. (2005), *A Brief History of Neoliberalism*, Oxford: Oxford University Press.

Hayek, F.A. (1960), *The Constitution of Liberty*, London: Routledge.

Hayhoe, R. (1989), 'China's universities and Western academic models', in P. Altbach and V. Selvaratnam (eds.), *From Dependence to Autonomy: The Development of Asian Universities*, 25–61, Singapore: Springer.

Hayhoe, R. (1996), *China's Universities 1895–1995: A Century of Cultural Conflict*, New York and London: Garland Publishing.

Hayhoe, R. (2011), 'Introduction and acknowledgements', in R. Hayhoe, J. Li, J. Lin, and Q. Zha (eds.), *Portraits of 21st Century Chinese Universities*, 1–18, Hong Kong: Springer/CERC.

Hayhoe, R. (2016), *China's Universities and the Open Door*, London: Routledge.

Hayhoe, R., J. Li, J. Lin, and Q. Zha (2012), *Portraits of 21st Century Chinese Universities: In the Move to Mass Higher Education*, Singapore: Springer.

Hazelkorn, E. (2015), *Rankings and the Reshaping of Higher Education: The Battle for World-class Excellence*, London: Springer.

Hazelkorn, E. and A. Gibson (2017), 'Public goods and public policy: What is public good, and who and what decides?' *Centre for Global Higher Education Working Papers, No.18*, London: UCL Institute of Education.

Hazelkorn, E. and A. Gibson (2018), 'Public goods and public policy: What is public good, and who and what decides?' *Higher Education*, 78: 257–71.

Held, D. and P. Maffettone (2016), 'Legitimacy and global governance', in D. Held and P. Maffettone (eds.), *Global Political Theory*, 117–42, Cambridge: Polity Press.

Hobbes, T. ([1651] 2006), *Leviathan*, London: A&C Black.
Hobhouse, L.T. ([1911] 1964), *Liberalism*, Oxford: Oxford University Press.
Hofstede, G. (1980), *Culture's Consequences: International Differences in Work-related Values*, Beverly Hills: Sage.
Horkheimer, M. ([1972] 1981), *Gesellschaft im Übergang: Aufsätye, Reden und Vorträge 1942–1970*, Frankfurt: Fischer.
Horlacher, R. (2012), 'What is bildung? or: Why padegogik cannot get away from the concept of Bildung?' in P. Siljander, A. Kivelä, and A. Sutinen (eds.), *Theories of Bildung and Growth: Connections and Controversies between Continental Educational Thinking and American Pragmatism*, 135–47, Rotterdam: Sense Publisher.
Hou, D. (2011), 'Knowledge transfer in humanities and social sciences: Incubation of high-quality university think tank (Renwen shehui kexue de zhishi zhuanhua jizhi tanxi: Jianlun youzhi daxue zhiku de peiyu)', *Fudan Education Forum (Fudan Jiaoyu Luntan)*, 5: 33–8.
Howland, D. (2005), *Personal Liberty and Public Good: The Introduction of John Stuart Mill to Japan and China*, Toronto: University of Toronto Press.
Hsü, I.C.Y. (1983), *The Rise of Modern China*, Oxford: Oxford University Press.
Hu, S. (1918), 'The Yi Bushengism (Yi Busheng zhuyi)', *New Youth (Xin qing nian)*, 4 (6): 504–5.
Huang, C. (1991), *Ideas of Mencius* (Vol. 1), Taipei: Dongda Book.
Huang, C. (2005), 'East Asian scholars' exploration on divisions of 'public' and 'private' (Dongya jinshi ruizhe dui 'gong' 'si' lingyu fenji de sikao)', *Jianghai Academic Journal (Jianghai Xuekan)*, 4: 17–23.
Huang, C. (2010), 'East Asian conceptions of the public and private realms', In K. Yu and J. Tao (eds.), *Taking Confucian Ethics Seriously: Contemporary Theories and Applications*, 73–97, Albany: State University of New York.
Huang, C. and Y.-h. Jiang (2005a), 'Introduction', in C. Huang and Y.-h. Jiang (eds.), *A New Exploration of the Public and Private: A Comparison between Eastern and Western Ideas (Gongsi Lingyu Xintan: Dongya yu Xifang Guandian zhi Bijiao)*, ix–xxvi, Taipei: National Taiwan University Press.
Huang, C. and Y.-h. Jiang (2005b), *A new Exploration of the Public and Private: A Comparison between Eastern and Western Ideas (Gongsi Lingyu Xintan: Dongya yu Xifang Guandian zhi Bijiao)*, Taipei: National Taiwan University Press.
Huang, F. (2015), 'Building the world-class research universities: A case study of China', *Higher education*, 70 (2): 203–15.
Huang, F. (2017), 'From the former Soviet patterns towards the US model? Changes in Chinese doctoral education', *Centre for Global Higher Education Working Paper, No. 12*, London: UCL Institute of Education.
Huang, X. (2000), *The Republic of China (Minguo Juan)*, Beijing: Zhonggong Zhongyang Dangxiao Chubanshe.
Huff, T.E. (2009), *The Rise of Early Modern Science: Islam, China, and the West* (2nd edn.), Cambridge: Cambridge University Press.

Hüfner, K. (2003), 'Higher education as a public good: Means and forms of provision', *Higher Education in Europe*, 28 (3): 339–48.

Hui, W. (2003), *China's New Order: Society, Politics, and Economy in Transition*, Cambridge, MA: Harvard University Press.

Hui, W. (2017), 'From empire to state: Kang Youwei, Confucian universalism, and unity', in B. Wang (ed.), *Chinese Visions of World Order: Tianxia, Culture, and World Politics*, 49–64, Durham and London: Duke University Press.

Huntington, S.P. (1996), *The Clash of Civilizations and the Remaking of World Order*, New York: Simon & Schuster.

Jacobs, L. (2013), 'A vision of equal opportunity in postsecondary education', in J.H.-D. Meyer, E.P.S. John, M. Chankseliani, and L. Uribe (eds.), *Fairness in Access to Higher Education in a Global Perspective: Reconciling Excellence, Efficiency, and Justice*, 41–56, Rotterdam: Sense.

Jacques, M. (2012), *When China Rules the World: The Rise of the Middle Kingdom and the End of the Western World [Greatly Updated and Expanded]*, London: Penguin UK.

Jarvis, P. (2002), 'Globalisation, citizenship and the education of adults in contemporary European society', *Compare*, 32 (1): 5–19.

Jesson, J. and F. Lacey (2006), 'How to do (or not to do) a critical literature review', *Pharmacy Education*, 6 (2): 139–48.

Jia, K. (2007), 'Responsibilities of governments and policy rationality in distribution: A distinction between equality and equalization (Lun fenpei wenti shang de zhengfu zeren yu zhengce lixing: Cong qufen gongping yu junping shuoqi)', *Research on Economics and Management (Jingji yu guanli yanjiu)*, 2: 11–15.

Jia, Q. and D.P. Ericson (2017), 'Equity and access to higher education in China: Lessons from Hunan province for university admissions policy', *International Journal of Educational Development*, 52: 97–110.

Jin, J. and S.J. Ball (2019), 'Precarious success and the conspiracy of reflexivity: Questioning the 'habitus transformation' of working-class students at elite universities', *Critical Studies in Education*. doi:10.1080/17508487.2019.1593869

Johnson, G.E., D. Davis, and S. Harrel, eds (1993), *Chinese Families in the Post-Mao Era*, Berkeley: University of California Press.

Jørgensen, T.B. and B. Bozeman (2007), 'Public values: An inventory', *Administration & Society*, 39 (3): 354–81.

Kalton, M.C. (2010), 'Confucian trajectories on environmental understanding', Ii W. Chang and L. Kalmanson (eds.), *Confucianism in Context: Classic Philosophy and Contemporary Issues, East Asia and Beyond*, 191–210, Albany: State University of New York Press.

Kant, I. ([1784] 1963), 'What is enlightenment?' Available online: https://pdfs.semanticscholar.org/e79f/f4968a9d58fae20890347698c548cdb81963.pdf (accessed 25 February 2021).

Kant, I. (1996), *The Metaphysics of Morals*, Cambridge: Cambridge University Press.

Karabel, J. (2006), *The Chosen: The Hidden History of Admission and Exclusion at Harvard, Yale, and Princeton*, Boston: Houghton Mifflin Harcourt.

Kasfir, N. (1998), 'The conventional notion of civil society: A critique', *Commonwealth & Comparative Politics*, 36 (2): 1–20.

Kassimir, R. (2009), 'Introduction: Academic freedom and regime transition', *Social Research*, 76 (2): 623–6.

Kaul, I., P. Conceicao, K.I. Goulven, and R.U. Mendoza (2003), *Providing Global Public Goods*, New York and Oxford: Oxford University Press.

Kaul, I., I. Grunberg, and M. Stern (1999a), 'Defining global public goods', in I. Kaul, I. Grunberg, and M. Stern (eds.), *Global Public Goods: International Cooperation in the 21st Century*, 1–19, Oxford: Oxford University Press.

Kaul, I., I. Grunberg, and M. Stern, eds (1999b), *Global Public Goods: International Cooperation in the Twenty-first Century*, Oxford: Oxford University Press.

Kehm, B.M. (2014), 'Beyond neo-liberalism: Higher education in Europe and the global public good', in P. Gibbs and R. Barnett (eds.), *Thinking about Higher Education*, 91–108, Basel: Springer.

Kelly, E., P. J. O'Connell and E. Smyth (2010), 'The economic returns to field of study and competencies among higher education graduates in Ireland', *Economics of Education Review*, 29 (4): 650–7.

Kennedy, K.J., G.P. Fairbrother, and Z. Zhao (2014), *Citizenship Education in China: Preparing Citizens for the "Chinese Century"*, New York and London: Routledge.

Kerr, C. (2003), *The Gold and the Blue: A Personal Memoir of the University of California 1949–1967* (Vol. 2. Political Turmoil), Berkeley: University of California Press.

Kerr, C. (2011), *The Gold and the Blue: A Personal Memoir of the University of California, 1949–1967* (Vol. 1), Berkeley: University of California Press.

Kim, S. (2008), 'The origin of political liberty in Confucianism: A Nietzschean interpretation', *History of Political Thought*, 29 (3): 393–415.

King, A.Y. (2018), *China's Great Transformation: Selected Essays on Confucianism, Modernization, and Democracy*, Hong Kong: The Chinese University Press.

King, D.S. (1987), *The New Right: Politics, Markets and Citizenship*, Basingstoke: Palgrave Macmillan.

King, R.E. (2000), *The Lexical Basis of Grammatical Borrowing: A Prince Edward Island French Case Study (Vol. 209)*, Amsterdam: John Benjamins Publishing.

Kipnis, A. (2007), 'Neoliberalism reified: Suzhi discourse and tropes of neoliberalism in the People's Republic of China', *Journal of the Royal Anthropological Institute*, 13 (2): 383–400.

Kivelä, A. (2012), 'From Immanuel Kant to Jahann Gottlieb Fichte: Concept of education and German idealism', in P. Siljander, A. Kivelä, and A. Sutinen (eds.), *Theories of Bildung and Growth: Connections and Controversies Between Continental Educational Thinking and American Pragmatism*, 59–86, Rotterdam: Sense Publisher.

Kivelä, A., P. Siljander, and A. Sutinen (2012), 'Between Bildung and growth: Connections and controversies', in P. Siljander, A. Kivelä, and A. Sutinen (eds.), *Theories of Bildung and Growth: Connections and Controversies Between Continental Educational Thinking and American Pragmatism*, 303–12, Rotterdam: Sense Publisher.

Kleingeld, P. and E. Brown (2019), 'Cosmopolitanism', in E.N. Zalta (ed.), *The Stanford Encyclopedia of Philosophy* (Winter 2018 edn.), Stanford: Metaphysics Research Lab, Stanford University. Available online: https://plato.stanford.edu/entries/cosmopolitanism/ (accessed 25 February 2021).

Kliemt, H. (2004), 'Contractarianism as liberal conservatism: Buchanan's unfinished philosophical Agenda', *Constitutional Political Economy*, 15 (2): 171–85.

Konrad, F.-M. (2012), 'Wilhelm von Humboldt's contribution to a theory of Bildung', in P. Siljander, A. Kivelä, and A. Sutinen (eds.), *Theories of Bildung and Growth: Connections and Controversies between Continental Educational Thinking and American Pragmatism*, 107–24, Rotterdam: Sense Publisher.

Kraus, R.C. (1976), 'The limits of Maoist egalitarianism', *Asian Survey*, 16 (11): 1081–96.

Labaree, D.F. (1997), 'Public goods, private goods: The American struggle over educational goals', *American Educational Research Journal*, 34 (1): 39–81.

Labaree, D.F. (2016), 'An affair to remember: America's brief fling with the university as a public good', *Journal of Philosophy of Education*, 50 (1): 20–36.

Lauwerys, J.A. (1965), 'General education in a changing world', *International Review of Education*, 11 (4): 385–403.

Lee, H. (2017), 'The soft power of the constant soldier: Or, why we should stop worrying and learn to love the PLA', in B. Wang (ed.), *Chinese Visions of World Order: Tianxia, Culture, and World Politics*, 237–66, Durham and London: Duke University Press.

Lee, J. and Y.-P. Zhu (2006), 'Urban governance, neoliberalism and housing reform in China', *The Pacific Review*, 19 (1): 39–61.

Lee, S. (2014), 'Traces of a lost landscape tradition and cross-cultural relationships between Korea, China and Japan in the early Joseon period (1392–1550)', Ph.D. diss., University of Kansas, Lawrence.

Lee, T.H.C. (2000), *Education in Traditional China: A History*, Leiden: Brill.

Lee, Y.-J. and Z. Xiao (1998), 'Children's support for elderly parents in urban and rural China: Results from a national survey', *Journal of Cross-cultural Gerontology*, 13 (1): 39–62.

Lerner, M. (1974), 'The justice motive: "Equity" and "parity" among children', *Journal of Personality and Social Psychology*, 29 (4): 539–50.

Letizia, A. (2015), 'Revitalizing higher education and the commitment to the public good: A literature review', *InterActions: UCLA Journal of Education and Information Studies*, 11 (2). Available online: http://www.escholarship.org/uc/item/6c41r85j (accessed 25 February 2021).

Levenson, J.R. (1968), *Confucian China and Its Modern Fate: A Trilogy*, Berkeley: University of California Press.

Li, A. (2014), 'Towards building direct educational partnership: The foundation of Shanxi University in 1902', *Frontier of Education in China*, 9 (2): 188–210.

Li, C. (2012), 'Equality and inequality in Confucianism', *Dao*, 11 (3): 295–313.

Li, C. (2014), 'The Confucian conception of freedom', *Philosophy East and West*, 64 (4): 902–19.

Li, D. (1919), 'My opinions on Marxism (Wode makesi zhuyiguan)', *New Youths (Xinqingnian)*, 6 (5): 529.

Li, H., P. Loyalka, S. Rozelle, B. Wu, and J. Xie (2015), 'Unequal access to college in China: How far have poor, rural students been left behind?' *The China Quarterly*, 221: 185–207.

Li, J. (2006), 'Confucian ideas on morality cultivation and modern university education (Rujia xiushen sixiang yu xiandai daxue jiaoyu)', *Tsinghua Journal of Education (Qinghua Daxue Jiaoyu Yanjiu)*, S1: 10–15.

Li, J. (2012), 'World-class higher education and the emerging Chinese model of the university', *Prospects*, 42 (3): 319–39.

Li, W. (2008), 'Education inequality in China: Problems of policies on access to higher education', *Journal of Asian Public Policy*, 1 (1): 115–23.

Li, W., K. Yan, and Y. Wang (2016), 'Types and growth factors of college students from impoverished rural areas: An empirical study of "elf-improvement Program" participants (Gaoxiao nongcun pinkun xuesheng de leixing fenxi yu chengzhang yinsu yanjiu: "Ziqiang Jihua" xuesheng diaocha)', *Tsinghua Journal of Education (Tsinghua Daxue Jiaoyu Yanjiu)*, 37 (1): 99–104.

Liang, Q. (1989a), *General Discussions on Reformation (Bianfa Tongyi)* (Vol. 1), Beijing: Zhonghua Shuju.

Liang, Q. (1989b), *A Study on Parliament (Gu Yi Yuankao)* (Vol. 1), Beijing: Zhonghua Shuju.

Liang, S. (1990), *Main Ideas of Chinese Culture* (Vol. 3), Jinan: Shandong Renmin Chubanshe.

Liang, T. (2018), 'The evolution of the "center-periphery" game from the perspective of imperialism and China's responses (Meiyuan baquan xia de 'zhongxin-waiwei' boyi dui zhongguo de yingxiang yu yingdui,') *Finance & Economics (Caijing Kexue)*, 7: 25–36.

Light, D. and J.P. Spiegel (1977), *The Dynamics of University Protest*, Chicago: Nelson Hall.

Lin, T. and Q. Zhou (1995), 'The dynamism and tension in the anthropocosmic vision of Mou zongsan:-A reflection on Confucian concept of tianren heyi', *Journal of Chinese Philosophy*, 22 (4): 401–40.

Lin, Y.-m. (2011), 'Transformation of work in post-1978 China', in X. Zang (ed.), *Understanding Chinese Society*, 142–55, Oxford: Routledge.

Lindbeck, A. and J.W. Weibull (1993), 'A model of political equilibrium in a representative democracy', *Journal of Public Economics*, 51 (2): 195–209.

Liu, C. (2011), 'Contested ground: Community and neighbourhood', in X. Zang (ed.), *Understanding Chinese Society*, 67–82, Oxford: Routledge.

Liu, T. (2009), 'Key factors of China's higher education massification in financial crisis (Jinrongweiji xia woguo gaodeng jiaoyu guimo kuozhang de yinsu fenxi)', *University Education Science (Daxue Jiaoyu Kexue)*, 6: 45–50.

Liu, Y. (2013), 'Meritocracy and the Gaokao: A survey study of higher education selection and socio-economic participation in East China', *British Journal of Sociology of Education*, 34 (5-6): 868–87.

Liu, Y. (2015), 'Geographical stratification and the role of the state in access to higher education in contemporary China', *International Journal of Educational Development*, 44: 108–17.

Liu, Y. (2016), *Higher Education, Meritocracy and Inequality in China*, Singapore: Springer.

Locatelli, R. (2019), *Reframing Education as a Public and Common Good: Enhancing Democratic Governance*, London: Palgrave Macmillan.

Locke, J. ([1689] 1976), *Second Treatise of Government (An Essay Concerning the True Original, Extent and End of Civil Government) and A Letter Concerning Toleration*, Oxford: Basil Blackwell.

Lomonaco, J. (1999), *The Government of Civil Society and the Self: Adam Smith's Political and Moral Thought*, Baltimore: Johns Hopkins University Press.

Løvlie, L., K.P. Mortensen, and S.E. Nordenbo (2003), *Educating Humanity: Bildung in Postmodernity*, Oxford: Blackwell.

Lu, Q. (2007), 'The study and comparison on realization of ancient qualification and right to education: Take "avoiding priviledge" as the clue', Ph.D. diss., East China University of Political Science and Law, Shanghai.

Lu, Y., A. Huang, and W. Huang (2015), 'Cost study of admissions system based on the right to autonomous enrollment and university choice: With American universities as a reference [Kaohou shuangxiang zizhu xuanze de zhaosheng tixi chengben yanjiu: yi Meiguo daxue wei canzhao]', *Tsinghua Journal of Education (Tsinghuaua Daxue Jiayu Yanjiu)*, 36 (1): 111–17.

Lu, Y. and G. Jover (2019), 'An anthropocosmic view: What Confucian traditions can teach us about the past and future of Chinese higher education', *Higher Education*, 77: 423–36.

Lu, Y. and X. Yu (2014), 'How to reform the university admission system in China? (Daxue zhaokao zhidu ruhe gaige?)', *Social Outlook (Shehui guancha)*, 3: 42–5.

Lucy, J.A. (1994), 'The role of semantic value in lexical comparison: Motion and position roots in Yucatec Maya', *Linguistics*, 32 (4-5): 623–56.

Lukes, S. (1973), *Individualism*, Oxford: Blackwell.

Luo, Y., F. Guo, and J. Shi (2018), 'Expansion and inequality of higher education in China: How likely would Chinese poor students get to success?' *Higher Education Research & Development*, 37 (5): 1015–34.

Lv, X. (1997), 'Minor public economy: The revolutionary origins of the danwei', in X. Lv and E.J. Perry (eds.), *Danwei: The Changing Chinese Working Place in a Comparative Perspective*, 21–41, New York: ME Sharpe Inc.

Maçaes, B. (2019), *Belt and Road: A Chinese World Order*, Oxford: Oxford University Press.

Manent, P. (1996), *An Intellectual History of Liberalism*, Princeton: Princeton University Press.

Mansbridge, J. (1998), 'On the contested nature of the public good', in W.W. Powell and E.S. Clemens (eds.), *Private Action and the Public Good*, 3–19, New Haven: Yale University Press.

Mao, Z. (2004), 'On the new stage', in S. Schram (ed.), *Mao's Road to Power: Revolutionary Writings, 1912–1949*, New York: M. E. Sharpe.

Marginson, S. (1997), *Markets in Education*, Sydney: Allen & Unwin Sydney.

Marginson, S. (2006), 'Putting "public" back into the public university', *Thesis Eleven*, 84 (1): 44–59.

Marginson, S. (2007), 'The public/private divide in higher education: A global revision', *Higher Education*, 53 (3): 307–33.

Marginson, S. (2011a), 'Equity, status and freedom: A note on higher education', *Cambridge Journal of Education*, 41 (1): 23–36.

Marginson, S. (2011b), 'Higher education and public good', *Higher Education Quarterly*, 65 (4): 411–33.

Marginson, S. (2011c), 'Higher education in East Asia and Singapore: Rise of the Confucian model', *Higher Education*, 61 (5): 587–611.

Marginson, S. (2013a), 'Higher education and public good', in P. Gibbs and R. Barnett (eds.), *Thinking about Higher Education*, 53–69, Basel: Spinger.

Marginson, S. (2013b), 'The impossibility of capitalist markets in higher education', *Journal of Education Policy*, 28 (3): 353–70.

Marginson, S. (2014a), 'Academic freedom: A global comparative approach', *Frontiers of Education in China*, 9 (1): 24–41.

Marginson, S. (2014b), 'Emerging higher education in the post-Confucian heritage zone', in D. Araya and P. Marber (eds.), *Higher Education in the Global Age: Education Policy, Practice and Promise in Emerging Societies*, 89–112, New York: Routledge.

Marginson, S. (2014c), 'Higher education and public good: A global study', in G. Goastellec and F. Picard (eds.), *Higher Education in Societies: A Multi-scale Perspective*, 51–72, Rotterdam: Sense Publisher.

Marginson, S. (2014d), 'Student self-formation in international education', *Journal of Studies in International Education*, 18 (1): 6–22.

Marginson, S. (2016a), *The Dream is Over: The Crisis of Clark Kerr's California Idea of Higher Education*, Berkeley: University of California Press.

Marginson, S. (2016b), 'Foreword: The partial shift from public to private goods in UK higher education', *London Review of Education*, 14 (1): 4–10.

Marginson, S. (2016c), *Higher Education and the Common Good*, Melbourne: Melbourne University Publishing.

Marginson, S. (2018a), 'Equity', in B. Cantwell, S. Marginson, and A. Smolentseva (eds.), *High Participation Systems of Higher Education*, 151–83, Oxford: Oxford University Press.

Marginson, S. (2018b), 'Global cooperation and national competition in the world-class university sector', in Y. Wu, Q. Wang, and N.C. Liu (eds.), *World-Class Universities*, 13–53, Netherlands: Brill Sense.

Marginson, S. (2018c), 'High participation systems of higher education', in B. Cantwell, S. Marginson, and A. Smolentseva (eds.), *High Participation Systems of Higher Education*, 3–38, Oxford: Oxford University Press.

Marginson, S. (2018d), *Higher Education as Self-formation*, London: UCL IOE Press.

Marginson, S. (2018e), 'Higher education, economic inequality and social mobility: Implications for emerging East Asia', *International Journal of Educational Development*, 63: 4–11.

Marginson, S. (2018f), 'National/global synergy in the development of higher education and science in China since 1978', *Frontiers of Education in China*, 13 (4): 486–512.

Marginson, S. (2018g), 'The new geo-politics of higher education: Global cooperation, national competition and social inequality in the World-Class University (WCU) sector', *Centre for Global Higher Education Working Papers, No. 34*, London: UCL Institute of Education. Available online: https://www.researchcghe.org/publications/working-paper/the-new-geo-politics-of-higher-education/ (accessed 25 February 2021).

Marginson, S. (2018h), 'Public/private in higher education: A synthesis of economic and political approaches', *Studies in Higher Education*, 42 (2): 322–37.

Marginson, S. (2018i), 'World higher education under conditions of national/global disequilibria', *Centre for Global Higher Education Working Papers, No. 42*, London: UCL Institute of Education. Available online: https://www.researchcghe.org/publications/working-paper/world-higher-education-under-conditions-of-nationalglobal-disequilibria/ (accessed 25 February 2021).

Marginson, S. (2019), 'Limitations of human capital theory', *Studies in Higher Education*, 44 (2): 287–301.

Marginson, S. and L. Yang (2020), 'China meets Anglo-America on the New Silk Road: A comparison of state, society, self and higher education', in M. van der Wende, W.C. Kirby, N.C. Liu, and S. Marginson (eds.), *China and Europe on the New Silk Road: Connecting Universities across Eurasia*, 255–83, Oxford: Oxford University Press.

Marginson, S. and L. Yang (2021), 'Individual and collective outcomes of higher education: A comparison of Anglo-American and Chinese approaches', *Globalisation, Societies and Education*, https://doi.org/10.1080/14767724.2021.1932436

Maskus, K.E. and J.H. Reichman (2004), 'The globalization of private knowledge goods and the privatization of global public goods', *Journal of International Economic Law*, 7 (2): 279–320.

Mazzarol, T. and G.N. Soutar (2002), '"Push-pull" factors influencing international student destination choice', *International Journal of Educational Management*, 16 (2): 82–90.
McCormick, C.T. and K.K. White (2011), *Folklore: An encyclopedia of Beliefs, Customs, Tales, Music, and Art* (2nd edn.), Santa Barbara: ABC-CLIO.
McCowan, T. (2016), 'Three dimensions of equity of access to higher education', *Compare: A Journal of Comparative and International Education*, 46 (4): 645–65.
McMahon, W.W. (2009), *Higher Learning, Greater Good: The Private and Social Benefits of Higher Education*, Baltimore: Johns Hopkins University Press.
Mill, J.S. ([1825] 1996), 'Law of liber and liberty of the press', in J.M. Robson (ed.), *The Collected Works of John Stuart Mill (Vol. Essays on Equality, Law, and Education)*, 3–34, London and New York: Routledge.
Mill, J.S. ([1859] 2015), *On Liberty, Utilitarianism, and Other Essays*, Oxford: Oxford University Press.
Mill, J.S. ([1861] 2015), *On Liberty, Utilitarianism, and Other Essays*, Oxford: Oxford University Press.
Mill, J.S. ([1869] 1996), 'The subjection of women', in J.M. Robson (ed.), *The Collected Works of John Stuart Mill (Vol. Essays on Equality, Law, and Education)*, 261–340, London and New York: Routledge.
Miller, F.D. (1997), *Nature, Justice, and Rights in Aristotle's Politics*, Oxford: Oxford University Press.
Moindjie, M.A. (2006), 'A Comparative Study of Literary Translation from Arabic into English and French', Ph.D. diss., Universiti Sains Malaysia, Penang.
Mok, K.H. (2013), *Centralization and Decentralization: Educational Reforms and Changing Governance in Chinese Societies* (Vol. 13), Singapore: Springer Science & Business Media.
Molloy, J.C. (2011), 'The open knowledge foundation: Open data means better science', *PLoS biology*, 9 (12): e1001195.
Monks, J. (2000), 'The returns to individual and college characteristics: Evidence from the National Longitudinal Survey of Youth', *Economics of Education Review*, 19 (3): 279–89.
Montgomery, C. (2010), *Understanding the International Student Experience*, London: Macmillan International Higher Education.
Moon, R.J. and J.-W. Koo (2011), 'Global citizenship and human rights: A longitudinal analysis of social studies and ethics textbooks in the Republic of Korea', *Comparative Education Review*, 55 (4): 574–99.
Morales, M.H. (1996), *Perfect Equality: John Stuart Mill on Well-constituted Communities*, Lanham: Rowman and Littlefield.
Mou, Z. (1999), *The Mind and Dispositions (Xin ti yu xing ti)*, Shanghai: Shanghai Gu Ji Chu Ban She.
Mueller-Vollmer, K.M. (2017), 'Wilhem von Humboldt', in E.N. Zalta (ed.), *The Stanford Encyclopedia of Philosophy* (Spring 2017 edn.), Stanford: Metaphysics Research Lab,

Stanford University. Available online: https://plato.stanford.edu/entries/wilhelm-humboldt/ (accessed 25 February 2021).

Muhlhahn, K. (2019), *Making China Modern: From the Great Qing to Xi Jinping*. Cambridge: The Belknap Press of Harvard University Press.

Mullis, E.C. (2008), 'Ritualized exchange: A consideration of Confucian reciprocity', *Asian Philosophy*, 18 (1): 35–50.

Nagel, T. (1989), *The View from Nowhere*, Oxford: Oxford University Press.

Naidoo, R. (2004), 'Fields and institutional strategy: Bourdieu on the relationship between higher education, inequality and society', *British Journal of Sociology of Education*, 25 (4): 457–71.

Naidoo, R. and J. Williams (2015), 'The neoliberal regime in English higher education: Charters, consumers and the erosion of the public good', *Critical Studies in Education*, 56 (2): 208–23.

Narveson, J. (1984), 'Equality vs. liberty: Advantage, liberty', *Social Philosophy and Policy*, 2 (1): 33–60.

Needham, J. (1969), *The Grand Titrantion: Science and Society in East and West*, Toronto: University of Toronto Press.

Nelson, C. (2010), *No University is an Island: Saving Academic Freedom*, New York and London: New York University Press.

Neubauer, D. (2008), 'The historical transformation of public good', *Journal of Asian Public Policy*, 1 (2): 127–38.

Neumayer, E. (2006), 'Unequal access to foreign spaces: How states use visa restrictions to regulate mobility in a globalized world', *Transactions of the Institute of British Geographers*, 31 (1): 72–84.

Newman, J.H. ([1852] 1996), 'Discourse VII: Knowledge view in relation to professional skill', in F.M. Turner (ed.), *The Idea of A University*, 108–26, New Haven and London: Yale University Press.

Niu, G. (2011), 'Liberalism and Confucianism: Rights and virtues', *Core Ethics*, 7: 235–48.

Nixon, J. (2011), *Higher Education and the Public Good: Imagining the University*, London: Bloomsbury Publishing.

Nonini, D.M. (2008), 'Is China becoming neoliberal?' *Critique of anthropology*, 28 (2): 145–76.

Novelli, M. (2013), *The New Geopolitics of Educational Aid: From Cold wars to Holy Wars?* Netherlands: Brill Sense.

Nuyen, A.T. (2001), 'Confucianism and the Idea of Equality', *Asian Philosophy*, 11 (2): 61–71.

Nybom, T. (2003), 'The Humboldt legacy: Reflections on the past, present, and future of the European university', *Higher Education Policy*, 16 (2): 141–59.

Nyborg, P. (2003), 'Higher education as a public good and a public responsibility', *Higher Education in Europe*, 28 (3): 355–9.

O'Sullivan, K., J. Robson, and N. Winters (2019), '"I feel like I have a disadvantage": How socio-economically disadvantaged students make the decision to study at a prestigious university', *Studies in Higher Education*, 44 (9): 1676–90.

Olson, M. (1965), *The Logic of Collective Action: Public Goods and the Theory of Groups*, Cambridge, MA: Harvard University Press.

Ophuls, W. (1973), 'Leviathan or oblivion', in H.E. Daly (ed.), *Toward a Steady State Economy*, 215-30, San Francisco: Freeman.

Osgood, C.E. (1964), 'Semantic differential technique in the comparative study of cultures', *American Anthropologist*, 66 (3): 171-200.

Östling, J. (2018), *Humboldt and the Modern German University: An Intellectual History*, trans. L. Olsson, Lund: Lund University Press.

Ostrom, E. (1990), *Governing the Commons: The Evolution of Institutions for Collective Action*, Cambridge: Cambridge University Press.

Ostrom, E. (2010), 'Beyond markets and states: Polycentric governance of complex economic systems', *American Economic Review*, 100 (3): 641-72.

Ouyang, Z. (1992), 'Family education in ancient China', *Journal of Nanchang University: Humanities and Social Science*, 1: 55-60.

Palfreyman, D. (2007), 'Is academic freedom under threat in UK and US higher education?' *Education and the Law*, 19 (1): 19-40.

Pan, S.Y. (2007), 'Intertwining of academia and officialdom and university autonomy: Experience from Tsinghua University in China', *Higher Education Policy*, 20 (2): 121-44.

Pan, S.Y. (2009), *University Autonomy, the State and Social Change in China*, Hong Kong: Hong Kong University Press.

Parsons, T. and E.A. Shils (1951), 'Values, motives, and systems of action', *Toward A General Theory of Action*, 33: 247-75.

Pasque, P. (2010), *American Higher Education, Leadership, and Policy: Critical Issues and the Public Good*, New York: Palgrave Macmillan.

Paulsen, M.B. and J.C. Smart (2001), *The Finance of Higher Education: Theory, Research, Policy, and Practice*, New York: Algora Publishing.

Peterson, A. (2011), *Civic Republicanism and Civic Education: The Education of Citizens*, New York: Palgrave Macmillan.

Pink, T. (2004), *Free Will: A Very Short Introduction*. Oxford: Oxford University Press.

Plato and A. Bloom ([1968] 1991), *The Republic of Plato (Translated with Notes and Interpretive Essay by Allan Bloom)* (2nd edn.), New York: BasicBooks.

Popadiuk, S. and C.W. Choo (2006), 'Innovation and knowledge creation: How are these concepts related?' *International Journal of Information Management*, 26 (4): 302-12.

Pring, R. (2002), *Philosophy of Educational Research*, London: Continuum.

Pritchard, R.M.O. (1998), 'Freedom and autonomy in the United Kingdom and Germany', *Minerva*, 36 (2): 101-24.

Pusser, B. (2006), 'Reconsidering higher education and the public good', in W.G. Tierney (ed.), *Governance and the Public Good*, 11-28, Albany: State University of New York Press.

Qi, H. and D. Shen (2015), 'Chinese traditional world citizenship thoughts and its impact on the cultivation of Chinese world citizenship awareness', *Citizenship Studies*, 19 (3-4): 267-84.

Qi, Q. (2012), *The Evolutionary History of Chinese Society in the late Qing Dynasty (Wanqing shehui sichao yanjinshi)*, Beijing: Zhonghua Shuju.

Qian, M. ([2005] 2016), *Discussions on Modern China's Academy (Xiandai Zhongguo Xueshu Lunheng)*, Beijing: Joint Publishing (Sanlian Shudian).

Qin, X. (1981), *A History of Cultural Development in the Republic of China (Zhonghua Minguo Wenhua Fazhanshi)*, Taipei: Taiwan Jindai Zhongguo Chubanshe.

Qu, Z. (2014), 'Building the governance system of higher education with Chinese characteristics (Jianshe zhongguo tese gaodeng jiaoyu zhili tixi)', *China Higher Education Research (Zhongguo Gaojiao Yanjiu)*, 1: 1–4.

Ramirez, F.O. and Y.-K. Cha (1990), 'Citizenship and gender: Western educational developments in comparative perspective', *Research in Sociology of Education and Socialization*, 9, 153–73.

Randall, A. (1983), 'The problem of market failure', *Nature Resources Journal*, 23 (1): 131–48.

Ranson, S. (2003), 'Public accountability in the age of neo-liberal governance', *Journal Education Policy*, 18 (5): 459–80.

Rao, J.M., E.B. Kapstein, and A. Sen (1999), 'Equity and Justice', in I. Kaul, I. Grunberg, and M. Stern (eds.), *Global Public Goods: International Cooperation in the 21st Century*, 66–7, Oxford: Oxford University Press.

Rawls, J. ([1971] 2001), *Justice as Fairness* (Original edn.), Cambridge, MA: The Belknap Press of Harvard University Press.

Rawls, J. ([1971] 2005), *A Theory of Justice* (Original edn.), Cambridge, MA: Harvard University Press.

Rawls, J. ([1993] 2004), *Political Liberalism*, New York: Columbia University Press.

Reischauer, E.O. (1974), 'The Chinese world in perspective', *Foreign Affairs; an American Quarterly Review*, 52 (2): 341.

Ren, K. and J. Li (2013), 'Academic freedom and university autonomy: A higher education policy perspective', *Higher Education Policy*, 26 (4): 507–22.

Retter, H. (2012), 'Dewey's progressive education, experience and instrumental pragmatism with particular reference to the concept of Bildung', in P. Siljander, A. Kivelä, and A. Sutinen (eds.), *Theories of Bildung and Growth: Connections and Controversies between Continental Educational Thinking and American Pragmatism*, 281–302, Rotterdam: Sense Publishers.

Rhoads, R.A. (2011), 'The US research university as a global model: Some fundamental problems to consider', *InterActions: UCLA Journal of Education and Information Studies*, 2. Available online: https://escholarship.org/content/qt8b91s24r/qt8b91s24r.pdf (accessed 20 December 2019).

Rieckmann, M. (2012), 'Future-oriented higher education: Which key competencies should be fostered through university teaching and learning?' *Futures*, 44 (2): 127–35.

Riley, J. (1988), *Liberal Utilitarianism: Social Choice Theory and J. S. Mill's Philosophy*, Cambridge: Cambridge University Press.

Robertson, S.L. (2010), 'Corporatisation, competitiveness, commercialisation: New logics in the globalising of UK higher education', *Globalisation, Societies and Education*, 8 (2): 191–203.

Rohstock, A. (2012), 'Some things never change: The invention of Humboldt in Western higher education systems', in P. Siljander, A. Kivelä, and A. Sutinen (eds.), *Theories of Bildung and Growth: Connections and Controversies between Continental Educational Thinking and American Pragmatism*, 165–82, Rotterdam: Sense Publishers.

Rosemont Jr, H. (2015), *Against Individualism: A Confucian Rethinking of the Foundations of Morality, Politics, Family, and Religion*, London: Lexington Books.

Ryan, A. (2012), *The Making of Modern Liberalism*, Princeton and Oxford: Princeton University Press.

Sadiq, S. (2010), *A Comparative Study of Four English Translations of Surat Ad-Dukhan on the Semantic Level*, Cambridge: Cambridge Scholars Publishing.

Samuelson, P.A. (1954), 'The pure theory of public expenditure', *The Review of Economics and Statistics*, 36 (4): 387–9.

Sayer, A. (2011), *Why Things Matter to People: Social Science, Values and Ethical Life*, Cambridge: Cambridge University Press.

Scalapino, R.A. (1988), *Asian Communism: Continuity and Transition* (Vol. 15), Berkeley: University of California Inst of East.

Schendel, R. and T. McCowan (2016), 'Expanding higher education systems in low-and middle-income countries: The challenges of equity and quality', *Higher Education*, 72 (4): 407–11.

Schumann, C. (2019), 'Aversive education: Emersonian variations on "Bildung"', *Educational Philosophy and Theory*, 51 (5): 488–97.

Schumpeter, J. (1980), *Methodological Individualism*. Brussels: European Institute.

Schwartz, B. (1965), 'Modernisation and the Maoist vision—some reflections on Chinese communist goals', *The China Quarterly*, 21: 3–19.

Schwartz, B. (1987), 'The primacy of the political order in East Asian societies: Some preliminary generalizations', in S.R. Schram (ed.), *Foundations and Limits of State Power in China*, 1–10, Hong Kong: The Chinese University Press.

Schwenk, B. (1996), 'Bildung', in D. Lenzen (ed.), *Padagogische Grundbegriffe*, Hamburg: Rowohlt Taschenbuch Verlag.

Secada, W. (1989), 'Educational equity versus equality of education: An alternative conception', in W. Secada (ed.), *Equity and Education*, 68–88, New York: Falmer.

Sen, A. (1985), 'Well-being, agency and freedom: The Dewey Lectures 1984', *The Journal of Philosophy*, 82 (4): 169–221.

Sen, A. (1992), *Inequality Reexamined*, Oxford: Clarendon Press.

Sen, A. (1993), 'Positional objectivity', *Philosophy & Public Affairs*, 22 (2): 126–45.

Sen, A. (1999), *Development as Freedom*, Oxford: Oxford University Press.

Sen, A. (2002), *Rationality and Freedom*, Cambridge, MA: The Belknap Press of Harvard University Press.

Sen, A. (2006), *The Idea of Justice*. Cambridge, MA: The Belknap Press of Harvard University Press.

Sen, A. and B. Williams (1982), 'Introduction: Utilitarianism and beyond', in A. Sen and B. Williams (eds.), *Utilitarianism and Beyond*, 1–21, Cambridge: Cambridge University Press.

Shahjahan, R.A. and A.J. Kezar (2013), 'Beyond the "national container" addressing methodological nationalism in higher education research', *Educational Researcher*, 42 (1): 20–9.

Shao, Q. (2015), 'American academic freedom and Chinese nationalism: An H-Asia debate', *Positions: East Asia Cultures Critique*, 23 (1): 41–8.

Shavit, Y. (2007), *Stratification in Higher Education: A Comparative Study*, Stanford: Stanford University Press.

Shelton, L.J. and C.W. Yao (2019), 'Early career professionals' perceptions of higher education and student affairs graduate programs: Preparation to work with international students', *Journal of College Student Development*, 6 (2): 156–72.

Shils, E. (1991), 'The virtue of civil society', *Government and Opposition*, 26 (1): 3–20.

Siljander, P., A. Kivelä, and A. Sutinen (2012), *Theories of Bildung and Growth: Connections and Controversies between Continental Educational Thinking and American Pragmatism*, Rotterdam: Sense Publishers.

Siljander, P. and A. Sutinen (2012), 'Introduction', in P. Siljander, A. Kivelä, and A. Sutinen (eds.), *Theories of Bildung and Growth: Connections and Controversies between Continental Educational Thinking and American Pragmatism*, 1–18, Rotterdam: Sense Publishers.

Slaughter, S. and L.L. Leslie (1997), *Academic Capitalism: Politics, Policies, and the Entrepreneurial University*, Baltimore: The Johns Hopkins University Press.

Smith, A. ([1790] 2010), *The Theory of Moral Sentiments*, London: Penguin.

Smith, A. ([1827] 2000), *An Inquiry into the Nature and Causes of the Wealth of Nations*, New York: The Moder Library.

Smith, R.J. (1981), 'Resolving the tragedy of the commons by creating private property rights in wildlife', *CATO Journal*, 1: 439–68.

Spann, R.M. (1974), 'Collective consumption of private goods', *Public Choice*, 20 (1): 63–81.

Stiglitz, J.E. (1999), 'Knowledge as a global public goods', in I. Kaul, I. Grunberg, and M. Stern (eds.), *Global Public Goods: International Cooperation in the 21st Century*, 308–25, Oxford: Oxford University Press.

Strauss, L. (1959), 'The liberalism of classical political philosophy', *The Review of Metaphysics*, 12 (3): 390–439.

Sun, P. (2001), 'Studies of early modernization of Chinese education (Zhongguo jiaoyu zaoqi xiandaihua yanjiu)', Ph.D. diss., East China Normal University, Shanghai.

Swales, K. (2016), *Understanding the Leave Vote*. Available online: http://natcen.ac.uk/media/1319222/natcen_brexplanationsreport-final-web2.pdf (accessed 5 May 2018).

Szadkowski, K. (2019), 'The common in higher education: A conceptual approach', *Higher Education*, 78: 241–55.

Tan, C. (2017), 'A Confucian perspective of self-cultivation in learning: Its implications for self-directed learning', *Journal of Adult and Continuing Education*, 23 (2): 250–62.

Tang, Y. (2015), *Confucianism, Buddhism, Daoism, Christianity and Chinese Culture*, Heidelberg: Springer.

Tawney, R.H. (1938), *Equality* (3rd edn.), London: George Allen & Unwin LTD.

Taylor, C.A. (2017), 'Is a posthumanist Bildung possible? Reclaiming the promise of Bildung for contemporary higher education', *Higher Education*, 74 (3): 419–35.

Taylor, I. (2014), 'Distributive justice and global public good', DPhil diss., University of Oxford, Oxford.

Thorens, J. (1993), 'Proposal for an international declaration on academic freedom and university autonomy', in E.C.F.H.E.U. Autonomy (ed.), *Academic Freedom and University Autonomy*, Bucharest: UNESCO European Centre for Higher Education.

Tian, L. and N.C. Liu (2018), 'Local and global public good contributions of higher education in China', *Centre for Global Higher Education Working Paper, No. 37*, London: UCL Institute of Education. Available online: https://www.researchcghe.org/publications/working-paper/local-and-global-public-good-contributions-of-higher-education-in-china/ (accessed 25 February 2021).

Tierney, W.G. and M. Lanford (2014), 'The question of academic freedom: Universal right or relative term', *Frontiers of Education in China*, 9 (1): 4–23.

Tierney, W.G. and Q. Zha (2014), 'The changing nature of academic freedom in an age of globalization', *Frontiers of Education in China*, 9 (1): 1–3.

Tilak, J.B. (2008), 'Higher education: A public good or a commodity for trade?' *Prospects*, 38 (4): 449–66.

Traianou, A. (2015), 'The erosion of academic freedom in the UK higher education', *Ethics in Science and Environmental Politics*, 15: 39–47.

Tran, L.T. (2016), 'Mobility as 'becoming': A Bourdieuian analysis of the factors shaping international student mobility', *British Journal of Sociology of Education*, 37 (8): 1268–89.

Triventi, M. (2013), 'The role of higher education stratification in the reproduction of social inequality in the labor market', *Research in Social Stratification and Mobility*, 32: 45–63.

Tröhler, D. (2012), 'The German idea of *Bildung* and the anti-Western ideology', in P. Siljander, A. Kivelä, and A. Sutinen (eds.), *Theories of Bildung and Growth: Connections and Controversies between Continental Educational Thinking and American Pragmatism*, 149–64, Rotterdam: Sense Publishers.

Trow, M. ([1973] 2010a), 'Problems in the transition from elite to mass higher education', in M. Burrage (ed.), *Martin Trow, Twentieth-Century Higher Education: Elite to Mass to Universal*, 86–142, Baltimore: The Johns Hopkins University Press.

Trow, M. ([1976] 2010b), 'Elite higher education: An endangered species?' in M. Burrage (ed.), *Twentieth-Century Higher Education: Elite to Mass to Universal*, 143–75, Baltimore: The Johns Hopkins University Press.

Trow, M. ([1991] 2010c), 'Federalism in American higher education', in M. Burrage (ed.), *Twentieth-Century Higher Education: Elite to Mass to Universal*, 175–207, Baltimore: The Johns Hopkins University Press.
Tu, W.-M. (1979), 'Ultimate self-transformation as a communal act: Comments on modes of self-cultivation in traditional China', *Journal of Chinese Philosophy*, 6: 237–46.
Tu, W.-M. (1985), *Confucian Thought: Selfhood as Creative Transformation*, Albany: State University of New York Press.
Tu, W.-M. (1989), 'The rise of industrial East Asia: The role of Confucian values', *The Copenhagen Journal of Asian Studies*, 4 (1): 81.
Tu, W.-M. (1994), 'The historical significance of the Confucian discourse', *The China Quarterly*, 140: 1131–41.
Tu, W.-M. (1998a), 'Confucius and Confuciansim', in W.H. Slote and G.A. DeVos (eds.), *Confucianism and the Family*, 3–36, Albany: State University of New York Press.
Tu, W.-M. (1998b), 'Probing the "three bonds" and "five relationships" in Confucian humanism', in W.H. Slote and G.A. DeVos (eds.), *Confucianism and the Family*, 121–36, Albany: State University of New York Press.
Tu, W.-M. (2013), 'Confucian humanism in perspective', *Frontiers of Literary Studies in China*, 7 (3): 333–8.
Turner, R.S. (2008), *Neo-liberal Ideology: History, Concepts and Policies*, Edinburgh: Edinburgh University Press.
UNESCO (2015), *Rethinking Education: Towards A Global Common Good?* Paris: UNESCO.
UNESCO (2018), UNESCO Institute for Statistics data on education. Available online: http://data.uis.unesco.org/ (accessed 24 December 2019).
UNESCO (2020), UNESCO Institute for Statistics data on education. Available online: http://data.uis.unesco.org/ (accessed 6 April 2022).
Unterhalter, E. (2008), 'Cosmopolitanism, global social justice and gender equality in education', *Compare: A Journal of Comparative and International Education*, 38 (5): 539–53.
Viner, J. (1960), 'The intellectual history of laissez faire', *The Journal of Law and Economics*, 3: 45–69.
Vogel, E.F. (2011), *Deng Xiaoping and the Transformation of China* (Vol. 10), Cambridge, MA: Belknap Press of Harvard University Press.
von Humboldt, W. (2000), 'Theory of Bildung', in I. Westbury, S. Hopmann, and K. Riquarts (eds.), *Teaching As A Reflective Practice: The German Didaktik tradition*, 57–62, New York: Routledge.
Walberg, H.J. and S.-L. Tsai (1983), 'Matthew effects in education', *American Educational Research Journal*, 20 (3): 359–73.
Wang, B. (2017), 'Introduction', in B. Wang (ed.), *Chinese Visions of World Order: Tianxia, Culture, and World Politics*, 1–24, Durham and London: Duke University Press.

Wang, H. (1991), *A Study of Village Chinese Family Culture in Contemporary China (Dangdai Zhongguo Cunluo Jiazu Wenhua)*, Shanghai: Shanghai People's Press.

Wang, H. (2011), 'Access to higher education in China: Differences in opportunity', *Frontiers of Education in China*, 6 (2): 227–47.

Wang, H. (2014), 'The nature and mission of higher education (Lun gaodeng jiaoyu de benzhi shuxing jiqi shiming)', *Journal of Higher Education (Gaodeng jiaoyu yanjiu)*, 35 (6): 1–7.

Wang, J.C. (2012), *John Dewey in China: To Teach and to Learn*, Albany: State University of New York Press.

Wang, L. (2010), 'Higher education governance and university autonomy in China', *Globalisation, Societies and Education*, 8 (4): 477–95.

Wang, R. (2012), *Yinyang: The Way of Heaven and Earth in Chinese Thought and Culture*, Cambridge: Cambridge University Press.

Wang, S. (1915), 'The problem of the new and the old (Xinjiu wenti)', *Youths' Magazine (Qingnian zazhi)*, 1 (1): 1G4.

Weber, M. ([1922] 1968), *Economy and Society*, eds., G. Roth and C. Wittich, Berkeley: University of California Press.

Wei, Y. and H. Chen (1998), *Illustrated Annals of Overseas Countries (Haiguo tuzhi)* (Vol. 2), Changsha: Yuelu Shushe Chubanshe.

Williams, G. (2016), 'Higher education: Public good or private commodity?' *London Review of Education*, 14 (1): 131–42.

Williams, J. (2014), 'Defending knowledge as the public good of higher education', in G. Goastellec and F. Picard (eds.), *Higher Education in Societies: A Multi-scale Perspective*, 73–86, Rotterdam: Sense Publishers.

Williams, J. (2016), 'A critical exploration of changing definitions of public good in relation to higher education', *Studies in Higher Education*, 41 (4): 619–30.

Wills, R. (2017), 'Exploring the ethics of agency through the lens of Bildung', *International Journal of Children's Spirituality*, 22 (3–4): 317–28.

Wolff, R.P. (1992), *The Ideal of the University*, New Brunswick: Transaction Publishers.

Wu, H. and M. Li (2021), 'Three phases of De Facto quasi-decentralization of higher education in China since 1949', *Higher Education Policy*, 34: 685–705.

Wu, L. (2005), 'The impact of Keju to education in ancient China', *Journal of Southwest Minzu University (Humanities and Social Science)*, 26 (5): 350–2.

Xia, G. (2014), 'China as a "civilization-state": A historical and comparative interpretation', *Procedia-Social and Behavioral Sciences*, 140: 43–7.

Xian, L. (2009), 'Two universities and two eras of Catholicism in China: Fu Jen University and Aurora University, 1903–1937', *Christian Higher Education*, 8 (5): 405–21.

Xie, M. (2018), 'Internationalizing Social Sciences in China: The Disciplinary Development of Sociology at Tsinghua University', Ph.D. diss., The University of Hong Kong, Hong Kong.

Xu, C. (2013), 'The commentary of Heilongjiang higher education during the period of the Republic of China (Minguo Shiqi Heilongjiang Gaodeng Jiaoyu Shulun)', Ph.D. diss., Jilin University, Changchun.

Xu, J. (2000), 'Educational institutions in ancient China', *Knowledge of Classic Literature*, 4: 112–19.

Xu, J. (2017), *Family, Nation and All under Heaven (Jiaguo tianxia)*, Shanghai: Shanghai People's Publishing (Shanghai Renmin Chubanshe).

Xu, X. (2020), 'The hunt for a coronavirus cure is showing how science can change for the better', Available online: https://theconversation.com/the-hunt-for-a-coronavirus-cure-is-showing-how-science-can-change-for-the-better-132130 (accessed 25 February 2021).

Xu, Z. (2018), 'Family, state, and tianxia: China and the world in peace', *Literature, History, and Philosophy (Wen, Shi, Zhe)*, 1: 14–19.

Xun, Y. (2002), 'The transition of Chinese higher education: An investigation of Chinese higher education between 1901 and 1936 (Zhongguo Gaodeng Jiaoyu cong Chuantong dao Xiandai de Zhuanxing)', Ph.D. diss., East China Normal University, Shanghai.

Yan, X. (2011), 'Xunzi's interstate political philosophy and its message for today (E. Ryden, Ttrans.)', in D.A. Bell and S. Zhe (eds.), *Ancient Chinese Thought, Modern Chinese Power*, 70–106, Princeton and Oxford: Princeton University Press.

Yan, Y. (2003), *Private Life under Socialism: Love, Intimacy, and Family Change in A Chinese Village, 1949–1999*, Stanford: Stanford University Press.

Yang, D. (2006), 'From equality of right to equality of opportunity: the slot of educational equity in new China (Cong quanli pingdeng dao jihui jundeng: Xinzhongguo jiaoyu gongping de guiju)', *Peking University Education Review (Beijing Daxue Jiaoyu Pinglun)*, 2: 2–11.

Yang, L. (2017), 'The public role of higher learning in Imperial China', *Centre for Global Higher Education Working Papers, No. 28*, London: UCL Institute of Education. Available online: https://www.researchcghe.org/publications/working-paper/the-public-role-of-higher-learning-in-imperial-china/ (accessed 25 February 2021).

Yang, R. (2000), 'Tensions between the global and the local: A comparative illustration of the reorganisation of China's higher education in the 1950s and 1990s', *Higher Education*, 39 (3): 319–37.

Yang, R. (2011), 'Self and the other in the Confucian cultural context: Implications of China's higher education development for comparative studies', *International Review of Education*, 57 (3): 337–55.

Yang, R. (2015), 'The concept of Tianxia and its impact on Chinese discourses on the West', in C. Halse (ed.), *Asia Literate Schooling in the Asian Century*, 44–55, Abington: Routledge.

Yang, R. (2018), 'Emulating or integrating? Modern transformations of Chinese higher education', *Journal of Asian Public Policy*, 12 (3): 294–311.

Yang, R. and Y. Shen (2020), 'Integrating Chinese and Western bodies of knowledge is an important pursuit of Chinese higher education (Ronghui zhongxi zhishi tixi shi woguo gaodengjiaoyu de zhongyao zhuiqiu)', *Guangming Daily (Guangming Ribao)*, 21 April 2020. Available online: https://news.gmw.cn/2020-04/21/content_33755308.htm (accessed 25 February 2021).

Yang, R., M. Xie, and W. Wen (2019), 'Pilgrimage to the west: Modern transformations of Chinese intellectual formation in social sciences', *Higher Education*, 77: 815–29.

Yang, W. (2011), 'A study on the school system of renxu (Renxu xuezhi yanjiu)', Ph.D. diss., Nanjing University, Nanjing.

Yu, K. and H. Ertl (2010), 'Equity in access to higher education in China: The role of public and nonpublic institutions', *Chinese Education & Society*, 43 (6): 36–58.

Yuan, X. (2012), 'Reflections on the social role of contemporary Chinese universities in the reform era', *Frontiers of Education in China*, 7 (2): 232–52.

Zang, X. (2011a), 'Family and marriage', in X. Zang (ed.), *Understanding Chinese Society*, 36–52, Abington: Routledge.

Zang, X. (2011b), 'Government and changing state-society relations', in X. Zang (ed.), *Understanding Chinese Society*, 170–83, Abington: Routledge.

Zha, Q. (2010), 'Academic freedom and public intellectuals in China', *International Higher Education*, 58: 17–18.

Zha, Q. and R. Hayhoe (2014), 'The "Beijing Consensus" and the Chinese model of university autonomy', *Frontiers of Education in China*, 9 (1): 42–62.

Zha, Q. and W. Shen (2018), 'The paradox of academic freedom in the Chinese context', *History of Education Quarterly*, 58 (3): 447–52.

Zhang, B. and Y. Sun (2004), 'Privileges of medieval universities in Western Europe (Xiou zhongshiji daxue de tequan)', *Journal of Beijing Normal University (Social Sciences) (Beijing Shifan Daxue Xuebao, Shehui Kexueban)*, 4: 16–23.

Zhang, D. (1985), 'An analysis of 'the unity of heaven and humanity' in Chinese philosophy (zhong guo zhe xue zhong 'tian ren he yi' si xiang pou xi)', *Journal of Peking University (Humanities and Social Sciences) (Bei Jing Da Xue Xue Bao, Zhe Xue She Hui Ke Xue Ban)*, 22 (1): 3–10.

Zhang, D. (1996), *The Collection of Works of Zhang Dainian (Zhang Dainian quanji)* (Vol. 1), Shijiazhuang: Hebei Remin Publishing (Hebei Renmin Chubanshe).

Zhang, D. (2002), *Key Concepts in Chinese Philosophy (translated by Edmund Ryden)*, Connecticut: Yale University Press.

Zhang, E. (2010), 'Community, the common good, and public healthcare—Confucianism and its relevance to contemporary China', *Public Health Ethics*, 3 (3): 259–66.

Zhang, G. (1979), *The Self-strengthening Movement and China's Recent Companies (Yangwu Yundong yu Zhongguo Jindai Qiye)* (Vol. 1), Beijing: Zhongguo Shehui Kexue Chubanshe.

Zhang, K. (2016), 'Research on the Relations between Public Universities of and the Government of the Republic of China: 1912–1937 (Minguo gongli daxue yu zhengfu guanxi yanjiu)', Ph.D. diss., Xinan University, Chongqing.

Zhang, L. (2008), 'The collapse of the Chinese imaginary of China as the Celestial Empire in the late Qing (Shilun tianchaoshangguo guannian zai wanqing de bengkui)', *Guangxi Shehui Kexue*, 7: 109–12.

Zhang, W. (2012), *The China Wave: Rise of A Civilizational State*, Singapore: World Scientific.

Zhang, W. and M. Bray (2017), 'Micro-neoliberalism in China: Public-private interactions at the confluence of mainstream and shadow education', *Journal of Education Policy*, 32 (1): 63–81.

Zhang, Y.B., M.-C. Lin, A. Nonaka, and K. Beom (2005), 'Harmony, hierarchy and conservatism: A cross-cultural comparison of Confucian values in China, Korea, Japan, and Taiwan', *Communication Research Reports*, 22 (2): 107–15.

Zhao, S. (1993), 'Deng Xiaoping's southern tour: Elite politics in post-Tiananmen China', *Asian Survey*, 33 (8): 739–56.

Zhao, T. (2003), 'The tianxia system: Empire and the world system (Tianxia tixi: diguo yu shijie zhidu)', *World Philosophy (Shijie Zhexue)*, 5: 2–33.

Zhao, T. (2011), *The Tianxia System: An Introduction to the Philosophy of World Institution (Tianxia tixi: Shijie zhidu zhexue daolun)*, Beijing: Renmin University Press (Zhongguo Renmin Daxue Chubanshe).

Zhao, T. (2018), 'The new tianxia-ism (Xin tianxia zhuyi zonglun)', *Literature, History, and Philosophy (Wen, Shi, Zhe)*, 1: 5–13.

Zhao, T. (2019), 'Tianxia: Between idealism and realism (Tianxia: Zai lixiangzhuyi yu xianshizhuyi zhijian)', *Exploration and Free Views (Tansuo yu zhengming)*, 9: 100–8.

Zheng, Y. (2010), 'Society must be defended: Reform, openness, and social policy in China', *Journal of Contemporary China*, 19 (67): 799–818.

Zhou, F. (1961), *Dong Zhongshu's thoughts (Lun Dong Zhongshu sixiang)*, Shanghai: Shanghai People's Publishing House (Shanghai Renmin Chubanshe).

Zhu, X. and Z. Lv ([1175] 2001), *Reflections on Things at Hand (Jinsi Lu)*, Jinan: Shangdong Youyi Press.

Zürcher, E. (2007), *The Buddhist Conquest of China: The Spread and Adaptation of Buddhism in Early Medieval China* (Vol. 11), Leiden: Brill.

Index

Page numbers followed with "n" refer to footnotes.

academic freedom   52, 55, 73, 83, 84, 98,
    127, 168, 199, 207–9, 221
  Chinese universities   139–40
  in higher education   136–40
  legal protection   138
  and university autonomy   141–3
  US and UK   138–9
agency   112
  free   195–8, 206–9
  human   202
  individual   196–8, 204, 221
  student   198
Altbach, P.G.   143
American universities   138, 141, 142, 189
Anglo-American traditions   5, 17, 27, 28,
    103, 124–5, 137, 162, 164, 195,
    199, 207, 218. *See also* Chinese
    traditions
  academia   209
  Bildung in   193, 195–8
    Dewey's idea of growth/
      education   99–101
    Sen's concept of capability   101–2
  communication sphere   156–7
  communicative inclusive public   212
  communicative public   146–7
  comparative methodology with
      Chinese tradition   13–14
  equality of freedom to achieve   201–4
  equity in   109–10, 199–201
    democracy   110
    social justice   110–15
    social order   115
  freedom to act   208–9
  global common goods in   174–5,
    177–8
  global public goods in   174–8
  higher education   11–12, 74
  individual autonomy in   206
  liberalism   6, 16, 60

liberty in   49, 81, 114, 132–4
market in   154–5
normative values   157–8
public   210–15
  and private   153–8
public-as-state   212
of public good   4, 6–7, 16
public/private dualism in   153–4
public spiritedness   197
scholarship examined for   8
self-determination in   129
society sphere   80–1
spheres of social action   63, 64
state sphere   81
university autonomy   141–2, 209
world sphere   81
anthropocosmic worldview   89–91, 162,
    178, 189, 195
atomic individualism   60, 103, 158
autonomy
  of higher education   168
  individual   34, 130, 135, 206–7
  institutional   52, 55, 73, 83, 84, 98
  moral   58, 93, 104, 128–30, 207, 209
    and individual   206
  university   17, 21, 73, 74, 207–9, 221

Bary, W.T.   9
basic liberties   55, 56, 65
Beiyang Gongxue   39
Bell, D.A.   9
Bellah, R.   95
Bell, D.A.   9
Belt and Road Initiative   148, 182
benchmarking   142–3
Berdahl, R.O.   140, 208
Berlin, I.   114
Biesta, G.   105
Bildung   3, 17, 21, 82–4, 87–9, 91, 92,
    96–7, 129, 136, 137, 208

    in Anglo-American traditions 99–102
    comparison of *xiushen* (self-
        cultivation) with 193, 195–8
    Dewey's idea of growth/
        education 99–101
    dualistic worldview 97–8
    environmental prerequisites
        of 101–2
    external emphasis 206
    higher education in 102–6
    public spiritedness in 197
    Sen's concept of capability 101–2
    as socially nested self-formation 99,
        100, 102, 103
Bodycott, P. 152
Bowen, W.G. 112

Cai Yuanpei 40
Calhoun, C. 169
California Master Plan 171
Callahan, W.A. 182
callous meritocratic society 93, 112,
    114, 121
Cantwell, B. 107
capability 63, 66–7, 89, 101–2, 104,
    114–15, 126, 134, 166, 185,
    197, 202
capitalist 43–5, 148–9
    society 4, 213, 215, 216, 220
Cardinal Principles 116–18
CCP. See Chinese Communist Party
    (CCP)
Chang, W. 9
Chan, J. 128, 130
Chang, W. 9
Chen, H. 108
Chen Duxiu 40
Cheng, C. 128
Cheng, K. 146
Cheng Yi 130
Chen, H. 108
Chinese civilization 30, 152
Chinese Communist Party (CCP) 37,
    40–3, 148
Chineseisation of Marxism 41–2
Chinese Lexicon 76–7
Chinese traditions 5, 7–10, 17, 31, 103,
    124, 125, 137, 162–4, 195, 218
    anthropocosmic worldview of 25–6
    collectivist 147–51

equality
    of potential to self-cultivate 201–3
    of rights and status in 110
gong (public) in 144–7, 150, 207
gongping (equity) in 116–20,
    199–200
higher education 7–11
    in Imperial times 25–34
higher learning 32–4
individuals 80
    and society 31–2
liberalism in 6
moral quality 197
of public good 6–7, 16
scholarship examined for 8
si (private) in 144–7, 150, 207
social equity 201
state sphere 81
university 209
Western influence on 34–8
whole and unity 25–9
world sphere 81
xiushen (self-cultivation) in 89–96,
    193, 195–8, 202
Chinese universities
    academic freedom 139–40
    governance 143
    lack of autonomy 142–3
citizenship education 199, 214
civic republican tradition 6, 157,
    157 n.2, 161, 162, 210, 212
civil equality 116, 119, 120, 201, 202
civilization 7, 9, 30, 35, 152
civilizational state 30–1, 42, 148, 179,
    210, 212, 220
civil society 50–1, 58, 59, 69–70, 80–1
    social values of 70–1
    spontaneous formation of 70
Clark, B.R. 170
classical Confucianism 117, 150
classical liberalism 49, 50
classic Confucianism 10–11
classic Greek philosophy 6, 11–12, 28
classic utilitarianism 62
collective good(s) 1, 13, 44, 74, 129, 138,
    155, 159, 163–4, 206, 207, 209,
    214–18
    common 161–3
    common and public 161–3
    economic public goods 159–63

governmental public goods 160–3
   normative 163–4, 166–8
   production 165–71
   of *tianxia* (all under heaven) 180, 184, 186
   understanding of 169–71
collective spheres 148–50, 156, 158, 206
collectivism 17, 20, 37, 41–2, 147–8, 150
   in Chinese higher education 151–2
collectivist tradition 147–51
combination 17–18, 20, 193, 198, 207
commercial society 51
the common good 28, 79, 159, 161, 177
common goods 161–3, 184, 212–14, 216, 217, 219
   UNESCO's notion of 159, 161–2, 177, 184, 185, 213, 216
communication sphere 156
communicative inclusive public 156, 161, 163, 212
communicative public 146–7, 157
communicative universal public 156–7
comparative methodology 13–14
   two-step trans-positional 16–18
comparison 16–17
   gong and public 210–11
   gongping and equity 199–202
   tianxia weigong (all under belongs to/ is for all) and global public/common goods 211, 212–15
   xiushen (self-cultivation) and *Bildung* 193–7
   zhi (the free will) and liberty 204–7
competition 105, 112
complementarity 18–20, 194, 196, 202–4
   of *xiushen* (self-cultivation) and *Bildung* 198
comprehensive freedom 63
Confucianism/Confucian 6–11, 26–8, 34, 36, 37, 41, 80, 89, 91–5, 120, 137–8, 179, 180, 195–7, 199
   collective good 163
   collectivism 41
   gongping (equity) in 116–19
   individualism 20, 37–8, 57, 103, 147–8
   inequity 116
   liberal tradition in 127–32

moral
   autonomy 130
   equality 118, 120, 201
   perfectionism 128–31
   qualities 129–30
   system 30–1, 116–18
   self-cultivation 203
   social equity 118–19
Confucius 28, 33, 93, 119, 145
contemporary China
   gongping (equity) in 119–20
   higher education 151
   rise of the autonomous individual in 150–1
   since 1949
      capitalist influence since 1978 43–5
      higher education system 45–7
      Mao era 41–3
contemporary university autonomy 143
contractarianism 49
corruption of values 167
cosmopolitanism 177, 181, 183
cross-border higher education 84
cultura animi (spiritual cultivation/refining of the soul) 97

dao (the way) 10, 27
Daodejing 27
Daoism 9–11, 26
daru 145
datong (the great harmony) 90
dawo (larger self) 32, 146, 148, 151, 180, 182
de (virtues or morals) 163–4
de Bary, W.T. 8, 128
democracy 59, 110, 113, 114, 116, 124, 134, 181–2
Deneulin, S. 177
Deng Xiaoping 43–6, 120, 148
denial of rights 62
Development as Freedom (Sen) 61, 213
Dewey, J. 28, 31, 34, 49, 94–6, 103, 155, 158
   concept of the world 71–2
   definition of the public 153–4
   ideal form of the government 68–9
   idea of growth/education 99–101
   on liberty and equality 59–61
   public/private dualism 153, 160
   social values of civil society 71

distribution of wealth and income 112
diverse individuality 132, 195–6, 198, 204
diversity 132–3, 185
Dong Zhongshu 117–18
dual-governance system 143
dualistic worldview 173–4, 195
Duara, P. 181
Dupré, L., common goods definition 161

Earley, P.C. 147
economic equality 116, 119–21, 201, 202
economic externalities 166
economic inequality 52, 55–6, 111, 113, 119
economic liberalization 43, 44
economic public goods 159–64, 169, 213–14
education 3, 123
  citizenship 199, 214
  and growth 99–101
  higher (*see* higher education)
elite institutions 122–5, 143
environment 100–1, 196–8
epistemology in *yin-yang* 18–20
equality 48, 50, 61, 65, 109, 118–20, 199–201
  of achievement 114
  of agent formation 126
  of basic liberties 110–11
  Confucian 126
    moral 118, 120
  constitutes of 115–16
  and equity 107
  of freedom 20, 114–15
    to achieve 114, 116, 201–3
  liberty and (*see* liberty: and equality)
  in morality and capacity 91
  of opportunity 55–7, 111, 112, 114–16, 120, 121, 124, 125, 201–3
  of political liberty 59
  of potential and freedom to achieve 203–4
  of potential to self-cultivate 120, 201–3
  of rights and status 110
  social justice and 110–15
  Western 37–9
equal rights 67
equity 3, 17, 28, 83, 84, 108–9, 119–20, 198–202, 221

of access to higher education 121, 122, 124–5
  advancement of 124–5
  in Anglo-American tradition 109–16
  Confucian 118, 119
  equality and 107
  global 187
  in higher education 202–4
  participation and 121–2
  self-formation as 125–6
Ericson, D.P. 124
Espinoza, O. 107, 108
European Union 181
European university 136
executive power 67–8
externalities of higher education 155, 165–6
external kinglihood 90–2

fair distribution of wealth and income 112
fair equality of opportunity 55–7, 111, 112, 115, 116, 201
family 26, 30–3, 36, 37, 44, 63, 89, 149, 158, 213
  backgrounds 122, 123
  higher education and 152
  inequality 121, 123–5
  social and economic capitals 122
fan ai zhong (affection for all humanity) 180
Fei, X. 182–3
Fichte, J.G. 98
formation 4, 10, 70, 126, 167
'for the sake of one self' 128
free agency 195–8, 206–9
free development of individuality 132–3
freedom 98–100, 114–15
  academic 136–40, 207–9, 221
  to act 130–2, 206, 207–9
  of discussions 52, 131, 133–4, 198–9, 208
  of expression 53, 131–4, 137–8, 156, 206, 207
  individual 101
  to make choice 197
  Sen, A. 61–3
  of speech 61
  of thought 52, 56–7, 137–8, 156
Friedman, M. 165
Fu, C.W.-h. 42

gaokao (Chinese college entrance
    examination) 124–6
Ge, Z. 183
Geng, Y. 38
Ge, Z. 183
Gibson, A. 165
Gibson, C.B. 147
global collective goods 172–3, 178, 183,
    185–7
  international mobility as 188
  knowledge as 186, 189
global common challenges 176
global common goods 79, 84, 162–3,
    174–5, 177–8, 213
global equity 187
global governance 176
global government 176
global normative collective goods 185
global public goods 84, 174, 177, 178
  defined 175–6
Goldin, K.D. 169
gong (public) 3, 17, 22, 76, 84, 108,
    144–7, 150, 163, 164, 207, 215
  comparison with public 210–11
  -as-state 212, 214
  -as-*tianxia* 214
gongde 163
gonggong chanpin/gonggong wupin 213
gongping (equity) 3, 17, 21, 83, 84,
    107–8, 199
  in Chinese traditions 116–20
  in Confucianism 116–19
  constitutes of 120
  in contemporary China 119–20
  and higher education 121–6
gong/public-as-state/government 216
governance 3, 131
  university 9, 142–3
governmental deregulation 46, 171
governmental public goods 160–4, 169
government's ideal form 67–8
Graham, J. 140
guanxi (social networks/
    relationships) 149–50
guojia (state) 78

Habermas, J.
  communicative public 146–7
  public sphere 157, 212
Hahm, C. 127–8

Han, S.-J. 183
harmonious world 185, 195, 197, 199
Hayek, F.A. 165
Hayhoe, R. 40, 140, 143
Hazelkorn, E. 165
heaven 26–9, 31
heer butong (harmony without
    conformity) 20, 180
higher education 3–4
  academic freedom 136–40, 207–9
  Anglo-American tradition 11–12, 74
  China 170–1
  Chinese, collectivism in 151–2
  Chinese traditions 7–11
  collective goods production 165–71
  collective outcomes 215–17
  competition 112
  equal opportunity to 111–12
  equity in 202–4
  equity of access to 121, 122, 124–5
  externalities of 155, 165–6
  global equity 187
  gong (public) 168
  gongping (equity) and 121–6
  history in China 223
  knowledge in 186–7
  location of activity 165
  marketization of 46, 47, 167, 171
  modern 38–41
  national and global
      perspectives 187–9
  nature of the activity 165
  privatization of 46, 47, 167, 171
  public funding for 165, 168–70
  quality of 126
  si (private) 168
  social access 169
  spheres of social action influence
      on 82–4
  student 185–6
    development 198–9
  system 45–7
  United Kingdom and the United
      States 73–4, 170
  university autonomy 140–3, 207–9
  xiushen (self-cultivation) and *Bildung*
      in 102–6
higher learning 32–4
Hofstede, G. 147
the home state 187

Horlacher, R.   104, 123
Huang, C.   146
Hui Shi   26
human beings   26–9, 91–2
human capital theory   74, 88, 89, 105
humanity   26–8
Humboldtian university   73, 87–8, 97, 103, 136
Huntington, Samuel   5
Hu Shi   40
hybridization   17–18, 207, 215. See also synergy

Imago Dei (God's image)   97
impartial observations   14
Imperial China   29–31, 133
  higher learning in   32–4
  liberty in   131
the inclusive public   212
individual(s)   31–2, 38, 52–4, 152–8, 213
  agency   196–8, 204, 221
  autonomy   34, 130, 135, 150–1, 206–7
  capability of   63, 66–7
  freedom   101
  and private   151
  public spirit of   65–6, 100
  rational autonomy   97–8
  self-respect and mutual respect of   64–5
  sphere of   80, 82–3
individual-community interactions   94–6
individualism   17, 20, 44, 60, 147, 158
  Western   36–8
individuality, free development of   132–3
individualized goods   217, 219
individual liberty   195, 197
information base   61–3
institutional autonomy   52, 55, 73, 83, 84, 98
intellectual authority   140
intellectual freedom   140
Intellectual Property Rights regime   188
internal sagehood   90–2
international agreements   174
international mobility   185, 188–9
inward perfectionism   90, 91, 93–5, 195–7, 199. See also outward perfectionism

Jia, K.   119
Jia, Q.   124

jiaguo tonggou (family state)   30
Jia, K.   119
Jiang, Y.-h.   146
jianguan   132, 147
Jiang, Y.-h.   146
Jia, Q.   124
Jingshi Daxuetang   40
Jover, G.   26
justice   69

Kalmanson, L.   9
Kant, I.   91, 99, 208
  sympathy in humanity   180
Kaul, I.   175
keju (the civil service examination)   33, 39, 151
King, A. Y.   30
kinship systems   149
knowledge   28, 186–7
  acquisition   103–4
  as global collective goods   186, 189
  privatization of   188, 189
  production   166

Labaree, D.F.   125
labour market   108–9
Lai, A.   152
Lanford, M.   136
Lauwerys, J.A.   88
Law School   9–11
Lee, T. H. C.   128
legal liberties   56, 57
legislative power   67–8
Leninist party system   42, 44
lexical basis   17, 21, 225
  Anglo-American terms in Chinese   77–9
  Chinese terms into English   76–7
li (propriety)   76, 94, 117
Li, C.   129
Liang, S.   31
Liang Qichao   36
Liang, S.   31
liberal education   88
liberal individualism   38, 74, 103, 157–8, 214
liberalism   6, 11–12, 16, 36–7, 41, 48–50, 91, 95, 110, 129, 196, 198
  Western   129, 131
libertarianism   62

liberty 3, 6, 21, 39, 48–9, 67, 68, 81, 83, 84, 113, 114, 127–8, 131, 156, 195, 204–7, 209, 220
  in Anglo-American tradition 132–4
  of conscience 56–7
  and equality
    Dewey, J. 59–61
    Locke, J. 58–9
    Mill, J.S. 52–5
    Rawls, J. 55–7
    Sen, A. 61–3
    Smith, A. 50–2
  individual 195, 197
  of thought and discussion 133
  and university autonomy 141
  Western 35–7
Li, C. 129
limited liberal state 160
Liu, N.C. 160, 162, 216
lizhi 129
Locatelli, R. 176
Locke, J. 49, 50, 52, 55, 56
  ideal form of the government 67–8
  on liberty and equality 58–9
  responsibility of the state 69
Løvlie, L. 96
Lu, Y. 26, 125
Lufrano, R. 9
Lukes, S. 158
Luo, Y. 122
Lu, Y. 26, 125

Mao era 41–4, 46, 119, 120, 148, 149
Marginson, S. 9, 102, 104, 109, 111, 121, 144, 148, 154, 160, 165, 170, 186
  public goods 159, 160
market 51, 63, 154–5, 176
  failure 155, 160
marketization of higher education 46, 47, 167, 171
Marxism-Leninism 37, 41–2, 110, 119
materialism 150
'Matthew effects' 122
May, T. 180
Mencius 28, 30, 91, 145
Messling, M. 97
methodological individualism 158, 168
methodological limitation 226
methodological nationalism 174, 184, 189, 214, 220

methodological reflections 224–6
military technology of the West 34–5
Mill, J.S. 49, 50, 56, 62, 98, 132–3
  freedom of thought, discussion and expression 133
  ideal form of the government 68
  on liberty and equality 52–5
  principle of self-protection 130, 133, 208–9
  public spirit of individuals 65–6
  social values of civil society 71
modern liberalism 49–50
modern universities in China 38–41
moral
  autonomy 58, 93, 104, 128–30, 206, 207, 209
  education 66, 103, 199, 214
  equality, Confucian 118
  perfectionism 91, 128–31, 164
  qualities 91, 94, 128–30, 197–9, 206–7, 209
  values 71
Morales, M.H. 54
Mortensen, K.P. 96
Mou, Z. 90
Mueller-Vollmer, K.M. 97
Muhlhahn, K. 149
multilateralism 174–5
mutual respect 64–5
mutual trust 138, 139, 183, 208, 209, 220

Nagel, T. 14
nation-states 174–5, 178
natural sympathy 50, 70, 117, 180
Needham, J. 152
negative externalities 155
neisheng (internal sagehood) 90–2
Nelson, C. 138
neo-Anglo-American 113
neo-Confucianism 6, 10
neoliberal 105, 113
neoliberalism 113–14
neoliberal state 113
New Confucianism 6, 10
Newman, J.H. 12
Nixon, J. 167
non-elite institutions 123, 143
non-state dimension 160–1
Nordenbo, S.E. 96
Nordic 112–13

normative collective goods   163–4, 166–8, 185, 214, 217
normative values   160, 163–4
Nuyen, A.T.   117

objectivity   14–15
Olson, M.   155, 164
On Liberty (Mill)   52, 153
open impartiality   72
opportunity   219–20
  equality of   55–7, 111, 112, 114–16, 120, 121, 124, 125, 201–3
original position   55
Orthodox Confucianism   10
outward perfectionism   90, 91, 94, 95, 100, 103, 195–6
ownership of property   57

Pan, S.Y.   142
Park, Y.-D.   183
People's Republic of China   148
perfect freedom   58
Persoenlichkeit   105
ping (fair and equal)   108
pingdeng (equality)   108
Piper, D.R.   140
Plato   28
political control   101
political
  equality   58, 59, 116, 119, 120, 201, 202
  inequality   54
  liberty   56, 58, 59
  participation   65–6
political control   101
positive externalities   155
pragmatism   49, 140
pre-Qin period   9, 10
Pritchard, R.M.O.   139
private good(s)   4, 44, 74, 152–4, 156, 166, 170
privatization   155
  of higher education   46, 47, 167, 171
  of knowledge   188, 189
prosperity   51
public   72, 153–4, 210–15
  consequences   71, 73
  definition of   153–4
  discussion   198–9
  funding   165, 168–70
  influence   72

  -as-non-market   213
  reasoning   99
  service   69
  sphere   136, 141–2, 146, 156–7, 167, 212
  -as-state/government   154, 213, 214
  -as-*tianxia*   215
  transactions   153
public/and private dualism   153–6, 161, 163, 165, 212, 213
the public good   2–5, 15–17, 20–2, 38, 48, 50, 54, 63, 69, 72, 75, 84, 95, 137, 140, 145, 152, 159, 165, 170, 209, 218, 221, 223–6
  concept of   13, 16
  of higher education
    Anglo-American traditions   4, 6–7, 16
    Chinese tradition   6–7, 16
public goods   1, 7, 63, 70, 113, 138, 152, 154, 156, 159, 160, 162, 170, 209, 216, 217, 219
  defining   160
  economic   159–64, 169, 213–14
  externalities as   165–6
  governmental   160–3, 169
public spirit/spiritedness   65–6, 100, 197–9, 208
pure knowledge   152

Qi, Q.   35
Qian, M.   29
qin qin (affection for one's kin)   117, 180
Qi, Q.   35

rational autonomy   97–8
Rawls, J.   49, 50, 59, 62, 119, 124
  callous meritocratic society   93, 112, 114
  equality of basic liberties in   110–11
  fair equality of opportunity   201
  freedom of thought and expression   134
  on liberty and equality   55–7
  mutual respect of individuals   64–5
  self-respect of individuals   64–5, 115
  social and economic equality   116
  social justice   110–12
realpolitik of *tianxia* (all under heaven)   181–3, 212

Reform and Opening-up Policy (1978)   43
reinterpretations   93
ren (benevolence)   26, 31, 76, 94, 164
rendao (way of humanity)   10, 27–9, 89–90
renlei   26
Robbins Report   138–9, 170
Rosemont Jr, H.   38
Russian October Revolution   41
Ryan, A.   49

sameness of personhood   91, 92, 195, 204
Samuelson, P.A.   4, 156
    concept of public goods   152
    market   176
    public/ private formula   154
Schwenk, B.   97
science
    and higher education   46
    and technology   45
scientific knowledge   187
Secada, W.   107
self   80, 94–5
self-determination   129
self-formation
    Bildung as socially nested   99, 100, 102, 103
    as equity   125–6
self-governance   143
self-protection principle   53, 133
self-respect   64–5, 115
Self-strengthening Movement *(ziqiang/ yangwu yundong)*   35, 37
Sen, A.   49, 50, 157, 201, 206, 213, 225
    concept of capability   66–7, 89, 101–2, 104, 114–15, 126, 197, 202
    concept of the world   71–2
    equality of freedom to achieve   203, 204
    equity   108–10, 114, 115
    freedom   61–3
    heterogeneities of society   133–4
    on liberty and equality   61–3
    social justice   114, 116
    trans-positional analysis   2, 14–16
sex equality   54
shadow education   149
shangxian   117

Shanxi University   40
Shavit, Y.   125
shehui (society)   78
Shim, Y.-H.   183
si (private)   3, 17, 22, 84, 144–7, 150, 164, 207, 210, 215, 217
Siljander, P.   96, 97
Si Maguang   145
sixiang quanwei (intellectual authority)   140
sixiang ziyou (intellectual freedom)   140
Smith, A.   49, 50, 121, 153, 155
    civil society   80
    on liberty and equality   50–2
    natural sympathy   50, 70, 117, 180
    responsibility of the state   69
    social values of civil society   70
    spontaneous formation of civil Society   70
social
    accessibility of higher education   169
    contractarianism   58
    control   52–3, 101
    equality   116, 119–21, 201, 202
    externalities   166
    inequality   52, 55–6, 111, 119
    justice   110–16, 118, 124, 201
    nexuses   149–51
    order   115, 117–19, 134, 201
    structure   121
socially nested self-formation   195–6
society   26, 31–2, 42–4, 51, 71, 78, 89, 109, 115
    heterogeneities of   133–4
    market and non-market sector of   155
    sphere of   80–1, 83
    trust between higher education and   138
spheres of social action   1–3, 75, 77, 82, 84, 144, 146–9, 158, 164, 213, 218
    key thinkers on   63–73
    public and private   153–7
state   26, 32, 42–4, 71–3, 89, 112, 159–60, 174–5, 212
    and higher education   151–2
    ideal form of   67–8
    Imperial Chinese   29–31
    legislative and executive powers   67–8
    neoliberal   113

public and   154
responsibility of   69
and society   138, 139
sphere of the   81, 83
state-university relationship   141–2
stratification of higher education   123
students
 development   198–9
 higher education for   185–6
 as national citizens   188, 189
The Subjection of Women (Mill)   54
supreme power   67
Sutinen, A.   97
synergy   17–18, 207, 215
systemic stratification   123

taiji   19
Taylor, C.A.   104
Taylor, I.   175
The Theory of Moral Sentiments
 (Smith)   50–1, 70
ti (fraternity)   31
tian (heaven)   76
Tian, L.   160, 162, 216
tiandao (way of heaven)   10, 27–9, 89
tianren heyi (the unity of heaven and
 humanity)   26
tianxia (all under heaven)   7, 22, 76,
 81, 89, 148, 162, 175, 178, 207,
 210, 212
 Callahan's critique   182
 collective goods of   180, 184, 186
 defined   179
 as a normative appeal   179–81
 in realpolitik   181–3, 212
tianxia weigong (all under belongs to/is for
 all)   3, 17, 22, 76, 84, 162, 178,
 179, 184, 189, 214
 comparison with global public/
  common goods   214–15
Tierney, W.G.   136
Townsend, N.   177
traditional Chinese public goods   162–3,
 210, 214, 216
traditions   5–6
'the tragedy of the commons'   155
Traianou, A.   139
trans-positional analysis   2, 14–17, 82–4,
 221, 225
Triventi, M.   123

Tröhler, D.   105
Trow, M.   138
 universal higher education   171
trust   138
Tsinghua University   40
Tu, W.-M.   94
Turner, R.S.   113
Tu, W.-M.   94
two-step trans-positional comparative
 methodology   16–18

Ulrich, B.   183
UNESCO's notion common goods   159,
 161–2, 177, 184, 185, 213, 216
United Kingdom (UK)
 academic freedom   138–9
 control over universities   209
 higher education in   73–4, 170
United Nations   176, 181
United States
 academic freedom   136, 138
 control over universities   209
 higher education in   73–4, 170
unity   25–9
the universal public   212, 214, 215
university(ies)   5, 12, 45–6, 73–4, 103,
 104, 124, 209
 American   141
 autonomy   17, 21, 73, 74, 127, 142,
  207–9, 221
  academic freedom and   141–3
  defined   140
  in higher education   140–3
 Chinese   142–3
 control   142
 governance   4, 9, 142–3
 history   136
 mission of   137
 modern   38–41, 142
 Western   38–41
University of California   171
utilitarianism   49, 56

values   164
 corruption of   167
 creation   157–8
 global common goods   177
 normative   157–8
 public   167
 of *tianxia* (all under heaven)   180

Western 35
    equality 37
    individualism 37–8
    liberty 36–7
veil of ignorance 55, 57
virtues 7, 26, 28, 29, 35, 51, 52, 68, 70, 94, 117, 126
Vogel, E.F. 45
Von Humboldt, W. 12, 97, 98, 136, 208

waiwang (external kinglihood) 90–2
Wang, B. 179, 183
Wang, H. 215
Wang, J. C. 163
The Wealth of Nations (Smith) 51–2, 70
Western
    learning 34–6
    liberalism 129, 131
    university models in China 38–41
    values 35
world 26, 63, 174, 179–80, 184
    sphere of the 81, 84
World Health Organization 176
wuchang (five constant virtues) 94, 164

xiao (filial piety) 31
xiaowo (smaller self) 32, 146, 151, 180, 182
xin (integrity) 94
Xiong, C. 108
xiushen (self-cultivation) 3, 17, 21, 82–3, 87–9, 137, 148, 202
    in Chinese traditions 89–96
    comparison of *Bildung* with 193, 195–8
    Confucian anthropocosmic worldview and 89–91
    cultivation of moral qualities 91, 94

higher education in 102–6
individual-community interactions 94–6
internal emphasis 206
moral qualities in 197
process of 92
staying true to oneself 92–3
xueshu ziyou (academic freedom) 140
xueyi weiji 128

Yan, X. 182
Yang, L. 144, 148
Yang, R. 146
Yan, X. 182
yi (righteousness) 31, 94, 164
yiji zhisi 217
yin-yang 10, 17–20, 117
youjiao wulei 33
Yu, X. 125

Zha, Q. 139, 143
Zhang, E. 177
Zhao, T. 179, 181–2
Zha, Q. 139, 143
zhi (free will) 3, 17, 21, 77, 83, 84, 93, 94, 104, 127–30, 195–8, 204–9, 220
    separation of freedom to act and 130–2
zhong (loyalty) 31
Zhou, F. 117
Zhouli (*The Rites of Zhou*) 19
Zhu Xi 128, 145
zide 128
ziyou (liberty) 21, 127, 128
zizhi (self-governance) 143
zizhu (self-mastery) 143
zunxian 117–18
Zürcher, E. 9

www.ingramcontent.com/pod-product-compliance
Lightning Source LLC
Chambersburg PA
CBHW052219300426
44115CB00011B/1752